Teacher Preparation Classroom

TEACHER PREP

MERRILL
PRENTICE HALL

See a demo at
www.prenhall.com/teacherprep/demo

Your Class. Their Careers. Our Future. Will your students be prepared?

We invite you to explore our new, innovative and engaging website and all that it has to offer you, your course, and tomorrow's educators! Preview this site today at www.prenhall.com/teacherprep/demo. Just click on "go" on the login page to begin your exploration.

Organized around the major courses pre-service teachers take, the Teacher Preparation site provides media, student/teacher artifacts, strategies, research articles, and other resources to equip your students with the quality tools needed to excel in their courses and prepare them for their first classroom.

This ultimate on-line education resource will provide you and your students access to:

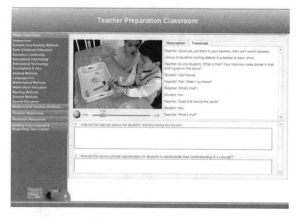

Online Video Library. More than 250 video clips—each tied to a course topic and framed by learning goals and Praxis-type questions—capture real teachers and students working in real classrooms.

Student and Teacher Artifacts. More than 200 student and teacher classroom artifacts—each tied to a course topic and framed by learning goals and application questions—provide a wealth of materials and experiences to help your students observe children's developmental learning.

Lesson Plan Builder. Step-by-step guidelines and lesson plan examples support students as they learn to build high-quality lesson plans.

Articles and Readings. Over 500 articles from ASCD's renowned journal *Educational Leadership* are available. The site also includes Research Navigator, a searchable database of additional educational journals.

Strategies and Lessons. Over 500 research-supported instructional strategies appropriate for a wide range of grade levels and content areas.

Licensure and Career Tools. Resources devoted to helping your students pass their licensure exam; learn standards, law, and public policies; plan a teaching portfolio; and succeed in their first year of teaching.

How to ORDER *Teacher Prep* for you and your students:

- For students to receive a *Teacher Prep* Access Code with this text, the instructor **must** provide a special value pack ISBN number on their textbook order form. To receive this special ISBN, please email: **Merrill.marketing@pearsoned.com** and provide the following information:
- Name and Affiliation
- Author/Title/Edition of Merrill text

Upon ordering *Teacher Prep* for their students, instructors will be given a lifetime *Teacher Prep* Access Code.

Meaningful Learning With Technology

THIRD EDITION

David Jonassen
University of Missouri

Jane Howland
University of Missouri

Rose Marra
University of Missouri

David Crismond
University of Missouri

PEARSON

Merrill
Prentice Hall

Upper Saddle River, New Jersey
Columbus, Ohio

Library of Congress Cataloging in Publication Data

Meaningful learning with technology/by David Jonassen . . . [et al.]. —3rd ed.
  p. cm.
  Prev. ed: Learning with technology/David Jonassen, Kyle L. Peck, Brent G. Wilson. 1999.
  ISBN 978-0-13-239395-9
    1. Educational technology. 2. Teaching—Aids and devices. 3. Learning. 4. Constructivism (Education)
  I. Jonassen, David H. Learning with technology.

LB1028.3 .J63 2008
371.33—dc22

2007014194

Vice President and Executive Publisher: Jeffery W. Johnston
Senior Editor: Darcy Betts Prybella
Production Editor: Kris Roach
Production Coordination: GGS Book Services
Photo Coordinator: Sandy Schaefer
Design Coordinator: Diane C. Lorenzo
Cover Designer: Ali Mohrman
Cover Image: Jupiter Images
Production Manager: Susan Hannahs
Director of Marketing: David Gesell
Marketing Coordinator: Brian Mounts

This book was set in Palatino by GGS Book Services. It was printed and bound by R.R. Donnelley & Sons Company. The cover was printed by R.R. Donnelley & Sons Company.

Photo Credits: SW Productions/Getty Images, Inc.—Photodisc, p. 1; Maria B. Vonada/Merrill, p. 13; Courtesy of Palm, Inc., p. 30; David Buffington/Getty Images, Inc. —Photodisc, p. 43; Scott Cunningham/Merrill, p. 61; Liz Moore/Merrill, p. 81; Anthony Magnacca/Merrill, p. 99; Pearson Learning Photo Studio, p. 139; Harry Sieplinga/HMS Images, The Image Bank, p. 169; Scott Cunningham/Merrill, p. 191; Author supplied, pp. 204, 205, 207, 213; Valerie Schultz/Merrill, p. 217; Image of Classroom Performance System courtesy of eInstruction Corporation, p. 231.

Pearson Education Ltd.
Pearson Education Singapore Pte. Ltd.
Pearson Education Canada, Ltd.
Pearson Education—Japan

Pearson Education Australia Pty. Limited
Pearson Education North Asia Ltd.
Pearson Educación de Mexico, S.A. de C.V.
Pearson Education Malaysia Pte. Ltd.

10 9 8 7 6 5 4 3
ISBN 13: 978-0-13-239395-9
ISBN 10:   0-13-239395-6

Preface

Implications of Learning With Technology

Welcome to the third edition of this book. Each edition, including this one, is based on the assumption that meaningful learning requires active engagement in authentic learning tasks, articulation and reflection on personally and socially constructed meaning, collaboration in those tasks whenever possible, and most importantly, an intention to learn. This assumption is grounded in a constructivist epistemology. Constructivism is a philosophy for describing processes of meaning making. Although it is a philosophy that is relatively new to educational practice, it has always existed. Since the beginning humans have interacted with the world and struggled to make sense out of what they have experienced. This is as natural to humans as breathing and explains why we have a relatively large cerebral cortex. People naturally construct their own meaning for experiences. Unfortunately, that is a problem in the industrial model of education, where learners are evaluated by high-stakes tests for learning the same thing. Regardless of what we teach students or the experiences they have, they will naturally construct their own interpretations of those experiences. They may learn what we teach them, but what they will remember and use in the future are their own personal and social relevant interpretations.

Like the first two editions, the purpose of this edition is to demonstrate ways that technology can be used to engage and support meaningful learning. However, the structure and treatment of the learning process in this edition are quite different from the previous editions. This edition is organized around learning processes, such as investigating, exploring, writing, modeling, community building, communicating, designing, visualizing, and assessing. That is, in each chapter, we describe how different technologies can be used to engage and support the learning processes stated above. The chapters describe the learning-with-technology processes conceptually. In most examples, we discuss specific software applications. It is likely that you may not have access to these specific applications, or that they are not compatible with your computer. If that is the case, read Chapter 2, Investigating With Technologies, and use those ideas to find similar applications that you may be able to use. We focus on how to use technologies to engage meaningful learning, not on cookbook lessons that you can apply tomorrow morning. If we took that approach (providing specific lesson plans), they probably would not work the way that we intended in your classrooms, because students naturally construct their own meaning from experiences. So, our purpose is not to demonstrate how to use these technologies, but rather to demonstrate how learners can use these technologies. The process may be more difficult, but the meaning that you and your students derive from it will be deeper. We believe this approach is worth the effort.

New Roles for Technology

As stated in Chapter 1, we believe that although technologies can be used to provide additional testing practice, when they are used to engage students in active, constructive, intentional, authentic, and cooperative learning, then students will derive more meaning. Throughout this book, we contend that learning takes place in environments where students truly understand the nature of the tasks they are undertaking. Only then, when individuals understand and freely invest the effort needed to complete a task or activity, does meaningful, authentic learning occur. When learning tasks are relevant and embedded in a meaningful context, students see them as more than simply busywork.

Using technologies to engage meaningful learning assumes that our conceptions of education will change, that schools or classrooms (at least those that use technologies in the ways that we describe) will rethink the educational process. Although few people would ever publicly state that schools should not emphasize meaningful learning, meaningful learning is not engaged or assessed using standardized tests. Meaningful learning presupposes that parents, students, and teachers will realize the implications and demand change, so that meaningful learning is valued as much as memorization. Technologies will not be the cause of the social change that is required for a renaissance in learning, but they can catalyze that change and support it if it comes.

Implications for Teachers

In order for students to learn *with* technology, teachers must accept and learn a new model of learning. Traditionally, teachers' primary responsibility and activity have been directly instructing students, where teachers were the purveyors of knowledge and students the recipients. That is, the teacher told the students what they knew and how they interpreted the world according to the curriculum, textbooks, and other resources they have studied. Teachers are hired and rewarded for their content expertise. This assumes that the ways that teachers know the world are correct and should be emulated by the students. Students take notes on what teachers tell them and try to comprehend the world as their teachers do. Successful students develop concepts similar to those of their teachers. In this kind of learning context, students will not be able to learn *with* technology because they will not be able to construct their own meaning and manage their own learning if the teacher does it for them.

So, first and foremost, teachers must relinquish at least some of their authority, especially intellectual. If teachers determine what is important for students to know, how they should know it, and how they should learn it, then students cannot become intentional, constructive learners. They aren't allowed. In those classroom contexts, there is no reason for students to make sense of the world—only to comprehend the teacher's understanding of it. We believe that the students' task should not be to understand the world as the teacher does. Rather, students should construct their own meaning for the world. If they do, then the teachers' roles shift from dispensing knowledge to helping learners construct more viable conceptions of the world. We said earlier that we believe that not all meaning is created equally. So the teacher needs to help students to discover what the larger community of scholars regards as meaningful concepts and to evaluate their own beliefs and understandings in terms of those standards. Science teachers should help students comprehend the beliefs of the scientific community. Social studies teachers should examine with their students the values and beliefs that societies have constructed. In this role, the teacher is not the arbiter of knowledge but rather is a coach that helps students to engage in a larger community of scholars.

Teachers must also relinquish some of their authority in their management of learning. They cannot control all of the learning activities in the classroom. If teachers determine not only what is important for students to know, but how they should learn it, then students cannot be self-regulated learners. They aren't allowed.

Finally, teachers must gain some familiarity with the technology. They must gain skills and fluency with the technology. However, they will be unsuccessful in helping students to learn *with* technology if they learn about the technologies in order to function as the expert. Rather, they should learn to coach the learning of technology skills. In many instances, teachers will be learning with the students. We have worked in many school situations where the students were constantly pushing our understanding of the technology. Often, we were barely keeping ahead of the students. They can and will learn *with* technologies, with or without the help of the teacher. That does not mean that as a teacher, you can abdicate any responsibility for learning the technologies. Rather, teachers should try not to be the expert all of the time.

These implications are very problematic for teachers. They require that teachers assume new roles with different beliefs than they have traditionally pursued. Most teachers in most schools will find these implications challenging. We believe that the results will justify the risks. And just as teachers must assume new roles, learning *with* technology requires that students also assume new roles.

Implications for Students

If teachers relinquish authority, learners must assume it. Learners must develop skills in articulating, reflecting on, and evaluating what they know; setting goals for themselves (determining what is important to know) and regulating their activities and effort in order to achieve those goals; and collaborating and conversing with others so that the understandings of all students is enriched. Many students are not ready to assume that much responsibility. They do not want the power to determine their own destiny. It is much easier to allow others to regulate their lives for them. How skilled are students at setting their own agendas and pursuing them? Many students believe in their roles as passive students. However, our experience and the experiences of virtually every researcher and educator involved with every technology project described in this book show that most students readily accept those responsibilities. When given the opportunity, students of all ages readily experiment with technologies, articulate their own beliefs, and construct, co-construct, and criticize each others' ideas. When learners are allowed to assume ownership of the product, they are diligent and persevering builders of knowledge.

Constructivist approaches to learning, with or without technology, are fraught with risks for students, parents, teachers, and administrators. Change always assumes risks. Many of the activities described in this book entail risks. We encourage you to take those risks. The excitement and enthusiasm generated by students while they construct their own understanding using technology-based tools is more than sufficient reward for taking those risks.

Standards

Teachers are challenged to ensure that students meet a myriad of required national, state, and local standards. It was impossible to tie each of our recommended activities to these myriad standards so we chose the most relevant national standards, National Educational Technology Standards (NETS), provided by the International Society for Technology in Education (ISTE), as our focus. NETS are designed to provide educators with frameworks and standards that guide them in creating rich, technology-supported learning environments. Teachers often become overwhelmed by the numerous indicators students are required to demonstrate in meeting state standards, see each of these indicators as discrete, and subsequently design disconnected instruction that isolates individual objectives. Instead, teachers should think broadly, recognizing that rich project-based learning that incorporates problem-solving and authentic tasks can meet many standards simultaneously. Rather than structure this book around specific, grade level lesson plans, we have offered ways that several types of technologies can be used to enhance a variety of learning activities and outcomes. The six general standards that comprise the NETS for students are demonstrated through ten separate, specific grade level performance indicators for students in Grades Pre-K–2, 3–5, 6–8, and 9–12.

Using the Arbor Day/Earth Day Tree Exploration field experiment in Chapter 2 as an example, let's examine how Suzanne Stillwell's fourth grade students could meet the NETS standards and performance indicators for third through fifth graders.

Each performance indicator (PI) is followed by the general standard being met in parentheses.

First, students spent time exploring technology, giving them an opportunity to meet PI 9: *Determine which technology is useful and select the appropriate tool(s) and technology resources to address a variety of tasks and problems. (5, 6)*

Students then used handheld and digital cameras to capture and record data about trees. PI 8: *Use technology resources (e.g., calculators, data collection probes, videos, educational software) for problem solving, self-directed learning, and extended learning activities. (5, 6)*

Next, students shared data with each other by beaming among handhelds and uploaded the data to computers, where they created graphs. In this process, they demonstrated PI 1: *Use keyboards and other common input and output devices (including adaptive devices when necessary) efficiently and effectively (1)* and PI 4: *Use general purpose productivity tools and peripherals to support personal productivity, remediate skill deficits, and facilitate learning throughout the curriculum. (3)*

The Arbor Day/Earth Day project could easily be extended to include student creation of a web site, meeting PI 5: *Use technology tools (e.g., multimedia authoring, presentation, Web tools, digital cameras, scanners) for individual and collaborative writing, communication, and publishing activities to create knowledge products for audiences inside and outside the classroom. (3, 4)*

This activity might also be one component of a larger project involving Internet research, with the potential of meeting PI 10: *Evaluate the accuracy, relevance, appropriateness, comprehensiveness, and bias of electronic information sources. (6)*

Students used resources from their state Department of Conservation; by connecting with experts at that organization, they would engage in the kind of activities indicated in PI 6: *Use telecommunications efficiently and effectively to access remote information, communicate with others in support of direct and independent learning, and pursue personal interests. (4)*

An interesting means for bringing additional collaboration into this project is by connecting with other classrooms in different parts of the country to share findings and create a joint product, such as a wiki, to publish results. In this way, students would meet PI 7: *Use telecommunications and online resources (e.g., e-mail, online discussions, Web environments) to participate in collaborative problem-solving activities for the purpose of developing solutions or products for audiences inside and outside the classroom. (4, 5)*

As you can see, it is possible within one well-designed, rich instructional activity to meet nearly all of the performance indicators and standards required for a grade level. With thoughtful planning, it is also just as feasible to simultaneously meet a number of content standards. This results in efficient use of students' time, but most important, it helps pull teachers away from an isolated standards model of teaching, where instruction is more likely to be prescriptive and disconnected from authentic learning activities. With a deeper focus, not only will teachers be helping students meet a multitude of standards, they will also be offering rich, interesting learning opportunities that engage students and compel them to think beyond the superficial. Challenging students' cognitive skills by providing motivating instruction that fulfills multiple standards is a worthy accomplishment—one that all teachers should strive for.

We encourage you to consider the complex learning outcomes described in this book as you design instruction for your students. Although authentic, complex, technology-supported activities may seem to be the antithesis of what is needed to prepare students for high achievement on tests, they are not. On the contrary, the meaningful learning that results from this work can not only encompass the knowledge needed for successful test taking, but will also develop individuals who are capable of real thinking.

Acknowledgments

We would like to thank the reviewers for their insightful comments and suggestions, They are Temba C. Bassoppo-Moyo, Illinois State University; Arthur Keith Dils, King's College; Cheryl Foltz, William Woods University and Southwest Baptist University; Kim Foreman, San Francisco State University; and Jennifer Richardson, Purdue University.

Brief Contents

Contents

What Is Meaningful Learning?

What drives learning, more than anything else, is the understanding of and effort invested in completing a task or activity. It is the nature of the task that students intend to perform that will best determine the nature of the learning that results. Unfortunately, the nature of the task that so many students most commonly experience in schools is completing standardized tests. Schools in America have become testing factories. Federal legislation has mandated continuous testing of K–12 students in order to make schools and students more accountable for their learning. In order to avoid censure and loss of funding, many K–12 schools have adopted test preparation as their primary curriculum. Perhaps the most unfortunate epiphenomenon of this process is the current generation of students who will complete their K–12 education knowing only how to take tests. Because the purpose of those tests and the preparation supporting them is to attain a passing score (relative to other schools), the students are seldom fully invested in the process, so they make no attempt to understand the knowledge being tested. The students do not ask to take the tests. The tests assess skills and knowledge that are detached from their everyday experience, so they have little meaning. The testing process is individual, so students are enjoined from cooperating with others. The tests represent only a single form of knowledge representation, so students are not able to develop conceptual understanding, which requires representing what you know in multiple ways. Simply stated, learning to take tests does not result in meaningful learning.

In order for students to learn meaningfully, they must be willfully engaged in a meaningful task. In order for meaningful learning to occur, the task that students pursue should engage active, constructive, intentional, authentic, and cooperative activities. Rather than testing inert knowledge, schools should help students to learn how to recognize and solve problems, comprehend new phenomena, construct mental models of those phenomena, and, given a new situation, set goals and regulate their own learning (learn how to learn). Tasks that require intentional, active, constructive, cooperative, and authentic learning processes (see Figure 1.1) will result in more meaningful learning. Although technologies can be used to provide additional testing practice, when they are used to engage students in active, constructive, intentional, authentic, and cooperative learning, the students will make more meaning. These attributes of meaningful learning will be used throughout the remainder of this book as the goals for using technologies as well as the criteria for evaluating the uses of technology. Let's examine these attributes a little more closely.

• **Active (Manipulative/Observant)** Learning is a natural, adaptive human process. Humans have survived and therefore evolved because they were able to learn about and adapt to their environment. Humans of all ages, without the intervention of formal instruction, have developed sophisticated skills and advanced knowledge about the world around them when they need to or want to. When learning about things in natural contexts, humans interact with their environment and manipulate the objects in that environment, observing the effects of their interventions and constructing their own interpretations of the

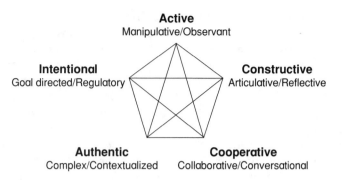

Figure 1.1 Characteristics of Meaningful Learning.

phenomena and the results of their manipulations. For instance, before playing sandlot baseball, do kids subject themselves to lectures and multiple-choice examinations about the theory of games, the aerodynamics of orbs, and vector forces applied to them? No! They start swinging the bat and chasing fly balls, and they negotiate the rules as they play the game. Through formal and informal apprenticeships in communities of play and work, learners develop skills and knowledge that they then share with other members of those communities with whom they learned and practiced those skills. In all of these situations, learners are actively manipulating the objects and tools of the trade and observing the effects of what they have done. The youngster who consistently hits foul balls will adjust his or her stance and handgrip on the bat in order to manipulate the path of flight and observe the effects of each manipulation. Meaningful learning requires learners who are active—actively engaged by a meaningful task in which they manipulate objects and parameters of the environment they are working in and observing the results of their manipulations.

• **Constructive (Articulative/Reflective)** Activity is necessary but not sufficient for meaningful learning. It is essential that learners articulate what they have accomplished and reflect on their activity and observations—to learn the lessons that their activity has to teach. New experiences often provide a discrepancy between what learners observe and what they understand. That is when meaningful learning begins. They are curious about or puzzled by what they see. That puzzlement is the catalyst for meaning making. By reflecting on the puzzling experience, learners integrate their new experiences with their prior knowledge about the world, or they establish goals for what they need to learn in order to make sense out of what they observe. Learners begin constructing their own simple mental models that explain what they observe, and with experience, support, and more reflection, their mental models become increasingly complex. Ever more complex models require that learners mentally represent their understanding in different ways using different thought processes. The active and constructive parts of the meaning making process are symbiotic. They both rely on the other for meaning making to occur.

- **Intentional (Goal-Directed/Regulatory)**   All human behavior is goal directed (Schank, 1994). That is, everything that we do is intended to fulfill some goal. That goal may be simple, like satiating hunger or getting more comfortable, or it may be more complex, like developing new career skills or studying for a master's degree. When learners are actively and willfully trying to achieve a cognitive goal (Scardamalia & Bereiter, 1994), they think and learn more because they are fulfilling an intention. Technologies have traditionally been used to support teachers' goals but not those of learners. Technologies need to engage learners in articulating and representing their understanding, not that of teachers. When learners use technologies to represent their actions and construction, they understand more and are better able to use the knowledge that they have constructed in new situations. When learners use computers to do skillful planning for doing everyday tasks or constructing and executing a way to research a problem they want to solve, they are intentional and are learning meaningfully.

- **Authentic (Complex/Contextual)**   Most lessons learned in schools focus on general principles or theories that may be used to explain phenomena that we experience. However, teachers and professors remove those ideas from their natural contexts in order to be able to cover the curriculum more efficiently. When they do, they strip those principles of the contextual cues that make them meaningful. Physics courses are a prime example. Teachers read a simplified problem and immediately represent the problem in a formula. Students may learn to get the correct answer, but what are they learning? Learning isn't meaningful because students learned to understand the ideas only as algorithmic procedures outside of any context, so they have no idea how to relate the ideas to real-world contexts. Everything physical that occurs in the world involves physics. Why not learn physics through baseball, driving, walking, or virtually any other physical process on earth?

   Most contemporary research on learning has shown that learning tasks that are situated in some meaningful real-world task or simulated in some case-based or problem-based learning environment are not only better understood and remembered but also more consistently transferred to new situations. Rather than abstracting ideas in rules that are memorized and then applied to other canned problems, learning should be embedded in real-life, useful contexts for learners to practice using those ideas.

- **Cooperative (Collaborative/Conversational)**   Humans naturally work together in learning and knowledge-building communities, exploiting each others' skills and appropriating each others' knowledge. In the everyday world, humans naturally seek out others to help them to solve problems and perform tasks. Then why do educators insist that learners work independently so much of the time? Schools generally function based on the belief that learning is an independent process, so learners seldom have the opportunity to "do anything that counts" in collaborative teams despite their natural inclinations. When students collaborate without permission, educators may even accuse them of cheating despite the fact that such cross-fertilization is encouraged in any self-respecting design studio. However, we believe that relying solely on independent methods of instruction cheats learners out of more natural and productive modes of thinking. Often, educators will promote collaborative methods of learning, only to resort to independent assessment of learning. Learners, they believe, must be accountable for their own knowledge, so even if you agree, at least in principle, with collaborative learning principles, the hardest part of applying your beliefs will be assessing learners in teams. Most of the technology-based activities described throughout this book are more effectively performed collaboratively in groups, so we must assess the performance of the groups as well as individuals. Learners are strategic enough to know "what counts" in classrooms, so if they are evaluated individually, collaborative learning activities will fail because students realize that their outcomes are not important.

Collaboration most often requires conversation among participants. Learners working in groups must socially negotiate a common understanding of the task and the methods they will use to accomplish it. That is, given a problem or task, people naturally seek out opinions and ideas from others. Technologies can support this conversational process by connecting learners in the same classroom, across town, or around the world (see chapters 6 and 7). When learners become part of knowledge-building communities both in class and outside of school, they learn that there are multiple ways of viewing the world and multiple solutions to most of life's problems. Conversation should be encouraged because it is the most natural way of meaning making.

As is depicted in Figure 1.1, these characteristics of meaningful learning are interrelated, interactive, and interdependent. That is, learning and instructional activities should engage and support combinations of active, constructive, intentional, authentic, and cooperative learning. Why? Because we believe that these characteristics are synergetic. That is, learning activities that represent a combination of these characteristics result in even more meaningful learning than the individual characteristics would in isolation.

There are many kinds of learning activities that engage meaningful learning, just as there are teachers who for years have engaged students in meaningful learning. We argue throughout this book that technologies can and should become the tools of meaningful learning. Technologies afford students the opportunities to engage in meaningful learning when they learn *with* the technology, not *from* it.

How Does Technology Facilitate Learning?

Learning From *Technology*

Some of the first educational technologies were illustrations in 17th-century books and slate chalkboards in 18th-century classrooms. Educational technologies in the 20th century include lantern-slide and opaque projectors, later radio, and then motion pictures. During the 1950s, programmed instruction emerged as the first true educational technology, that is, the first technology developed specifically to meet educational needs. With every other technology, including computers, educators recognized its importance and debated how to apply each nascent commercial technology for educational purposes. Unfortunately, educators have almost always tried to use technologies to teach students in the same ways that teachers had always taught. So information was recorded in the technology (e.g., the content presented by films and television programs), and the technology presented that information to the students. The students' role was to learn the information presented by the technology, just as they learned information presented by the teacher. The role of the technology was to deliver lessons to students, just as trucks deliver groceries to supermarkets (Clark, 1983). If you deliver groceries, people will eat. If you deliver instruction, students will learn. Not necessarily! We will tell you why later.

The introduction of modern computer technologies in classrooms has followed the same pattern of use. Before the advent of microcomputers in the 1980s, mainframe computers were used to deliver drill and practice and simple tutorials for teaching students lessons. When microcomputers began populating classrooms, the natural inclination was to use them in the same way. A 1983 national survey of computer uses showed that drill and practice was the most common use of microcomputers (Becker, 1985).

Later in the 1980s, educators began to perceive the importance of computers as productivity *tools*. The growing popularity of word processing, databases, spreadsheets, graphics programs, and desktop publishing was enabling businesses to become more productive. So students in classroom began word processing and using graphics packages and desktop publishing programs to write with (see chapter 4). This tool conception pervaded computer use according to a 1993 study by Hadley and Sheingold that showed that well-informed teachers were extensively using text processing tools (word processors), analytic and information tools (especially databases and some spreadsheet use), and graphics tools (paint programs and desktop publishing) along with instructional software (including problem-solving programs along with drill and practice and tutorials).

The development of inexpensive multimedia computers and the eruption of the Internet in the mid-1990s quickly changed the nature of educational computing. Communications tools (e.g., e-mail and computer conferences) and multimedia, little used according to Hadley and Sheingold, have dominated the role of technologies in the classroom ever since. But what are the students producing? Too often, they are using the technology to reproduce what the teacher or textbook told them or what they copy from the Internet.

Our conception of educational computing and technology use, described next, does not conceive of technologies as teachers or repositories of information. Rather, we believe that, in order to learn, students should teach the computer or use the technology to represent what they know rather than memorizing what teachers and textbooks tell them. Technologies provide rich and flexible media for representing what students know and what they are learning. A great deal of research on computers and other technologies has shown that they are no more effective at teaching students than teachers, but if we begin to think about technologies as learning tools that students learn *with*, not *from*, then the nature of student learning will change.

Learning With Technology

If schools are to foster meaningful learning, then the ways that we use technologies in schools must change from technology-as-teacher to technology-as-partner in the learning process. Before, we argued that students do not learn from technology but that technologies can support productive thinking and meaning making by students. That will happen when students learn *with* the technology. But how do students learn *with* technologies? How can technologies become intellectual partners with students? Throughout this book, we assume the following:

- Technology is more than hardware. Technology consists also of the designs and the environments that engage learners. Technology can also consist of any reliable technique or method for engaging learning, such as cognitive learning strategies and critical thinking skills.
- Learning technologies can be any environment or definable set of activities that engage learners in active, constructive, intentional, authentic, and cooperative learning.
- Technologies are not conveyors or communicators of meaning. Nor should they prescribe and control all of the learner interactions.
- Technologies support meaningful learning when they fulfill a learning need—when interactions with technologies are learner initiated and learner controlled and when interactions with the technologies are conceptually and intellectually engaging.
- Technologies should function as intellectual tool kits that enable learners to build more meaningful personal interpretations and representations of the world. These tool kits must support the intellectual functions that are required by a course of study.
- Learners and technologies should be intellectual partners, where the cognitive responsibility for performance is distributed by the part of the partnership that performs it better.

How Technologies Foster Learning

If technologies are used to foster meaningful learning, then they will not be used as delivery vehicles. Rather, technologies should be used as engagers and facilitators of thinking. Based on our conception of meaningful learning (Figure 1.1), we suggest the following roles for technologies in supporting meaningful learning:

- Technology as tools to support knowledge construction:
  - for representing learners' ideas, understandings, and beliefs
  - for producing organized, multimedia knowledge bases by learners
- Technology as information vehicle for exploring knowledge to support learning by constructing:
  - for accessing needed information
  - for comparing perspectives, beliefs, and worldviews

- Technology as authentic context to support learning by doing:
  - for representing and simulating meaningful real-world problems, situations, and contexts
  - for representing beliefs, perspectives, arguments, and stories of others
  - for defining a safe, controllable problem space for student thinking
- Technology as social medium to support learning by conversing:
  - for collaborating with others
  - for discussing, arguing, and building consensus among members of a community
  - for supporting discourse among knowledge-building communities
- Technology as intellectual partner (Jonassen, 2000) to support learning by reflecting:
  - for helping learners to articulate and represent what they know
  - for reflecting on what they have learned and how they came to know it
  - for supporting learners' internal negotiations and meaning making
  - for constructing personal representations of meaning
  - for supporting mindful thinking

How Technologies Foster Thinking

Why do these uses of technology foster meaningful learning? It is because they require that students think and reason. In this book, we argue that students do not learn from teachers or from technologies. Rather, students learn from thinking—thinking about what they are doing or what they did, thinking about what they believe, thinking about what others have done and believe, thinking about the thinking processes they use—just thinking and reasoning. Thinking mediates learning. Learning results from thinking. What kinds of thinking are fostered when learning *with* technologies?

Causal Causal reasoning is one of the most basic and important cognitive processes that underpin all higher-order activities, such as problem solving. Hume called causality the "cement of the universe" (Hume, 1739/2000). Reasoning from a description of a condition or set of conditions or states of an event to the possible effect(s) that may result from those states is called *prediction*. A baseball pitcher predicts where the ball will go by the forces that he or she applies when pitching the ball. When an outcome or state exists for which the causal agent is unknown, then an inference is required. That is, reasoning backward from effect to cause requires the process of inference. A primary function of inferences is diagnosis. For example, based on symptoms, historical factors, and test results of patients who are thought to be abnormal, a physician attempts to infer the cause(s) of that illness state. Thinking causally is also required for making explanations. Explaining how things work requires learner to identify all the causal connections among the things being explained.

Causal thinking is really more complex than learners understand. In order to be able to understand and apply causal relationships, learners must be able to quantify attributes of causal relationships (direction, strength, probability, and duration) as well as be able to explain the underlying mechanisms describing the relationship (Jonassen & Ionas, 2007). Why does a force applied to a ball cause it to move in certain direction?

Analogical If you distill cognitive psychology into a single principle, it would be to use analogies to convey and understand new ideas. That is, understanding a new idea is best accomplished by comparing and contrasting it to an idea that is already understood. In an analogy, the properties or attributes of one idea (the analogue) are mapped or transferred to another (the source or target). Single analogies are also known as synonyms or metaphors. One word conveys attributes to the other, often using the word "like" or "as" as a connector. Following Hurricane Katrina in 2005, New Orleans was said to be inundated with a "toxic gumbo." Gumbo is a complex New Orleans–style soup that contains a variety of ingredients. The waters that surrounded New Orleans contained a complex variety of toxic substances—thus metaphor as analogy.

People most commonly think of syllogism as analogies. A syllogism is a four-part analogy. For example, love is to hate as peace is to ———. The analogy makes sense only if the structural characteristics of the first analogy can be applied to the second.

In using technologies to represent their understanding, students consistently are required to engage in the comparison–contrast reasoning required to structurally map the attributes of one or more idea to others, that is, to draw an analogy.

Expressive Using technologies as tools to learn *with* entails learners representing what they know, that is, teaching the computer. To do so, learners must express what they know. Using different tools requires learners to express what they know in different ways. Chapter 4 describes how technologies can be used to help learners express themselves in writing. Chapter 5 illustrates how learners can express themselves using a variety of tools, such as databases, spreadsheets, and expert systems, each tool requiring different forms of expression. Chapters 6 and 7 show how technologies can support verbal expression, while chapter 9 focuses on visual expressions. Contrast these varieties of expressions to those required by state-mandated tests, where students' only form of expressions is the selection of answer a, b, c, or d.

Experiential Experiences result in the most meaningful and resistant memories. We can recall with clarity experiences that we have had many years before. The primary medium for expressing experiences is the story. Stories are the oldest and most natural form of sense making. Stories are the "means [by] which human beings give meaning to their experience of temporality and personal actions" (Polkinghorne, 1988, p. 11). Cultures have maintained their existence through different types of stories, including myths, fairy tales, and histories. Humans appear to have an innate ability and predisposition to organize and represent their experiences in the form of stories. Learning with technologies engages stories in a couple ways. First, the experiences that students have while using technologies to represent their understanding are meaningful and memorable. Second, students may seek out stories and use technologies to convey them (see chapters 5 and 9).

Problem Solving   Using technologies to express and convey learner knowledge all entail different kinds of problems solving. Learning with technologies requires that students make myriad decisions while constructing their representations. Deciding what information to include and exclude, how to structure the information, and what form it should take are all complex decision-making processes. Students also engage in a lot of design problem solving while constructing their interpretations. They also must solve rule-using problems in how to use software. When learners are solving problems, they are thinking deeply and are engaged in meaningful learning. What they learn while doing so will be so much better understood and remembered than continuously preparing to answer multiple-choice test questions.

Conclusion

An underlying assumption of this book is that the most productive and meaningful uses of technology will not occur if technologies are used in traditional ways—as delivery vehicles for instructional lessons. Technology cannot teach students. Rather, learners teach the technologies. Meaningful learning will result when technologies engage learners in the following:

- Knowledge construction, not reproduction
- Conversation, not reception
- Articulation, not repetition
- Collaboration, not competition
- Reflection, not prescription

We argue that technologies can support meaningful learning when students learn with the technology, not from it. When students use technologies to investigate (chapter 2), explore (chapter 3), write (chapter 4), build models (chapter 5), build communities (chapter 6), communicate with others (chapter 7), design (chapter 8), and visualize (chapter 9), then they are engaged in deeper levels of thinking and reasoning, including causal, analogical, expressive, experiential, and problem solving. Technologies are lousy teachers, but they can be powerful tools to think with. That is the theme that we describe in the remainder of this book.

Things to Think About

If you would like to reflect on the ideas that we presented in this chapter, consider your responses to the following questions.

1. If learners cannot know what the teacher knows because they do not share a common knowledge and experience base, how can we be certain that students learn important things? For instance, if you want to teach

students about the dangers of certain chemical reactions in the lab, how do we ensure that learners know and understand those important lessons?

2. What is your theory of learning? From your perspective, how do people learn? What are the important processes?

3. Is it possible to learn (construct personal meaning) without engaging in some activity; that is, is it possible to learn simply by thinking about something? What are you thinking about? Can you think of an example?

4. When learners construct knowledge, what are they building? How is it possible to observe the fruits of their labor, that is, the knowledge they construct?

5. Think back to your childhood. What can you remember from your early childhood? Where did your remembrance occur? What meaning did it have at the time? How has that meaning changed over time?

6. Think about a recent controversial topic that you have heard or read about. What are different sides arguing about? What do they believe? What assumptions do they make about what is causing the controversy? Where did those beliefs come from?

7. Radical constructivists argue that reality exists only in the mind of the knower. If that is true, is there a physical world that we live in? Prove it.

8. Some educators argue that we learn much more from our failures than from our successes. Why? They believe that we should put students in situations where their hypotheses or predictions fail. Can you think of a situation in which you learned a lot from a mistake?

9. Recall the last difficult problem that you had to solve. Did you solve it alone, or did you solicit the help of others? What did you learn from solving that problem? Can that learning be used again?

10. Can you learn to cook merely from watching cooking shows on television? What meaning do you make from the experiences that you observe? Will the experience you have when you prepare a dish be the same as that of the television chef? How will it be different?

11. Technology is the application of scientific knowledge, according to many definitions. Can you think of a teaching technology (replicable, proven teaching process) that does not involve machines?

12. Can you calculate the exact square root of 2,570 without a calculator? Does the calculator make you smarter? Is the calculator intelligent?

13. Describe the difference in thinking processes engaged by a short-answer versus a multiple-choice test question. Are they different? Are they assessing knowledge? Is that knowledge meaningful? Why or why not?

14. Can you think of an activity that makes you dumber, not smarter? Do you not learn anything from that activity?

15. Have you ever produced your own video, movie, slide show, or computer program? How did it make you think? How did it make you feel?

References

Becker, H. J. (1985). *How schools use microcomputers: Summary of a 1983 national survey.* (ERIC Document Reproduction Service No. ED 257448)

Clark, R. (1983). Mere vehicles. *Review of Educational Research, 53*(4), 445–459.

Hadley, M., & Sheingold, K. (1993). Commonalities and distinctive patterns in teacher interaction of computers. *American Journal of Education, 101*(3), 261–315.

Hume, D. (1739/2000). *A treatise of human nature.* Oxford, UK: Oxford University Press.

Jonassen, D. H. (2000). *Computers as mindtools in schools: Engaging critical thinking.* Columbus, OH: Merrill/Prentice Hall.

Jonassen, D. H., & Ionas, I. G. (2007). Designing effective supports for causal reasoning. *Educational Technology: Research and Development,* 55.

Polkinghorne, D. (1988). *Narrative knowing and the human sciences.* Albany: State University of New York Press.

Scardamalia, M. & Bereiter, C. (1994). Computer support for knowledge building communities. *Journal of the Learning Sciences, 3*(3), 265–283.

Schank, R. C. (1994). Goal-based scenarios. In R. C. Schank & E. Langer (Eds.), *Beliefs, reasoning, and decision making: Psycho-logic in honor of Bob Abelson* (pp. 1–33). Hillsdale, NJ: Lawrence Erlbaum.

Investigating With Technologies

Table 2.1 Internet Technology Trends

Moving From:	Moving To:
Narrowband	Broadband
Plain, single mode (e.g., text or speech)	Multimodal rich connectivity
Tethered (wired) access	Untethered (wireless) access
Users adapting to the technology	The technology adapting to the user

When teachers offer students opportunities for investigation, they create the potential for rich, meaningful learning experiences. Technology can provide the means for active, authentic learning through investigation both in the classroom and in the field.

Costa and Kallick (2000) include flexibility as one of the "habits of mind" that are required for effective thinkers. This flexible thinking is as necessary for teachers as it is for their students in today's shifting times. Emerging and rapidly changing technologies demand individuals who are prepared to experiment, adopt, or discard technology tools as they appear, evolve, become successfully entrenched, or fall by the wayside.

Several predictions made in a national report of the Web-Based Education Committee (2000) have come to pass. The report indicated the shifts shown in Table 2.1.

Ubiquitous computing, or access to hardware giving students the ability to continually interact with digital tools, is a growing trend. Small laptops and handheld devices allow ubiquitous computing. A valuable characteristic of these small devices is their portability. Students are no longer harnessed to a desktop, a classroom, or even a physical building. This freedom enables more authentic data collection, as students can take devices into the field to collect, record, and analyze information.

Internet technology is faster, multifaceted, and increasingly intelligent, as it remembers users' past actions, preferences, and history. Agents use data-mining techniques in order to learn and discover users' behaviors, and they interact with one another to share knowledge about their users. The Internet has become an almost unimaginable network of resources, and one can spend vast amounts of time cruising through Web sites. Learning to effectively harness those resources as true educational tools is a challenging task for educators. It is vital that we teach students the essential skills to become information literate citizens.

Let's take a look at how the Internet and mobile technologies can be used to support students' investigations, along with some of those essential skills they will need.

Information Gathering With Internet Resources

In the following sections, we explore how to use the Internet as a source of information for compelling, meaningful learning. Collaborative problem- and project-based learning activities often begin with online research as a first step.

The important thing to remember is that research is just a step—a means to a bigger end.

Too many educators tacitly equate information searching with learning. They believe that if students are busily searching for information online, they will naturally make sense out of what they find. Yet researchers have found (Fidel et al., 1999; Schacter, Chung & Dorr, 1998) that when students search for predetermined answers, they are not comprehending or reflecting on the meaning of what they have found. Their intention is to complete the assignment—to find the one answer that the teacher is looking for. Simply asking students to find information on the Web will probably not result in learning. Unless there is an intentional outcome, researching is a meaningless activity. Unfortunately, research often "ends with the harvesting of the data, rather than extending into the next stage of the process. While a Web hunt for close-ended questions from a Web site might technically be a form of research, it lacks the value of an active learning experience that can result if the information gathered is applied" (Kelly, 2000, p. 6).

Yet information searching is essential to meaning making and problem solving. In order to learn from information being sought, students must have an intention to find information that will help them solve a problem. They must have a purpose other than fulfilling the requirements of an assignment. Intentional information searching requires at least a four-step process: (a) plan, (b) use strategies to search the Web, (c) evaluate, and (d) triangulate sources (Jonassen & Colaric, 2001).

With the concept of "research as first step" firmly in mind, let's consider what it takes to become competent in using the Internet for information searches.

Searching for Information

Using the Internet as the vast online library that it is, requires multiple skills. Effective information gleaning from the Internet combines expertise in searching for information, evaluating the worth of that information, and then organizing the information to make it more readily usable.

Finding the information one needs on the Internet can be extremely challenging because of the billions of Web pages that are available. Among the concerns about the Internet as a learning tool is that there are so many interesting topics to explore and it is so easy to explore that students are often off task, following links that take them away from rather than toward their learning goal. In planning a search, students are required to identify what they need to know.

First, students should articulate their intention and verbalize what is being looked for as well as *why* that information is needed. This thought process activates knowledge that the learner already has and clarifies for the learner the dissonance that exists. Next, the learner must develop a conscious and intentional search strategy in order to locate information sources that may be useful. Selection of search terms can be a difficult process. It will be necessary for you, the teacher, to model the process of asking questions, such as who, where, when, and what, in order to identify search terms that are associated with the problem. These terms can then be developed into a search string that would be appropriate to use in a search engine.

Along with the technical skill of conducting an effective search, learners also need to develop awareness and self-regulatory skills in order to make the Internet a tool for effective learning. As they navigate the Internet, they must also be thinking about the information they encounter and how it relates to their existing knowledge. Understanding requires thinking. Browsing does not necessarily cause thinking.

A self-regulated learner who keeps his or her information-seeking goals in mind and makes good decisions can find the Web an essential information resource during intentional learning. That is, the educational secret to the Internet is intentionality. When students say, "I am looking for information to help me answer a question/build my own knowledge base/evaluate someone else's ideas/and so on," then they will likely learn from the experience. As your students visit Web sites that have been identified, they also need to evaluate whether the information they find there supports the students' purpose. That is, does the site contain the information that they need to fulfill their intention? Are there any ideas at the site that can be used to answer the questions they are seeking? This type of reflective thinking allows the learner to reevaluate what he or she really needs and what is missing. If the learner thinks the original search worked, then satisfaction is attained, and the searching stops. Otherwise, the learner can narrow the search by adding additional terms, expand the search by removing some of the terms, or simply scratch the original search and start over.

How can we support students in conducting intentional searches with the metacognition that keeps them focused and productive? Equipping students with the skills to search effectively is the first step in using the Internet as a source of information. The I-Search model (Tallman & Joyce, 2005) is structured to scaffold students throughout the research process. One strategy for effective searching is understanding the different types of search tools that are available, their unique characteristics, how they work, and when a specific type is appropriate.

We can divide search tools into two broad categories: search engines and directories. Both search engines and directories are databases of Web sites, but they are constructed differently. Search engines such as Google use automated scripts known as robots (also called spiders or crawlers) that travel the Internet, cataloging Web pages for search engine databases.

Rather than searching by key words, as search engines do, directories such as Yahoo and LookSmart are databases that use a hierarchical structure, listing Web pages in convenient categories and subcategories. Directories are an easy place to find information when you are looking on the Web since people review the sites on them and group the sites into appropriate categories. However, this takes quite a bit of time and effort, so only a small fraction of the available sites on the Web are listed with each directory.

The Open Directory Project (ODP), or dmoz (from directory.mozilla.org, its original domain name), is an attempt to solve the problem of populating directories (see Figure 2.1). ODP is an open-content, multilingual directory of Web links

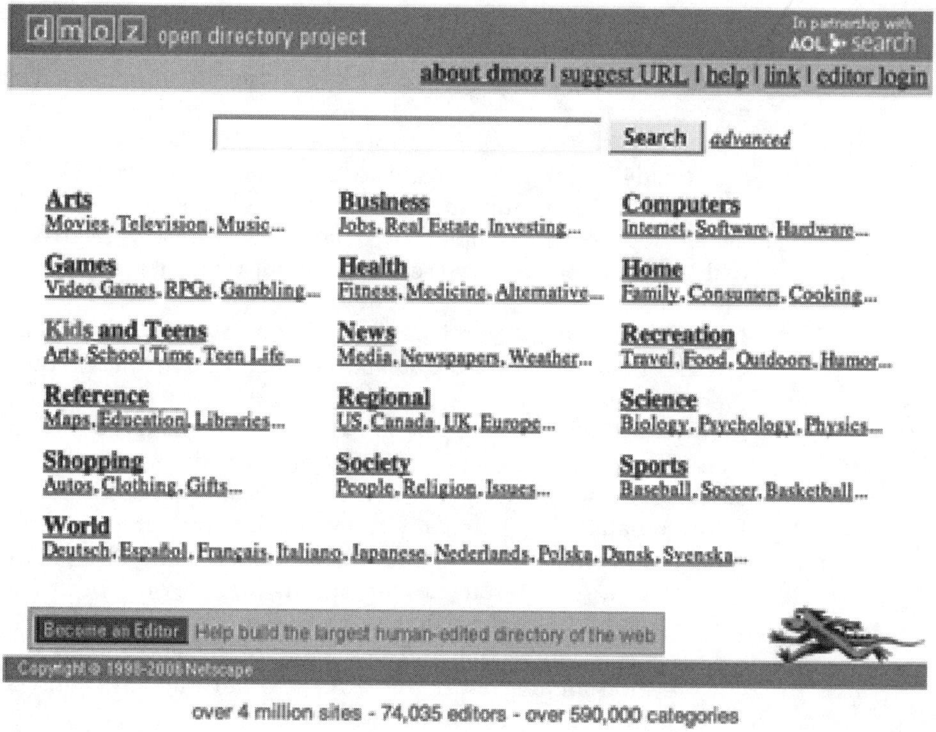

Figure 2.1 The dmoz Open Directory Project categories.

constructed and maintained by a global community of volunteer editors. By distributing responsibility for small portions of the Web among many people, ODP claims to be the largest, most comprehensive human-edited directory of the Web. We'll explore more social software applications like this in chapter 6.

To find obscure information or all the possible sites covering a subject, you need a more in-depth search. For this you need a search engine.

There are many search engines available on the Web, often using different methods of organizing and searching. Each search tool has specific features that may be best suited for particular information needs, as robots can use different methods for searching and indexing; therefore, the Web sites listed with each search engine may be different.

A subset of search engines is the meta–search engine. We can think of these powerful tools as a search engine clearinghouse. When a search is conducted in a meta–search engine, such as Dogpile, IxQuick, or Metacrawler, it is sent to a number of search engines, and the results from these multiple search engines are returned.

Other search engine subsets include specialized engines that hunt for specific types of Internet resources, such as Newslookup.com and WebMD for news and medical topics. Whatis.com is a specialized directory for technology topics, and ePals.com has a list of education-related Web directories and search engines.

You may notice "Sponsored Links" on some search results pages. These links are paid advertisements that have been purchased by companies or organizations who want to have their Web site links prominently displayed when you search for certain words or phrases.

Some search sites have integrated search engines and directories, along with customized features that individualize the search experience for users. For example, Yahoo's old directory structure exists alongside its newer, crawler search function. Other "Web portal" examples are Excite and Lycos. Most search engines include links with directions on advanced search techniques for that particular tool.

Invisible Web   Beyond the links found by popular search engines such as Google are many searchable databases that are sometimes known as the "invisible Web" because they aren't directly indexed by conventional search engines and require a direct query. Some are free (e.g., AskERIC and FindArticles), some charge for access (e.g., EBSCO, OVID, and Medline), and some have both free and subscription sections (e.g., New York Times and Wall Street Journal). Information in these databases is typically more specific, of better quality, and found more quickly and efficiently than information from general Web pages.

Here are some strategies for tapping into the deep or invisible Web:

- Consider the Web as just one part of the whole Internet
- Find an article title in ERIC or other databases and search for it with Google Scholar or other search tools
- Look for bibliographies on the Web that can be incorporated into searches for books, journal articles, or other documents
- Search for authors from books and journals
- Search for organizations and government reports
- Follow citations onto the Web
- Check e-mail addresses to contact authors for further information (Vidmar, 2003)

Feeds   It isn't always necessary to actively search out Web information, as feeds now allow published Web site content to be automatically delivered to a user. RSS (Really Simple Syndication) was the first syndication feed format; Atom is another.

Feeds use a technology called XML (Extensible Markup Language) to deliver headlines and summaries to your desktop or Web browser. A feed is a regularly updated summary of Web content along with links to full versions of that content. The feed's text file uses XML to include information describing the content and the location of this content on the originating Web site. This document is then registered with one of the directories that list syndication feed sites.

To subscribe to a feed and have it display in a readable format, you'll need what's called a feed reader or aggregator. Otherwise, when you click on an RSS or Atom feed link, your browser may display a page of unformatted gibberish. Feeds may be delivered to your desktop through a separate reader application (e.g., SharpReader, RSS Reader, NetNewsWire, or NewzCrawler) or through your Web browser (e.g., Google Reader, Bloglines, or NewsGator). There are many free and inexpensive feed readers, and most readers support both RSS and Atom formats. About.com has extensive information about feed readers and aggregators for Windows and Macintosh platforms (http://email.about.com/od/rssfeedreaders/). The Firefox browser supports Live Bookmarks, a system that detects RSS feeds and allows users to subscribe. If a Web site offers an RSS feed, the Live Bookmark icon can be clicked, and the feed will appear in your bookmark list.

Rocketinfo is an RSS search company with free tools, such as Rocket Researcher, an easy-to-use desktop search utility that searches news, headlines, RSS feeds, and weblogs. Rocket Researcher includes a built-in RSS reader, RSS channel, and alerting feature. The Rocket Searchbar, which resides on the desktop, searches over 16,000 news sources and maintains your search history, making it easy to repeat searches.

Individualizing and Organizing Searches   With the plethora of search tools available, choosing the most appropriate ones that will return resources best aligned with your needs can be daunting. After searching for relevant Web sites to gather information, some means of organizing and saving those sites is needed. Not surprisingly, with the exponential growth of Internet resources, new tools have been developed to meet these needs.

Over the past few years, many small search engines have disappeared, with Google becoming the most popular search engine on the Web. It is, in fact, so widely used that both the *Oxford English Dictionary* and the *Merriam-Webster Collegiate Dictionary* added "google" as a verb that means using the Google search engine to find information on the Internet (Bylund, 2006; Harris, 2006). The proliferation of Google tools continues, with several specialized search engines among them. For example, Google Scholar focuses searches on scholarly literature, such as articles, books, theses, and peer-reviewed papers from universities, academic publishing companies, and professional organizations. Google's preferences allow a user to define the number of desired results to be returned, what language(s) are included in the pages searched, and which of three filtering levels is used. When one creates a free Google account, the option for personalized searches is offered. Personalized searches find the results most relevant to you, based on what you've searched for in the past. This search feature also allows one to view and manage past searches and note trends in one's search activity, including top searches, most visited Web sites, and daily activity.

Several search tools, including Google, allow users to create bookmarks that can be accessed from any computer. Intelligent search and bookmark organizing is supported through tools such as A9.com, offered by Amazon. A9 personalizes searches by remembering what you've done and organizing your prior searches according to time, giving you the means to see and access results of searches you have done in the past. A9 also functions as a guide or mentor by suggesting new sites you might be interested in, based on previous searches you've done. Using A9 allows you to make notes about Web pages you visit, then automatically save those notes for subsequent searching and use. Bookmarks saved on A9 are retrievable from any computer.

One type of social software (see chapter 6) is exemplified in a growing number of social bookmarks managers. Social bookmarking sites are an increasingly popular way to locate, classify, rank, and share Internet resources. Social bookmarking services usually organize their content using tags, which can be used like key words to search for bookmarks that others have shared. These sites rank the resources according to the number of users who have bookmarked them.

Social bookmark managers allow one to easily add sites to a personal link collection and categorize those sites with key words. Collections can be shared and accessed on other computers as well as your own. When one registers for the service, a simple bookmarklet can be added to the browser. After finding a Web page you'd like to add to your list, simply select the bookmarklet, and you are prompted for information about the page. One may add descriptive terms to group similar links together, modify the title of the page, and add extended notes for oneself or for others.

One of the earliest social bookmarking sites was del.icio.us. Another site, Diigo (Digest of Internet Information, Groups and Other stuff), features "Social Annotation." In addition to sharing bookmarks with others, which is part of social bookmarking, Diigo enables a user to add the equivalent of a sticky note to Web pages. Diigo likens this to a giant transparency lying over all Web pages. Users can write on the transparency with either private notes or public comments; comments designated as public can been read by all, with interaction through subsequent responses. Another interesting tool Diigo offers is one that allows a user to highlight text from a Web page, then instantly add it to a personal blog post (see Figure 2.2).

The human involvement in adding and classifying Internet resources makes social bookmarking services function somewhat like directories. However, rather than having designated employees doing the work, it is distributed among all users, similar to the Open Directory Project model. Many social bookmarking

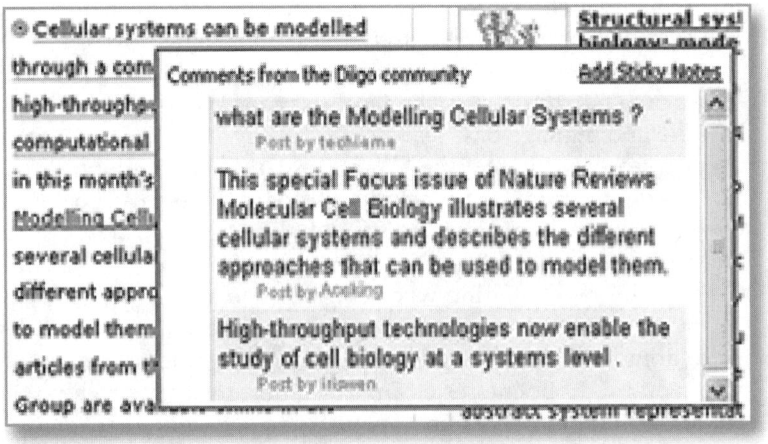

Figure 2.2 Diigo's highlight and sticky note feature.

services allow users to subscribe to syndication RSS feeds based on tags in order to learn of new resources for a given topic as they are noted, tagged, and classified by other users in this continual process.

Traditional Web-based bookmarking tools still exist, both as Web services and as built-in browser functions. Portaportal (http://portaportal.com/) and Backflip (http://backflip.com) are Web-based bookmarking utilities that allow users to store links online so they are accessible from any computer with Internet access. Internet browsers can offer useful features beyond the standard bookmark or favorites list. Firefox supports tabs, wherein subsequent Web sites can be opened in a new tab within the same window. When saving to Firefox's bookmark folder, the option for saving all tabs into one folder is given, enhancing organization. Another organization strategy is using the browser's history feature to track searches. Firefox organizes searches in daily history folders, allowing a user to trace the progression of searched sites and backtrack if needed.

Other tools for managing links are directories for educators such as eThemes (http://ethemes.org) and TrackStar (http://trackstar.hprtec.org/), which are two collections of Web sites that are organized thematically. Finally, NoodleTools is a set of online tools that supports research—including NoodleQuest, a wizard that suggests search strategies based on your answers to several questions.

Evaluating

Once information has been located, what next? Anyone who has access to a server can create and post Web pages. Students, often with teachers' and parents' blessings, construct their own representations by appropriating information and graphics from other Web sites without evaluating the viability of the ideas. There are no Internet police. Anyone can put anything on an Internet server (propaganda, pornography, and perjury), and they often do. Commercial sites are the fastest growing on the Internet. Organizations committed to hatred are finding new voice on the Internet. It is vital that students learn how to discriminate fact from fiction, information from opinion, and reality from fantasy. So how do we determine what is or is not accurate? Knowing whether a Web site is reputable and contains accurate information is the next essential step in using the Internet as a source of information.

When Web sites are located, the information contained in them must be evaluated. That evaluation process should engage the learner in two separate aspects of evaluation: relevancy and credibility. First, is the information on the site related to the problem? Does it contribute to the intention of the search? That is, does the site contain information that pertains to the learner's expressed intention? Does it provide an explanation, examples, alternative perspectives, or other pieces of information that the learner can use to construct his or her own knowledge?

Second, it is necessary that learners evaluate the credibility of the information. Evaluation of credibility usually involves two processes: evaluating the source of the information and evaluating the treatment of the subject. The teacher can model for the students the process of dissecting a Web site and should provide guiding questions to help students identify what to look for. Examples of questions to evaluate the source of the information include the following:

- Who provided this information? Why?
- Does the site author have authority in that field?
- If the site is published by an organization, is it one you recognize?
- Does the organization have a vested interest or bias concerning the information presented?
- Is the site owner affiliated with an organization (such as an educational institution or a government agency) that has authority in the stated subject area?
- Is it clear when the site was developed and last updated?
- Is a bibliography or resource list included?
- Are the references used in the bibliography credible?
- How can we validate the information provided? Can we check the sources?

Examples of questions to evaluate the treatment of the subject include the following:

- Is someone trying to sell us a product or point of view?
- What kind of site did it come from (.com = commercial, .gov = government, .edu = educational institution, and .org = nonprofit organization). How might the source affect the accuracy? Can we believe everything that comes from the government or an educational institution?
- Is the content factual or opinion? Does the information represent theory or evidence, fact or fiction, and so on? How do we distinguish between these?
- Does it follow a logical presentation of sequence?
- Is the intended audience clear?
- Are there any gaps in logic, or is there missing information that is relevant to the subject?
- Are there political or ideological biases?
- Is this primarily an advertising or a marketing site?
- If quotes or data are provided, are they properly referenced?
- Is the language used inflammatory or extreme?
- Is the text well written? Are there misspellings, or is poor grammar used?
- How do the visuals, sound, or animation influence how we interpret the information? Do visuals and text convey the same meaning?

In asking the learner to evaluate for relevancy and credibility, you are asking him or her to engage in reflective thinking about what is really needed and what is missing. You are also asking the student to question the authority of the documents and to become more information literate by critically evaluating sources of information. A final step in this process is to triangulate the search—identify at least two other sources that verify the information found.

Learning these critical information literacy skills should be mandatory for any students using the Internet to collect information. They are the first step as students investigate with Internet resources.

Things to Consider

Access Versus Safety   Many schools, concerned about students encountering offensive or objectionable material on the Web, employ Internet filtering software that screens for certain words or phrases and blocks access to that site. Unfortunately, filtering software is not perfect. First, it isn't very effective in blocking sites that promote hatred, violence, or illegal drugs (Consumer Reports Staff, 2005). Second, filtering software does not consider context when deciding whether a word such as "breast" is considered objectionable. Therefore, a student researching breast cancer would find many legitimate Web sites unavailable.

Two avenues of thought exist about the usefulness and appropriateness of installing filtering software in schools. The first line of reasoning goes something like, "The Internet, while offering valuable information, contains dangerous and inappropriate material from which students must be protected. Filtering software will prevent them from exposure to objectionable Web sites." Those holding the opposite viewpoint realize that students will not be shielded forever and believe that children should be taught what to do when they inadvertently run across offensive Web sites. They also see an opportunity to teach effective search skills that will increase the odds of obtaining useful, legitimate sites.

However, in 2000, the Children's Internet Protection Act (CIPA) was passed, requiring public libraries that receive federal funding to install and use Internet filtering software. Following the Supreme Court's 2003 upholding of a challenge to CIPA, the Center for Democracy and Technology published a set of guidelines to assist libraries in complying with CIPA requirements in a manner promoting free speech and robust access to information. By 2003, 96% of all public schools used some type of blocking software (Kleiner & Lewis, 2003). Librarians express concern over blocked sites that are clearly legitimate, citing the time and inconvenience of adults manually unblocking sites and fearing that students will not alert them to sites that are inadvertently blocked. They also voiced concern about the process of deciding which sites should be withheld, stating that technology specialists and software companies, rather than educators, were the decision makers (Consumer Reports Staff, 2005).

Finding moderate ground is a sensible solution. Filters allow one to set levels and types of content to filter. Search sites may have built-in filters (e.g., Google's SafeSearch filtering tool). For younger students, maximum protection may be required, with less interference desired for older students. Adjusting browser settings to disallow pop-up windows can reduce unwanted Web content. Perhaps the most important principle is that information literacy is an essential skill, one that teachers and parents are obligated to impart to children. Resources such as NetSmartz (http://www.netsmartz.org/) may be useful in helping students understand critical issues of Internet use.

Privacy   There are trade-offs between features, functionality, an individualized experience when using the Internet, and divulging personal information. When a search engine notes the searches one performs, this enables the tool to personalize your future service, such as suggesting searches based on your past queries, yet your privacy is compromised. The more personal information you divulge to search engines or any Web sites, the more vulnerable you are to possible misuse of that information. Students should be aware that information they choose to share on the Internet might also be shared with others, resulting in multiple databases containing that information.

Privacy issues are critical, and users don't always have control over the confidentiality of their data or actions. In May 2006, America Online (AOL) made an unauthorized release of about 20 million key word searches conducted by hundreds of thousands of its subscribers from March to May. The data were posted on a special AOL research Web site designed for the company to learn more about people's Internet searching habits. Although no names were attached to the search requests, some of the data were revealing enough to figure out the identities of the people behind the queries (Nakashima, 2006). At the time of this writing, privacy groups were urging the Federal Trade Commission to investigate and possibly penalize AOL (Associated Press, 2006), while top officials had resigned (Zeller, 2006).

Using Information to Build Knowledge With Open-Ended, Student-Directed Research Projects

In open-ended and student-directed research projects, students harvest the Internet's vast information bank to learn about topics, generally to produce some original work using their new knowledge. *Open ended* refers to the fact that the students are encouraged to learn as much as they can about the topic rather than simply finding answers to questions posed by the teacher. Good teachers use these projects to help students develop strategies to determine what information is important—to develop their own set of questions. *Student directed* implies that the students are in charge, making key decisions about search strategies, about which sites from the search returns look most promising, about what to collect, and about when to initiate conversations with information providers.

The Internet is a tool for facilitating knowledge exploration by learners. Although the Internet contains a wealth of information, it is little more than a virtual depository unless that information is transformed into knowledge through meaningful, reflective, active learning activities. Sending students on scavenger hunts or providing them with collections of Web sites does little to promote learning unless students are searching as a means to specific outcomes. When information is purposefully manipulated and reconstructed in authentic, meaningful learning tasks, the Internet becomes a powerful educational tool.

Building in complex learning goals strengthens the value of Internet-based learning. Exploration is most effective when learners articulate a clear purpose for their explorations—that is, exploring to find information to solve a problem, resolve an argument, construct an interpretation, and so on.

The Internet can be used as a tool to develop critical thinking skills as well as provide access to a variety of information and human resources. Riel (2000) argues, "The challenge of the knowledge-centered dimension of learning is to balance knowledge construction activities with activities that help students develop the suite of mental tools needed for this task".

Focusing Searches Using WebQuests and Student-Created WebQuests

One common instructional technique for using Internet information is the WebQuest. Unfortunately, the strong inquiry-based foundation for WebQuests as envisioned by their creator, Bernie Dodge, has often been ignored, with many WebQuests resembling little more than electronic worksheets. Well-designed WebQuests incorporate cooperative learning, consideration of multiple perspectives, analysis and synthesis of information, and creation of original products that demonstrate knowledge gained. A good WebQuest is an open-ended and student-directed research project.

Searching for information to be used in a WebQuest activity typically begins with a list of Web sites that have been previously selected. While a great deal of the information search and evaluation processes have already been done for students participating in a WebQuest, when students create WebQuests they take the lead in selecting and researching a topic of their choice. Engaging in a well-designed teacher-created WebQuest can be a terrific learning experience, but student-created WebQuests can be of even greater value. Students in two Chemistry 1 Advanced Placements classes brainstormed the topic "Nuclear Issues in the 21st Century" and identified a problem (Peterson & Koeck, 2001). After teacher-led brainstorming, responses were categorized to meet the teacher's instructional objectives. Student teams chose a category to develop, with the final WebQuest being a compilation of the categories.

To develop the WebQuest, students first evaluated existing WebQuests to understand the structure. They were introduced to the GAP model (Caverly, 2000 in Peterson & Koeck):

- **G**athering information
- **A**rranging information into meaningful formats
- Using technology tools to **P**resent that new knowledge to others

Searching for and critically analyzing information were seen as especially valuable for science students developing inductive thinking. As teams decided what to include in their portion of the WebQuest, they engaged in further critical thinking as individuals presented and defended the information they had found. When consensus was reached, teams used Inspiration software to create concept maps of their section. Each team had one person with Web development skills whose responsibility was creating the actual Web file for the WebQuest. When the WebQuest was completed, these students presented it to university faculty and preservice teachers. This type of authentic project whereby students actually

Table 2.2 WebQuest Task Comparison: Developing Versus Doing

Tasks for Developing a WebQuest	Tasks for Learning From a WebQuest
Define a problem	Respond to a problem
Develop questions	Respond to questions
Search for and evaluate resources	Evaluate information within preselected resources
Design a site with an audience in mind	Navigate within a site
Work on a team for project creation	Work on a team for problem solution
Synthesize information	Synthesize information
Apply logical thinking	Apply logical thinking
Consider and accept multiple possible solutions	Arrive at a possible solution to the problem

Source: Courtesy of Cynthia L. Peterson and Deborah C. Koeck

create a WebQuest rather than simply participate in one raises the WebQuest concept to a new level (see Table 2.2). The cognitive and social skills required to construct WebQuests offer a motivating, deep learning experience. Students made interdisciplinary connections and were challenged intellectually. At the same time, they gained experience with technology and presentation skills—and had fun!

Student-produced WebQuests engage problem solving. Developing a WebQuest requires a lot of purposeful information searching to fulfill a task that is designed by the students. Producing the WebQuest requires designing the task, the activities, the interface, and the procedures. These activities demand a lot of decision making, as does evaluation of the Internet resources that will be embedded within the WebQuest. We believe that even more valuable and constructive learning occurs when students produce a WebQuest than when they participate in a WebQuest.

Scientific Inquiry and Experimentation   An amazing number of Web sites are available to support students' diverse interests, with applications such as Flash animations offering highly interactive learning experiences. The Edheads Web site, for example, uses Flash to support investigations of force and simple machines, weather, and the human body.

The Web-based Inquiry Science Environment (WISE) is a free online science learning environment for students in grades 5 to 12. This Web site, supported by the National Science Foundation, offers a learning environment for students to examine real-world evidence and analyze current scientific controversies. Free teacher registration generates a student registration code that identifies a class, allows students to register, and creates a class account on WISE. Teachers may create original projects, copy and use existing projects, and access management tools for student assessment and feedback. WISE can be a good starting place for generating ideas and sparking areas of interest for students.

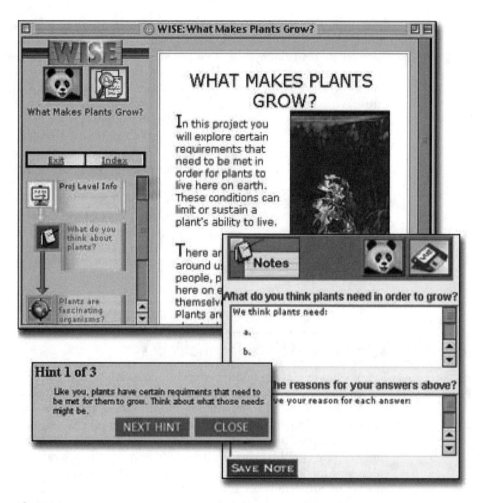

Figure 2.3 Images of the Essential Features of WISE, as Seen in the "What Makes Plants Grow?" project for grades 4 to 6. A browser window with the WISE inquiry steps and evidence about plants (background); reflection notes and a hint (foreground). *Source:* wise.berkeley.edu. Used with permission.

Using only a Web browser, special WISE software guides students through "evidence" Web pages that provide content, "notes" and "hints" that encourage students to reflect, and other tools for data visualization, causal modeling, simulations, online discussion with classmates, and assessment (see Figure 2.3). WISE engages students in searching for information to use in authentic, problem-solving situations.

Other WISE projects include "Cycles of Malaria," where students learn about the biology of the disease, where it is prevalent, and how it is spread. They compare three different strategies for controlling the spread of malaria. In "How Far Does Light Go?" students consider competing hypotheses about whether light goes on forever or eventually dies out. After examining a number of scenarios supporting each hypothesis, students debate the issue with their classmates. "Wolves in Your Backyard" involves students learning about wolf biology and predator–prey relationships. They survey different perspectives on wolf population control, including issues of depredation, hunting, and wildlife management (http://wise.berkeley.edu/pages/intro/wiseIntro03.html).

Teachers who used WISE projects with students report that it increases classroom interaction, reveals science as it is in the real world, and offers exciting resources that motivate kids to learn. One teacher said, "Students who were unmotivated at first demonstrated a tremendous amount of knowledge on the subject matter as they presented their evidence for the debate." Another teacher thought that WISE helped her students with critical thinking skills, causing them to ask, "'Does this make sense?'"—instead of kids tending to swallow everything and saying, 'Oh, there. It's all true.' I liked how [the project] seemed to intrigue them, and I heard some great questions from the kids [that] wouldn't have come up if they had been reading a textbook" (http://wise.berkeley.edu/pages/what_teachers_say.php).

Collecting Data With Mobile Technologies

Today's students are very different from those only a few years ago in terms of their experiences with and expectations of technology. This is a digital generation—one that has no memory of life without a multitude of technology tools. Cell phones, handheld computers, laptops, iPods and other mp3 players, digital cameras—all are part of daily life for many young people, and the lines of functionality between these devices are blurring. Cell phones and handhelds take pictures and have calendar functions; iPods play videos and podcasts transferred from a laptop or display pictures transferred from a cell phone. Wireless technology augments the increasing number of things one can do with these devices, as easy access to the Internet allows one to upload and download data anywhere there is an accessible wireless access point.

Prensky (2001, 2003, 2005) has labeled this generation "digital natives" and cautions those who were not born into but later adopted digital technology (the "digital immigrants") about the different language spoken by natives versus immigrants. His point is well taken—we must understand the fundamental differences between the way natives and immigrants perceive, value, and use technologies. Otherwise, we risk designing learning experiences with little relevance, interest, or meaning for students.

Wireless Internet learning devices, or WILDs, come in several forms. They may be handheld computers, small tablet notebooks, or even cell phones. Other countries, notably Europe, China, Japan, and the Phillipines, have already begun using cell phones as learning tools (Prensky, 2005). Prensky states, "Cell phones have enormous capabilities these days: voice, short messaging service (SMS), graphics, user-controlled operating systems, downloadables, browsers, camera functions (still and video), and geopositioning. Some have sensors, fingerprint readers, and voice recognition. Thumb keyboards and styluses as well as plug-in screens and headphones turn cell phones into both input and output mechanisms" (p. 12).

Prensky envisions cell phones as tools for accessing animations to support learning, for narrating guided tours, or to access language or vocabulary training. When one watches how quickly and effortlessly a teenager can key in a text message on a cell phone, it's not unreasonable to imagine a future where innovative educators take advantage of young people's familiarity with cell phones. The Pew Internet and American Life Project's "Teens and Technology" report found that almost half of teens (45%) own a cell phone and that 33% have used a cell phone to send a text message (Lenhart, Madden, & Hitlin, 2005). These numbers can be expected to increase as prices stabilize and cell phones become as commonplace as televisions and radios.

The relative low cost and small size of WILDs makes them ideal for ubiquitous learning and data collection in the field. Students can gather data and display and manipulate them to test predictions using WILDs in authentic environments.

Handhelds

Teachers have reported that handhelds are an effective tool for instruction and positively impact student motivation (Crawford & Vahey, 2002; Swan, van 't Hooft, & Kratcoski, 2005; Vahey & Crawford, 2002). Handheld computers (or "handhelds") are sometimes called personal digital assistants (PDAs) because of their organizing functions, such as calendar, task, and memo tools (see Figure 2.4). Like many small digital devices such as cell phones, there is great diversity with few standards, and companies sometimes merge or discontinue certain lines. Many handhelds used in education run on the Palm operating system, while Pocket PCs run a form of the Windows operating system. As with desktop Macs and PCs, these mobile systems are becoming more similar, and better compatibility should make them an increasingly viable option for schools.

Handheld features (and prices) can vary widely. High-end handhelds may include a digital camera, audio recording, USB port, and even an integrated Global Positioning Systems (GPS) receiver. Wireless Internet and cell phone service capability are common features, with additional costs for some service plans. In addition to using WiFi technology for wireless Internet access, Bluetooth or radio wave technology may be used. Bluetooth can connect a handheld with an Internet-capable cell phone, which is then used as the conduit for Internet access to the handheld.

Students can also use Bluetooth to "beam" or send applications and files from one handheld to another. Information, such as files or applications, is transferred, or synched, between a computer and handheld by using a WiFi or Bluetooth connection or by connecting the two devices with a cable.

Figure 2.4   The Palm Tungsten E2.

Many applications are available for handhelds, including freeware, share-ware, and sophisticated retail software. One widely used handheld application is Documents to Go, which allows users to transfer Microsoft Office files between a computer and handheld (see Figure 2.5). Files can be created and edited on either the computer or the handheld, then transferred wirelessly or by using the Hotsynch cable.

Count It (http://www.palmspot.com/software/detail/ps4244a_98104.html) is an inexpensive shareware program with 20 customizable counters that keep running totals, a timer, and an alarm. Saved data sets can be converted to .csv format and imported to a spreadsheet or database. Handheld animation soft-ware enables students to do such things as check sine waves and frequency when working on mathematical problems and then create a simulation. Data can also be represented in graphs and tables.

Perhaps the most commonly perceived problem with handheld use is the small screen size. While reading on a miniature screen seems unworkable for many adults, it appears that children don't regard it as difficult (Prensky, 2003). Many students, accustomed to the scale of Gameboys and other miniature devices, become quite proficient at using a handheld's small keys or writing on its screen with the stylus. However, the inexpensive keyboards that can be purchased for handhelds make them more closely resemble a computer and can make data input faster and easier.

Handhelds should be synched regularly with a computer to back up informa-tion. By giving each handheld a unique name, all students can synch their hand-helds on the same classroom computer. Other management issues include the need

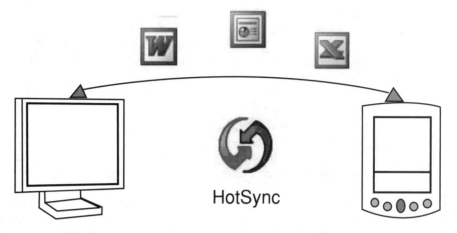

Figure 2.5   Microsoft Office files transfer between handhelds and computers.

for regular recharging, software compatibility with classroom computer operating systems, and physical use and storage of handhelds throughout the school day.

Sensor Technology

Many technologies are available to support scientific investigation. Sensor technology (probeware) can be combined with handhelds for highly interactive learning experiences. Probeware is a term that describes equipment and software used to gather and analyze data. Probeware systems can work with computers, handhelds, or graphing calculators. For example, Vernier's LabPro offers an assortment of sensors, software, and hardware interfaces that can be combined for collecting and analyzing data. This type of package might be used with a computer, graphing calculator, handheld, or GPS unit or on its own as a remote data collector.

Using probeware sensors and interfaces with handhelds facilitates interactive, inquiry-based learning by providing multiple representations of data as experiments are being conducted. Probes also make scientific experiments easier for students to perform and analyze (Tinker & Krajcik, 2001). Probeware is quite visual, with real-time data displayed as tables, graphs, meters, or values. Manipulating variables is easily accomplished, with instant visible results that graphically portray relationships, rules, and principles.

Probes can be used to support learning in chemistry, biology, math, and physics. They may measure such things as temperature, pH levels, voltage, pressure, force, motion, and magnetic fields. Probes use a transducer to convert the physical phenomena to an electrical signal, which is then converted to a number by analog interface circuitry and communicated to the computer. The analog interface may either be built into the sensor or be a separate piece of equipment in between the sensor and the computer.

Probes contain a microcomputer chip that can calibrate information and convert measurements to digital format. The sensor attaches to a handheld via the USB port, and additional software applications can extend what happens to data once they have been transferred. Built-in Bluetooth technology is replacing the hardwired method of data exchange between sensor and handheld. Bluetooth uses radio frequencies to transfer information between Bluetooth-compatible devices nearby, like computers, mobile phones, and other handhelds. For example, Palm's ImagiProbe Wireless Sensing System uses Bluetooth to connect sensors with handhelds from up to 10 meters away.

Wireless technology can also allow students to share data with other students as it is being collected. Imagine teams of students who are collecting information about water quality in a river. Team data can be combined through a handheld's wirelesss Internet connection, allowing students in the field to analyze data, look for trends, formulate hypotheses, and be guided toward other investigation. Student understanding of scientific and mathematic processes might then be demonstrated through NoviiAnimator or Sketchy, animation software for handhelds.

GPS

The GPS, a satellite-based navigation system comprised of a network of 24 satellites, was created by the U.S. Department of Defense for military applications but was made available for civilian use in the 1980s. GPS is free and works worldwide, anytime, in any type of weather.

Garmin, a navigation and communications equipment company, describes GPS functioning like this:

> GPS satellites circle the earth twice a day in a very precise orbit and transmit signal information to earth. GPS receivers take this information and use triangulation to calculate the user's exact location. A GPS receiver must be locked on to the signal of at least three satellites to calculate a 2D position (latitude and longitude) and track movement. With four or more satellites in view, the receiver can determine the user's 3D position (latitude, longitude and altitude). Once the user's position has been determined, the GPS unit can calculate other information, such as speed, bearing, track, trip distance, distance to destination, sunrise and sunset time and more.

Some handhelds are equipped with built-in GPS. In other cases, small GPS units, such as the Palm GPS Navigator, may work in conjunction with a handheld. Separately purchased GPS devices can be used in the field, with data transfer to a laptop or, later, to a desktop computer. A standard GPS receiver not only will place you on a map at any particular location but also will trace your path across a map as you move. If you leave your receiver on, it can stay in constant communication with GPS satellites to see how your location is changing.

GPS units can be used in an interesting activity known as geocaching. Like a treasure hunt, geocaching involves physically searching for a hidden cache whose location is given through GPS coordinates on a Web site. The cache container contains a logbook and items as rewards; finders are asked to leave something for the next person and to record the date and time in the logbook. On its own, geocaching utilizes students' problem-solving skills, mathematical thinking, and mapping abilities. Geocaching might be combined with a study of geology, the environment, or biology. As students navigate, they may encounter plants, animals, rocks, historical sites, and any number of things that lend themselves to additional learning. Teachers often find that nature guidebooks, digital cameras, audio and/or video recorders, and notepads are useful in GPS activities. Depending on the specific features it offers, a handheld can meet most of those needs. Sensor technologies are clearly another good fit when students take to the field for geocaching or other GPS work. There are many geocaching sites online; a good place to start is Geocaching—The Official Global GPS Cache Hunt Site at http://www.geocaching.com. GPS units and handhelds can also be used in conjunction with geographic information systems (GIS) (see chapter 9).

Conducting Field Experiments

Let's explore some uses of mobile technologies to see how they have been used with students in authentic learning situations.

Water Analysis Water quality evaluation is frequently conducted using handheld probes (Vahey & Crawford, 2002). Students take their Palms and probes to a nearby stream or other body of water. After individual students measure different points along the streambed, data are combined by beaming them to one another or aggregating them on one unit. When students return to the classroom, handhelds are used to graph and analyze the combined data set. For many teachers, finding nearby bodies of water to sample will be relatively easy. Depending on the results of the water analysis, students might research solutions for improving water quality, hypothesize about the effects on aquatic and amphibian life, determine where runoff is originating, or design a plan for filtering water.

NatureMapping The NatureMapping Program is combining GIS (see chapter 9) use with data collection in authentic work that connects schools with experts and communities. The program's vision is "to create a national network that links natural resource agencies, academia and land planners with local communities primarily through schools." NatureMapping incorporates species identification and data collection; data analysis, statistics, and graphics; and computers, remote sensing, GIS, local area networking, and the Internet.

Diane Petersen (2005) described NatureMapping work done in Waterville Elementary School in Waterville, Washington. Beginning in 1999, Petersen's fourth graders began working with local farmers to collect data about short-horned lizards, an at-risk species. Farmers, who were frequently in locations where these lizards might be spotted, logged information about when and where they were seen. Later, farmers and students worked together to locate fields on maps and create tables with data. Using aerial photographs of farmers' fields overlaid on digital maps, computer maps were then generated that depicted lizard sightings. Students also made spreadsheets to display related data. Students then generated a question, analyzed the data, and selected what was needed to graph information answering the question. Petersen describes this project as strengthening the school–community relationship. The serious, real-life contribution students are making has resulted in students who view themselves as scientists, with technology enhancing the work and partnerships. Initially, students collected data, but because the farmers were frequently in their fields and available to log information, they supplied most data in this particular case. However, students can do similar data collection, using handhelds or simple logging devices to record information.

Arbor Day/Earth Day Tree Exploration   Let's look next at an effective yet easy use of handhelds to collect field data. Suzanne Stillwell, a fourth grade teacher at a rural school in Hallsville, Missouri, described an Arbor Day/Earth Day activity using the school grounds as her students' laboratory. Before beginning the activity, students spent three 45-minute periods practicing with the technology so they would know how to use it. They also brainstormed data they could collect from trees on the school grounds. The information they decided to collect was girth of the tree (1 meter above the ground), height of the tree's shadow (correlated to the height of the tree, if measured at the right time of day), and types of leaf and tree identification. Students used this Web site to help understand the measurement of the tree's shadow: http://micro.magnet.fsu.edu/primer/java/scienceopticsu/shadows/.

Each partner team selected two trees on the school grounds and did the following:

1. Took a picture of the tree using the handheld cameras
2. Collected a leaf sample and took a picture of the leaf
3. Measured the girth of the tree in centimeters and recorded the information in an Excel table in Documents To Go on the handheld
4. Measured the shadow of the tree and recorded the information in an Excel table in Documents To Go on the handheld

After returning to the classroom, students beamed their information about the trees to two other teams. Each team then had information on six trees. Students uploaded the tree data to computers and made graphs showing the information of tree girth and height.

Students used their leaf samples and digital pictures to identify trees with the Missouri Department of Conservation tree manual and these online sources: http://www.grownative.org/index.cfm and http://www.mdc.mo.gov/nathis/plantpage/flora/motrees/.

Because this was one of the first projects done with handhelds, students were excited about the assignment. Some of the students figured out how to put the pictures of their trees on the Excel file with the graph and data table. There was strong motivation for students to record data and share information with each other through beaming between handhelds.

Denali National Park Fire Succession Study   This last example illustrates what can be done with the addition of sensor technology. In the summer of 2004, the Denali Borough School District teamed with the Eastern Area Fire Management of the National Park Service to study fire succession by monitoring the vegetation recovery in three burn areas in Alaska's Denali National Park and Preserve. Using Palm handhelds equipped with digital cameras and SmartList To Go, a program that allows one to create, view, and manage databases on a handheld, students first created a field guide of plants and animals they observed (see Figure 2.6).

Next, students used a Vernier temperature sensor (ImagiWorks) and software (ImagiProbe) to measure permafrost temperature and depth at each burn site. Documents To Go software enabled the creation of a Microsoft Excel spreadsheet recording temperature data and numbers of plant species found in each transect (see Figure 2.7).

Handhelds were synched with a laptop to transfer and combine data for a complete count of species coverage. Participants also represented their concept of fire succession by using handhelds to draw animations on their handhelds using Sketchy (see Figure 2.8).

In each of these instances, students are engaging in active, real-life work that goes beyond the classroom to involve data collection in the field. The use of technology enables students to measure, record, manipulate, share, and represent data as they are used to answer important questions. Activities such as these place

Figure 2.6   Field guide created by students. *Source:* Published by the Concord Consortium.

SheetToGo	▼ species_cove...

	E	H J K L M N P	AA
1			
2			
3			
4			
5	Species	2 4 5 6 7 8 10	Percent
6	Picea mariana (P. Mill.) B.S.P.	1 1	10
7	Picea glauca (Moench) Voss		0
8	Betula papyrifera Marsh.	1	5
9	Populus tremuloides Michx.	1	5
10	Populus balsamifera L.		0
11	Vaccinium uliginosum L.	1 1	10
12	Ledum palustre L.	1	5
13	Rosa acicularis Lindl.	1	5

✓ ✗

[Done] *fx* ◀ ◀ ◆ ▶ ▶   [Go]

Figure 2.7   Sheets To Go software for data collection.
Source: Published by the Concord Consortium.

Figure 2.8   Student's sketchy animation about fire succession. *Source:* Published by the Concord Consortium.

students in the role of investigating scientists and motivate them through interesting, authentic work that is relevant to their world.

Finding Opinions With Online Survey Tools

We live in a culture that is saturated with market research and opinion polls to find out what people think about all kinds of things. What is your opinion regarding this candidate, this issue, this media personality? What is your favorite (fill in the blank)? How often do you purchase this product, read this magazine, or eat at this restaurant? What do you think about the latest environmental problem? What are you willing to do or do without to solve it? Sampling is done via phone, paper questionnaires, and Web sites.

Online survey tools enable data collection opportunities across the curriculum. These tools range in functionality, ease of use, and cost. While there are perfectly acceptable free online survey Web sites (e.g., Free Online Surveys), frequent users may appreciate the added features that a subscription survey site offers. SurveyMonkey, illustrated in Figure 2.9, is one such site, as are Cool Surveys and Zoomerang. Free survey sites typically limit the number of questions, responses, and/or participants that are allowed. Subscription survey tools are more likely to allow unlimited surveys, customizing options, and data analysis tools that filter results to help users find patterns in the data. Other survey tool features can include sharing of results, downloadable files for export to spreadsheets, randomizing the order of answer choices to reduce bias, and requiring responses to questions the survey creator specifies (see Figure 2.9).

A third-grade teacher described using a simple online survey to begin a nutrition unit with her students. As students answered questions about their eating habits and knowledge of nutrition, they also learned math skills. After data

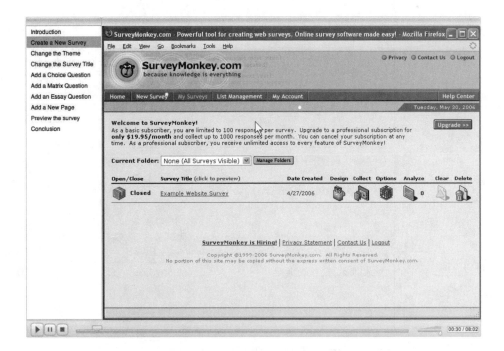

Figure 2.9 SurveyMonkey's free online survey tool. *Source:* SurveyMonkey.com

were collected, students created graphs depicting information such as the number of students who ate breakfast every day, how frequently students drank soda, and their favorite food selected from a list of 12 items. These results served as a springboard for discussions concerning reasons that students selected cookies as their favorite food, the influence of sugar in our diets, cause and effect, healthy eating, and how to make good food choices.

While the nutrition survey was conducted within a classroom, online surveys enable data collection from a wide audience. Students who are creating surveys themselves first need guidance in creating well-constructed survey questions. Timmerman (2003) suggests looking at examples of poorly and well-written questions, explaining the difference between open-ended and closed-ended questions, and considering how easily responses can be analyzed and graphed. Table 2.3 provides her rules and examples for writing good surveys.

Survey participants may be members of the originating class, students in other classes within the school or in other schools, students in other countries, teachers, or parents, depending on the purpose of the survey. Community groups

Table 2.3 Rules for Writing Good Surveys

Avoid bias	Biased: Do you think that using credit cards on the Internet is dangerous?
	Better: Which best describes how secure you think it is to shop on the Internet?
Avoid the words "and/or": one idea per question	More than one idea: Have you used a credit card for purchases on the Internet or in a store in the past month?
	Better: How many times in the past 6 months have you made a purchase with a credit card on the Internet?
Avoid long questions	Long: Given the complexity of balancing privacy and security when using credit cards on the Internet, do you think our laws adequately allow for both security and privacy?
	Better: Please indicate whether you agree or disagree with the following statement: There should be new laws to protect privacy on the Internet.
Avoid leading questions	Leading: Do you like shopping on the Internet better than shopping in a store?
	Better: Would you rather shop on the Internet, in a store, or it doesn't matter which?

Source: Courtesy of Annemarie Timmerman.

or organizations could be used to identify potential respondents. For example, students might contact the Audubon Society or World Wildlife Federation for an environmental survey needing expert opinions.

When students create surveys, they engage in learning that is intentional and authentic. Identifying the purpose of a survey, making decisions about the information that is needed, formulating well-designed questions that will elicit that information, and selecting the most appropriate respondents for gaining that information entail many cognitive processes. After data are collected, students must then analyze and evaluate the results, determining trends, possible causes and effects, and other phenomena that inform their purposes.

Conclusion

When students are given opportunities to investigate relevant, interesting phenomena and use the information they gather to solve problems, answer their questions, or inform others, they engage in learning that has significance and value. As we have seen, technologies can support and extend student investigations. Internet resources reach far beyond text files, with audio and video, graphics, and online simulations widely available. Tools such as online survey sites offer students a mechanism for data collection from a worldwide pool of participants.

Wireless devices can enable children to engage in flexible learning environments that permeate their daily lives (Inkpen, 1999; Soloway et al., 2001). Traditional lab settings that typically focus on the process of students collecting data are enhanced by the use of handhelds that encourage analysis and problem solving. Students can collect data and display and manipulate them to test predictions using WILDs and other handheld devices. While these technologies have much to offer, their value is determined largely by the way teachers integrate them into the curriculum. When thoughtfully used to promote active, reflective, complex learning, Internet and mobile technologies are at their best.

Things to Think About

Here are some questions to think about as you consider using Internet resources, handhelds, GPS units, and other WILDs with students.

1. What are the implications for teaching and learning when these tools are included in instruction?
2. What impact will handheld computers have on the curriculum?
3. How can WILDs be used to augment your existing curriculum?

4. Who will provide the support and training for use of handhelds and other WILDs?

5. Some people object to students using handhelds, arguing that these are unnecessary, frivolous, and little more than toys. How would you respond?

6. How can we evaluate the effectiveness of these devices?

7. How will we manage student use of WILDs?

8. What will happen if a student loses or breaks a WILD?

9. How will handhelds be physically cared for, especially if students take them home at night?

10. What information literacy skills do my students have?

11. What do my students need to know before engaging in Internet searches?

12. Are students' information searches conducted in a meaningful context?

13. How are students using the information they gain from Internet searches?

14. What is the Internet? Is it the computers, the programs, and multimedia documents that people store and make available, or is it the people who contribute the ideas? Or is the Internet "only minds."

15. Given the potential for students to encounter undesirable material on the Internet, what is the appropriate balance between protection and free access to information?

References

Associated Press. (2006, August 16). Group files FTC complaint Against AOL. *New York Times.* Retrieved August 16, 2006, from http://www.nytimes.com/aponline/technology/AP-AOL-Search-Privacy.html

Bylund, A. (2006, July 5). To Google or not to Google. Retrieved July 7, 2006.

Caverly, D. C. (2000). Technology and the "Knowledge Age." In D. B Lundell & J. L. Higbee (Eds.), Proceedings of the First Intentional Meeting on Future Directions in Developmental Education [Online] (pp. 34–36). Minneapolis: University of Minnesota, General College and The Center for Research on Developmental Education and Urban Literacy. Available: education.umn.edu/CRDEUL/pdf/proceedings/1-proceedings.pdf

Consumer Reports Staff. (2005, June). Filtering software: Better but still fallible. *Consumer Reports,* PDC 36–38. Retrieved August 22, 2006, from http://www.consumerreports.org/cro/electronics-computers/internet-filtering-software-605/overview/index.htm

Costa, A., & Kallick, B. (2000). *Habits of mind: A developmental series.* Alexandria, VA: Association for Supervision and Curriculum Development.

Crawford, V., & Vahey, P. (2002). *Palm Education Pioneers Program: March, 2002 Evaluation Report.* Menlo Park, CA: SRI International.

Fidel, R., Davies, R. K., Douglass, M. H., Kohlder, J. K., Hopkins, C. J., Kushner, E. J., et al. (1999). A visit to the information mall: Web searching behavior of high school students. *Journal of the American Society for Information Science, 50*(1), 24–37.

Harris, S. D. (2006, July 7). Dictionary adds verb: To Google. *San Jose Mercury News.* Retrieved July 7, 2006.

Inkpen, K. M. (1999). Designing handheld technologies for kids. *Personal Technologies Journal, 3*(1/2), 81–89.

Jonassen, D. H., & Colaric, S. (2001). Information landfills contain knowledge; searching equals learning; hyperlinking is good instruction; and other myths about learning from the internet. *Computers in Schools, 17*(3/4, Pt. I), 159–170.

Kelly, D. (2000) Online research skills for students. *Classroom Connect, 7*(2), 6.

Kleiner, A., & Lewis, L. (2003). *Internet access in U.S. public schools and classrooms: 1994–2002* (NCES 2004-011). Washington, DC: U.S. Department of Education, National Center for Education Statistics.

Lenhart, A. Madden, M., & Hitlin, P. (2005). Teens and Technology: Youth are Leading the Transition to a Fully Wired and Mobile Nation. Pew Internet and American Life Project. Available: http://207.21.232.103/PPF/r/162/report_display.asp

Linn, M., Tinker, R., Husic, F., & Chiu, J. (2006). Teaching and assessing knowledge integration in science. *Science, v 313, Aug.*, pp. 1049–50.

Nakashima, E. (2006, August 8). AOL takes down site with users' search data. *Washington Post*, p. D01. Retrieved August 16, 2006, from http://www.washingtonpost.com/wp-dyn/content/article/2006/08/07/AR2006080701150.html

Petersen, D. (2005, April/May). Leapin' lizards! *Edutopia*. Retrieved August 21, 2006, from http://edutopia.org/magazine/ed1article.php?id=art_1251&issue=apr_05

Peterson, C. L. & Koeck , D. C (2001). When students create their own webquests. Learning & Leading with Technology. v29nl.

Pownell, D., & Bailey, G. (2001). Getting a handle on handhelds. *Electronic School*. Retrieved June 19, 2006, from http://www.electronicschool.com/2001/06/0601handhelds.html

Prensky, M. (2001). Digital natives, digital immigrants. *On the Horizon, 9*(5), 1–2. Retrieved July 16, 2006, from http://www.marcprensy.com/ writing/

Prensky, M. (2003). "But the screen is too small . . ." Sorry, "digital immigrants"—cell phones—not computers—are the future of education. Retrieved July 16, 2006, from http://www.marcprensky.com/writing/

Prensky (2005). Learning in the Digital Age. Educational Leadership, 63(4), 8–13. Available: http://www.ascd.org/cms/objectlib/ascdframeset/index.cfm?publication=http://www.ascd.org/authors/ed_lead/el200512_prensky.html

Riel, M. (2000, September 11 & 12). New designs for connected teaching and learning. Paper presented at the Secretary's Conference on Educational Technology, Washington, DC. Retrieved April 8, 2002, from http://www.gse.uci.edu/mriel/whitepaper/

Roschelle, J. (2003). Keynote paper: Unlocking the learning value of wireless mobile devices. *Journal of Computer Assisted Learning, 19*, 260–272.

Schacter, J., Chung, G. K. W. K., & Dorr, A. (1998). Children's Internet searching on complex problem: Performance and process analyses. *Journal of the American Society for Information Science, 49*, 840–850.

Soloway, E., Norris, C., Blumenfeld, P., Fishman, B., Krajcik, J., & Marx, R. (2001). Log on education: Handheld devices are ready-at-hand. *Communications of the ACM, 44*(6), 15–20.

Staudt, C. (2004). Monday's lesson: handheld computers in the field. @ *Concord*, Concord Consortium, Fall edition, pp. 6–7.

Swan, K., van't Hooft, M., & Kratcoski, A. (2005). Uses and effects of mobile computing devices in K–8 classrooms. *Journal of Research on Technology in Education, 38*(1), 99–112.

Tallman, J., & Joyce, M. (2005, June). *What's new with the I-Search research/writing process?* Paper presented at the American Association of School Librarians 12th National Conference and Exhibition, Chicago, IL.

Timmerman, A. (2003). Survey says . . . online survey tools have rich instructional applications. *Learning & Leading with Technology, 31*(2), pp. 10–13, 55.

Tinker, R., & Krajcik, J. (Eds.) (2001). *Portable technologies: Science learning in context.* New York: Kluwer Academic/Plenum.

Vahey, P., & Crawford, V. (2002). *Palm Education Pioneers Program: Final evaluation report.* Menlo Park, CA: SRI International.

Vidmar, D. *Getting in Deep: After Google, the Invisible Web.* Campus Technology, 4/1/2003, http://www.campustechnology.com/article.asp?id=7477

Web-based Education Commission. (2000). The power of the Internet for learning: Moving from promise to practice (Report), Washington, DC: U.S Department of Education.

Zeller, T. (2006, August 22). AOL moves to increase privacy on search queries. *New York Times*. Retrieved August 22, 2006, from http://www.nytimes.com/2006/08/22/technology/22aol.html

Experimenting With Technologies

Learning to Reason Causally

In this chapter, we describe how students can experiment with technologies. Experimentation involves investigation or examination with the expectation of finding something important. As the headings in this chapter indicate, exploration requires hypothesizing, conjecturing, speculating, and testing. What do all these mental activities have in common?

Exploring, hypothesizing, conjecturing, experimenting, speculating, and testing all require that students reason causally, that is, apply their understanding of cause-and-effect relationships to generate hypotheses, conjectures, or speculations and test them. Causal reasoning supports three different kinds of thinking by students. Reasoning from set of conditions or states of an event to the possible effect(s) that may result from those states is called *prediction*. Predicting the effects of some changes in a set of conditions is the essence of scientific experimentation (hypothesis generation). The two primary functions of prediction are forecasting an event and testing hypotheses to confirm or refute scientific assumptions. Forecasting is used regularly by economists and meteorologists to predict changes in economic or meteorological conditions based on changes in the markets or in the weather conditions. Predictions also support experimentation; they are the hypotheses of experiments. A physicist, for example, predicts (hypothesizes) that the greater the application of a force to an object, the greater will be the change in the state of that object. Scientific predictions are empirically tested for their validity. A psychologist may predict that changes in environmental conditions, such as stress, will affect a person's behavior. Predictions assume a deterministic relationship between cause and effect, that is, that forces in the cause reliably determine an effect. Aristotle believed that everything is determined in accordance with causal rules. Prediction and hypothesizing are essential to the process of science inquiry as reflected in any science standards.

Another less deterministic form of prediction is to draw implications from a set of conditions or states on the basis of plausible cause-and-effect relationships. To imply is to entail or entangle events or to involve an effect as a necessary consequence of some cause without necessarily knowing what the effect will be. Drawing implications involves identifying potential effects or anticipated consequences from a causal antecedent. For example, the implications of any new law are politically, socially, and economically complex. The intended outcome of the law is often replaced by unintended outcomes. Implications of any causal event are often not known or could not have been hypothesized. As such, implications represent a conditional form of prediction that is less deterministic than a prediction. Implicational reasoning has received very little research, so little is known about implicational reasoning.

When an outcome or state exists for which the causal agent is unknown, then an inference is required. That is, reasoning backward from effect to cause requires the process of inference. A primary function of inferences is diagnosis. Diagnosis is the identification of a cause, an origin, or a reason for something that has occurred. In medicine, diagnosis seeks to identify the cause or origin of a disease or disorder as determined by medical diagnosis. For example, on the basis of symptoms, historical factors, and test results of patients that are thought to be abnormal, a physician attempts to infer the cause(s) of that illness state.

In chapter 1, we described some important kinds of thinking that can be fostered by technology use. Among those was causal reasoning. Causal reasoning is among the most important and commonly used kinds of thinking that exist. In this chapter, we describe a number of technologies (microworlds, virtual laboratories, virtual worlds, simulations, and games) that require that students think causally while making hypotheses, conjectures, speculations, and so on.

Hypothesizing With Microworlds

The term *microworld* was coined by Papert (1980) to describe explorational learning environments that used Logo turtles to learn principles of geometry. Logo is a simple computer programming language that provides learners with simple commands to direct the computerized turtles to create their own personal, visual worlds. Learners enter commands to manipulate a turtle on the screen in an effort to create more elaborate renderings, thus becoming familiar with "powerful ideas" underlying the turtle's operations, ideas such as variables, procedures, and recursion. The computer should be an "object to think with," according to Papert. Logo is, Papert argued, an ideal environment for creating microworlds, which are constrained problem spaces that resemble existing problems in the real world. These microworlds are generated by learners, so they are inherently interesting to learners (experimenting to "see if I can do that"). Students use simple commands to construct objects on the screen. They can also build more complex procedures that call on simple procedures which may call on other procedures. The resulting projects represent microworlds.

Although the theoretical rationale for Logo microworlds was strong, the procedures used to create Logo microworlds and the programming skills they require are not very generalizable. Although Logo is a syntactically simple language, it still requires several months of practice to develop skills sufficient for easily creating microworlds, and some students never become proficient. Further, many teachers are not comfortable teaching these "programming skills."

Nevertheless, the idea of microworlds as problem exploration and experimentation spaces is indeed a powerful idea. Many other microworld environments have been created that offer the exploratory advantages of Logo without the requirement of learning a programming language. They are constrained (or simplified) versions of reality that enable learners to manipulate variables and experiments within the parameters of some system. Although this kind of microworld does not always allow students to construct their own exploration spaces, they do enable learners to represent their own thinking in the ways that they explore, manipulate and experiment with the environment.

Microworlds can assume many forms in different knowledge domains. They are primarily exploratory learning environments often in the form of simulations of real-world phenomena in which learners manipulate or create objects and test their effects on one another. "Microworlds present students with a simple model of a part of the world" (Hanna, 1986, p. 197), allowing learners to control those phenomena and construct deeper-level knowledge of the phenomena they are manipulating. Microworlds provide learners with the observation and manipulation tools necessary for exploring and testing objects in their microworld. They have proven extremely effective in engaging learners in higher-order thinking, such as hypothesis testing and speculating.

There are many other fine examples of microworlds, such as ThinkerTools (White, 1993) and Bubble Dialog (McMahon & O'Neill, 1993), that are not described in this chapter. These environments share at least two important characteristics. They usually provide single representations of phenomena, and they provide immediate feedback when learners try something out. The learner generates predictions about how some object in the microworld will behave. On the basis of the prediction, the student manipulates the objects, and the microworld shows how the object behaves on the basis of that manipulation. The way the system performs functions as feedback that the learners must interpret and use to revise their conceptual model of the domain. It is important that this feedback comes about as a natural consequence of using the microworld.

Interactive Physics

Interactive Physics (http://www.design-simulation.com/IP/) is a microworld for exploring topics in physics, such as momentum, force, and acceleration. Each experiment in Interactive Physics is a microworld that simulates a physical phenomenon, allowing the learner to easily manipulate several attributes of the world, such as gravity, air resistance, elasticity of bodies, and various surface parameters. More important, it provides objects and tools that enable the learners to design their own experiments to model Newtonian phenomena. Having learners design their own experiments to test a hypothesis is a key aspect of the inquiry-based science-teaching paradigm currently being promoted by most science standards.

The experiment in Figure 3.1 was developed by students using the building blocks shown on the left side of the figure to test the effects of a one-kilogram projectile on a 10-kilogram pendulum. Learners can also change the views of the world by showing grids, rulers, vectors, axes, center of mass, and mass names. Students can turn on a tracker that shows the motion of objects. They can also select meters, such as velocity, acceleration, momentum, various forces (friction, gravity, and air), and rotation, in order to measure the effects of changes in the variables they designate. Interactive Physics is an excellent example of a microworld because the experiments are simple to create and use; students also get immediate feedback on their conceptual understanding when they run the experiment they constructed. Further, by simulating these experiments with

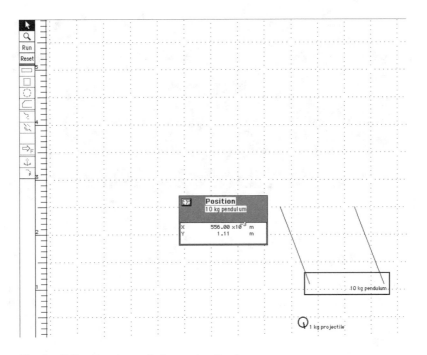

Figure 3.1 Experiment in Interactive Physics.

technology, teachers and schools don't need to invest in the thousands of dollars of equipment and many hours of work that would be required to set up the physics experiments that are contained in this environment.

SimCalc

The SimCalc project (http://www.simcalc.umassd.edu/) teaches elementary students calculus concepts through MathWorlds, which is a microworld consisting of animated worlds and dynamic graphs in which actors move according to graphs that are defined by mathematical functions. By exploring the movement of the actors in the simulations and seeing the graphs of their activity, students begin to understand important calculus ideas. In the MathWorlds activity illustrated in Figure 3.2, students match two motions. By doing so, they learn how velocity and position graphs relate to each other. Students must match the motion of the green and red graphs. To do this, they can change either graph. They iteratively run the simulation to see if they got it right. Students may also use MathWorld's link to enter their own bodily motion. For example, a student can walk across the classroom, and their motions can be entered into MathWorlds through sensing equipment. MathWorld will plot their motion, enabling the students to explore the properties of their own motion.

Microworlds are generally very specific to a content domain. SimCalc is useful only for supporting math learning, while Interactive Physics is useful only for

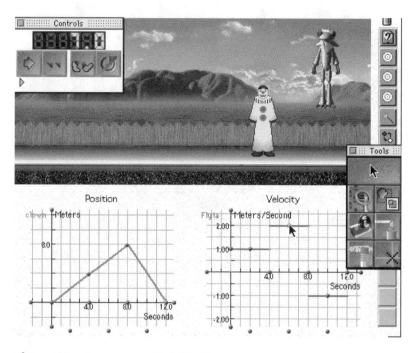

Figure 3.2 Experiment in Math World.

testing concepts in physics. They cannot be used for any other purpose. However, they are engaging, so students usually expend a great deal of effort experimenting with specific microworlds.

Experimenting With Simulations

The next two kinds of environments that we describe are forms of simulations. Simulations are imitations of some real thing, state of affairs, or process. Simulations imitate phenomena by allowing learners to manipulate key characteristics or variables within a physical or abstract system. Because of their computational capabilities, computers are frequently used to build simulations of real-life situations. The simulation designer builds a model of the phenomena or processes that enable learners to see how the system works. By changing variables, students make predictions about the behavior of the system, a form of causal reasoning (described previously in this chapter). You may be wondering how microworlds and simulations differ. The easy answer is not much. Microworlds are a form of simulation that addresses a fairly specific phenomenon. Microworlds often provide learners with the ability to represent their own models, though not always. Simulations, on the other hand, can be applied to a broader set of systems.

Simulations are used in a broad range of teaching and training operations. They vary tremendously in detail and complexity. A search of the Internet will produce hundreds of commercially available educational simulations. For instance, numerous medical simulations exist to support medical training. These simulations typically present a patient using video and allow the medical trainee to examine the patient, order tests, make diagnoses, and test those diagnoses (inference making) by treating the simulated patient. Those patients may be presented on a computer screen or in the form of a manipulable dummy. Some medical simulations are so complex that they allow medical personnel to conduct simulated surgery. Flight simulators are an important part of pilot training. Pilots can sit in simulated cockpits that even physically move on the basis of flight commands. These simulators can present complex and dramatic situations that the pilots must deal with. A number of planeloads of people have survived airline incidents because pilots had addressed those problems during simulator training. Such simulations are used extensively in the trucking industry and in the military.

Laboratory Simulations

Among the most commonly available educational simulations are laboratory simulations. Many of these, such as the physics lab simulation illustrated in Figure 3.3, are available on the Internet (e.g., http://www.myphysicslab.com/). This simulation allows learners to illustrate a double-pendulum experiment in which the learners may graph different angles in order to see the effects of the different pendulums.

A fascinating biology simulation has been developed by NASA's Classroom of the Future. BioBlast (see Figure 3.4; http://www.cet.edu/products/bioblast/

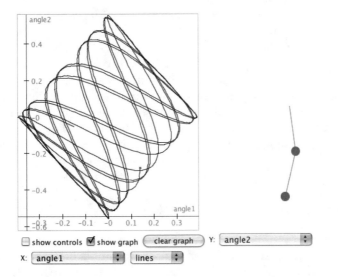

Figure 3.3 Online physics simulation.

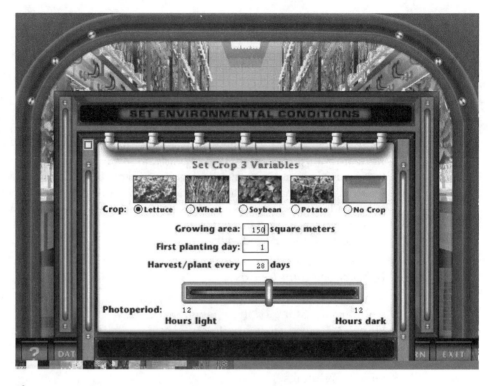

Figure 3.4 Setting environmental conditions in BioBlast simulation.

overview.html) is a simulation of plant biology laboratory in space where students become scientists trying to feed a space colony while recycling waste products in the process. In Figure 3.4, students set the environmental conditions under which different plants are grown. They have to balance the energy used to grow the plants with the biomass produced. Students receive results on water, oxygen, and energy used and biomass produced that they must compare with a database of human nutritional needs. Students must abandon preconceptions so that they can feed the space colony. It is important in all simulation use that the students suggest and justify their predictions before they test them. The worst thing that you can do is to provide a procedural list of actions that students should complete in order to get the right answer. Let them try out several options and fail. When an experiment fails, that is when real meaningful learning begins.

Urban Simulations

Among the most popular and effective simulations for use in schools (especially social studies) is the urban or city simulator. City simulators were first developed for urban planners to understand how cities are likely to evolve in response to various policy decisions. They often include aspects that we often think of occurring in

Figure 3.5   SimCity, a popular urban simulation.

computerized games (see the description of games later in this chapter). SimCity (http://simcity.ea.com/) was among the first urban simulations and is now available in several versions (Figure 3.5). Students make decisions about land use and transportation. While playing SimCity, students can create characters, known as Sims, who will engage other Sims and provide players with feedback on what is going on around the city. Your Sims also experience city life (e.g., they get stuck in traffic). Players can also create mountains, valleys, and forests to surround their city and cause tornadoes, volcanoes, or meteor showers to challenge the community. Students can also act as the mayor who runs the city and connect their city with others in the region that are sharing or competing for resources. The mayor also dispatches emergency vehicles to deal with the natural and unnatural disasters that you create. SimCity also allows group play, computer conferences, and chat lines through the Internet. The complexity of simulations such as SimCity helps students understand the systemic nature of organizations. Problems in SimCity are political, social, economic, historical, and cultural and cannot be solved using a single perspective. That is the nature of everyday problems that plague real cities throughout the world.

Simulation Builders

When simulations exist that meet your students' learning needs, they should be used judiciously to support meaningful learning. When they are not available (the more likely situation), then you may wish to create your own simulations.

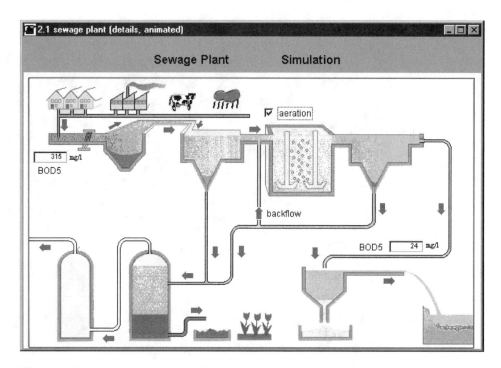

Figure 3.6 Simulation of sewage plant. *Source:* van Joolingen & de Jong (2003). SimQuest.

Building simulations can be a complex design and development activity, so we do not recommend the process for everyone. You need to be dedicated to the task to be successful. Fortunately, a number of systems have been created to help you to develop simulations. One of the best has been developed at the University of Twente in the Netherlands. Their simulation builder is called SimQuest (http://www.simquest.to.utwente.nl). Don't worry—there are instructions in English, and it's free of charge.

As an example, using SimQuest, authors have built a simulation of a sewage plant (Figure 3.6). The application is part of a series of courses about wastewater technology and can be used as starting and end point of such a course. The students in this simulation get to operate a working sewage plant. This simulation may be useful in learning how biological processes work.

Venturing Into Games

Games are among the oldest forms of entertainment in the world. In addition to sporting games, board games, and social games, newer kinds of video and computer-based games can be used to support meaningful learning in classrooms. In this brief section, we describe how different kinds of computer games can be used in classrooms.

Among the oldest forms of computer-based educational games are quiz games, where quizzes are embedded in a quiz show context. For example, Games2Train (http://www.games2train.com/games) produces a game maker called Pick-it! for teachers to construct quiz games (see Figure 3.7). The game maker resembles the television quiz show *Jeopardy*, allowing game players to select topics and values and play against others. The degree of meaningfulness of the learning from these games depends on the nature of the responses that are required. More often than not, quiz games require only memorization performance. While memorization of domain content may be important, these games do not readily engage students in deeper-level, meaningful learning activities (e.g., application and synthesis).

More complex games, such as the different versions of Sid Meier's Civilization (http://simcity.ea.com/), engage students in complex problem solving while trying to manage their civilization. Students can select different civilizations to explore, from Sumerians to the mystical Mayans. In the game, students can map the world using satellite images. They can form armies and attack other civilizations or forge alliances with them. They can choose the form of government they wish to impose on their civilization (e.g., fascism, feudalism, tribal council, or imperialism). They can also use a well-developed trade system to manage resources, trade routes, and

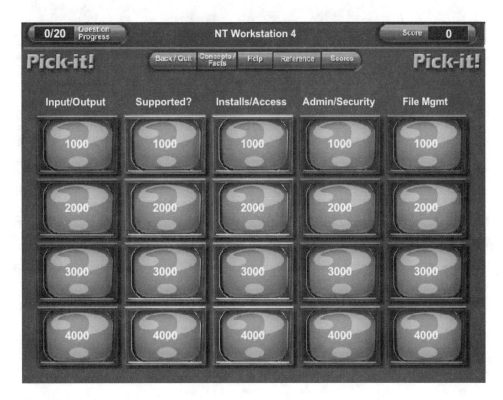

Figure 3.7 Pick-it! interface.

Figure 3.8   Different cities in Civilization. *Source:* © 2005 Sid Meier's Civilization III, Firaxis Games, Take-Two Interactive, Inc.

the spread of technology. Figure 3.8 shows a number of civilizations that must learn to interact with each other peacefully or pugilistically. Civilization is obviously appropriate for social studies classes in which the teacher wants students to understand the political, military, social, cultural, and historical complexities of the world.

Games, especially complex, interactive games such as Civilization interactive, can engage learners in very meaningful learning. Gee (2003) has identified a number of principles that underlie modern game design that can teach us a lot about learning. We list some of them here.

Active, Critical Learning Principle
All aspects of the learning environment (including the ways in which the domain is designed and presented) are set up to encourage active and critical, not passive, learning.

Semiotic Domains Principle
Learning involves mastering, at some level, semiotic domains and being able to participate, at some level, in the affinity group or groups connected to them.

"Psychosocial Moratorium" Principle
Learners can take risks in a space where real-world consequences are lowered.

Committed Learning Principle
Learners participate in an extended engagement (lots of effort and practice) as extensions of their real-world identities in relation to a virtual identity to which they feel some commitment and a virtual world that they find compelling.

Identity Principle
Learning involves taking on and playing with identities in such a way that the learner has real choices (in developing the virtual identity) and ample opportunity to meditate on the relationship between new identities and old ones. There is a tripartite play of identities as learners relate to and reflect on their multiple real-world identities, a virtual identity, and a projective identity.

Practice Principle
Learners get lots and lots of practice in a context where the practice is not boring (i.e., in a virtual world that is compelling to learners on their own terms and where the learners experience ongoing success). They spend lots of time on task.

Probing Principle
Learning is a cycle of probing the world (doing something); reflecting in and on this action and, on this basis, forming a hypothesis; reprobing the world to test this hypothesis; and then accepting or rethinking the hypothesis.

Situated Meaning Principle
The meanings of signs (e.g., words, actions, objects, artifacts, symbols, and texts) are situated in embodied experience. Meanings are not general or decontextualized. Whatever generality meanings come to have is discovered from the bottom up through embodied experiences.

Multimodal Principle
Meaning and knowledge are built up through various modalities (e.g., images, texts, symbols, interactions, abstract design, and sound), not just words.

Discovery Principle
Overt telling is kept to a well-thought-out minimum, allowing ample opportunity for the learner to experiment and make discoveries.

Not all computerized games represent these principles. Many games expose students to competition over an uninteresting task that may also engage only recall or memorization. These are good for filling classroom time, and it is likely that the students will even enjoy them. As with any technology-based activity, you must examine the nature of the task that you are engaging students in.

Immersing Into Virtual Worlds

Students may also learn to interact with virtual worlds that combine many aspects of simulations and games. A virtual world is a realistic, three-dimensional computer simulation in which users identify themselves as an avatar while interacting with other users. Many virtual worlds support multiple users playing with or against each other. The simulated world appears and functions similarly to the real world. Numerous commercial virtual worlds can be used in classrooms. For instance, Entropia Universe is an economic virtual world where Entropia currency can be traded with real-world funds or used to purchase virtual land and equipment or to support a virtual person (avatar) in the Virtual Universe. Because Entropia uses a cash economy, virtual items inside the Universe actually have a real cash value (they are frequently traded on the Internet), they can be bought and sold, and the proceeds may be saved in another form of currency. Numerous virtual worlds support complex user interactions.

One of the very best multiuser virtual environments available is Quest Atlantis (http://atlantis.crlt.indiana.edu/). Quest Atlantis is a virtual world that was designed to support a variety of learning tasks for 9- to 12-year-old students that are tied to academic standards in a three-dimensional immersive environment (Barab, Thomas, Dodge, Carteaux, & Tuzun, 2005; see Figure 3.9). Quest Atlantis combines attributes of commercial games with research-based educational practice. Quest Atlantis was designed on the basis of the belief that play can engage children in deeper-level thinking. Quest Atlantis includes three-dimensional worlds such as Unity World (emphasizing diversity issues), Ecology World, and Healthy World (emphasizing nutrition). Students use avatars to move through these worlds, meet other avatars, and participate in

Figure 3.9 Students on a quest in Quest Atlantis.

collaborative and socially responsible activities while completing different quests. A quest is an engaging curricular task designed to be entertaining yet educational. For example, a quest in Habitat Village in the Ecology World includes the following goals:

- Choose an animal that lives in your area but that you know little about
- Find out about the habits of that animal, where it lives, and what it uses for shelter
- Return to your personal digital assistant and submit a story about your animal and what it uses for shelter

Completing this quest requires that students engage in socially and educationally meaningful activities, such as conducting field studies, interviewing others, conducting research about community problems, examining current events from different perspectives, writing journals, and solving problems.

While fulfilling their quests, students converse with other students as well as with mentors. Thousands of students from all over the world regularly use Quest Atlantis in their classrooms.

Quest Atlantis is more than a computer game. It consists of a multiuser virtual environment that immerses children in educational tasks as part of an online adventure to save Atlantis from disaster, educational quests in that environment, unit plans for teachers, comic books, a novel, a board game, trading cards, a series of social commitments, and various characters using the environment. Research has shown that students learn a lot in the areas of science and social studies and gain a stronger sense of academic self-efficacy.

Conclusion

Experimenting with technologies requires that students learn to reason causally. That is important because causal reasoning is perhaps the most basic thinking skill that is tied to most science inquiry standards. Being able to reason causally enables students make predictions, inferences, and explanations; draw implications; and argue for (provide justifications) actions they have taken. Causal reasoning enables learners to generate hypotheses (a form of prediction) and test the accuracy of those predictions.

Causal reasoning is engaged by a number of technology-based learning environments, including microworlds, simulations, games, and virtual worlds. Microworlds provide simplified representations of the world that learners may manipulate and test. These are exploratory environments that focus on a limited number of causal relationships. Simulations share many characteristics with microworlds, although they tend to be more complex, often providing multiple variables that students may manipulate. The more complex environments require a more sophisticated model underlying the simulation, making them more difficult to design and implement. Games add competition with one's self or with others. At any time of the day, hundreds of thousands of people are playing Internet-based games. Some games (not typically first-person shooter games) can appropriately support classroom-learning goals. Virtual worlds combine the characteristics of microworlds, simulations, and games into educationally driven environments that allow students to explore distant worlds and pursue learning quests. Although there are few virtual worlds available to support educational goals, they possess the greatest potential for engaging students in meaningful learning.

Things to Think About

1. Are inferences and predictions two sides of the same coin? If you can generate predictions, do you believe that you will necessarily be able to makes inferences just as well? Will inferences transfer equally well to predictions?
2. Doctors make diagnoses, requiring inferential thinking. What other kinds of tasks require inferences?
3. We regularly talk about the implications of some event. Can you think of implications that students may need to draw that are relevant to your learning goals?
4. Microworlds are especially effective for allowing students to generate and test predictions (hypotheses). Can you think of how students can use microworlds to test inferences?
5. If SimCalc can help third graders understand the principles of differential calculus, what kind of microworld might you design to help learners understand supply and demand?
6. Simulations have been around from decades. How do computers make them more effective?
7. Simulations allow students to fail. One view of meaningful learning is "fast-forward failure." The sooner you put students into a situation where they try something and fail, the sooner they will begin learning. Why? How could you use that principle in your own class?
8. Good simulations are hard to build. If you were building a simulation for your class, what activity would you support? What variables could students manipulate? How would they affect each other?
9. Gee identified 36 principles about why games engage meaningful learning. Do those same principles apply to simulations? Microworlds?
10. One of Gee's principles states that learning involves taking on and playing with identities. Why do you think students like to assume and test other identities?
11. Gee's principle of probing states that learning is a cycle of probing the world (doing something) and reflecting in and on this action and forming a hypothesis. Donald Schön described the reflective practitioner in his book. What do you think the characteristics of a reflective practitioner are?

12. Gee's situated learning principle is similar to the authentic characteristics of meaningful learning described in chapter 1. How does a situation become an embodied experience?
13. Most games involve some kind of competition. When is competition good for learning? When is it harmful?
14. Virtual worlds allow students to escape their world and enter a new world with a different set of rules. Why is that so engaging?

References

Barab, S. A., Thomas, M., Dodge, T., Carteaux, R., & Tuzun, H. (2005). Making learning fun: Quest Atlantis, a game without guns. *Educational Technology Research and Development, 53*(1), 86–108.

Gee, J. P. (2003). *What video games have to teach us about learning and literacy.* New York: Palgrave Macmillan.

Hanna, J. (1986). Learning environment criteria. In R. Ennals, R. Gwyn, & L. Zdravchev (Eds.), *Information technology and education: The changing school.* Chichester: Ellis Horwood.

McMahon, H., & O'Neill, W. (1993). Computer-mediated zones of engagement in learning. In T. M. Duffy, J. Lowyck, & D. H. Jonassen (Eds.), *Designing environments for constructive learning* (pp. 37–58). Heidelberg: Springer-Verlag.

Papert, S. (1980). *Mindstorms: Children, computers, and powerful ideas.* New York: Basic Books.

Schön, D. A. (1983). *The reflective practitioner: How professionals think in action.* New York: Basic Books.

van Joolingen, W. R., & de Jong, T. (2003). SimQuest: Authoring educational simulations. In T. Murray, S. Blessing & S. Ainsworth (Eds.), *Authoring tools for advanced technology educational software: Toward cost-effective production of adaptive, interactive, and intelligent educational software,* pp. 1–31. Dordrecht: Kluwer Academic Publishers.

White, B. Y. (1993). ThinkerTools: Causal models, conceptual change, and science education. *Cognition and Instruction, 10*(1), 1–100.

Chapter 4

Supporting Writing With Technology

Although all the learning tasks we address in this book are important, teaching students to write well is fundamental not only to many school-based tasks but also to a myriad of everyday and work tasks, from personal communication with friends and family to written reports that are still common in the business world. And if this isn't enough of a reason to invest efforts into improving writing instructional activities, in our current climate of "accountability" and high-stakes testing, national and state standards alike place a high degree of emphasis on writing outcomes (National Council of Teachers of English, 1996).

As teachers are well aware, many students of all ages struggle with both learning to write well and learning to enjoy (or at least not dislike) writing. Technology tools for supporting both individual and collaborative writing are designed to address both of these outcomes.

Writing itself is a complex activity composed of many component tasks (Flower, Schriver, Carey, Haas, & Hayes, 1989):

- Setting goals
- Planning
- Idea organization
- Composition of text
- Editing

The technology tools we discuss address these tasks in varying ways. We address the various components of writing and how technology can support them in both individual and collaborative settings.

Supporting Writing Organization and Planning

Organizing ideas before beginning to write is commonly accepted as an important part of the writing process. This section describes several technology tools that support this activity.

Organizing Ideas With Concept Maps

Concept mapping is an activity that requires learners to draw visual maps of concepts connected to each other via lines (or links). These maps depict the semantic structure among concepts in a domain. Concept maps provide learners with a tool for representing the semantic structure of domain knowledge and in turn linkng those structures to existing mental structures (see chapter 5). Concept mapping is a process of identifying important concepts, arranging those concepts spatially, identifying relationships among those concepts, and labeling the nature of the relationships among those concepts. Concept maps can be drawn by hand using simple artifacts such as cards and string, paper and pencil, or sticky notes. However, a variety of computer-based semantic networking software enables much easier (and arguably more powerful) production of concept maps.

Several computer-based concept mapping tools (also referred to here as *semantic networking tools*) are available. Semantic networking programs are computer-based visualizing tools for developing representations of the semantic networks in memory. See Table 4.1 for a sample list of such tools.

These programs provide visual and verbal screen tools for developing concept maps (otherwise known as cognitive maps or semantic nets). Semantic nets or concept maps are spatial representations of ideas (concepts) and their interrelationships that are stored in personal memories. These tools enable learners to identify the important ideas or concepts in a knowledge domain and interrelate those ideas in multidimensional networks of concepts by labeling the relationships between those ideas. The tools vary in their features, and some—such as Semantica and Inspiration—are more focused on educational applications than others.

Semantic networks are composed of nodes (concepts or ideas) and links (statements of relationships) connecting them. In computer-based semantic networks, nodes are represented as information blocks or cards or in some cases with pictorial icons made available by the program (e.g., "Paleontologists" in Figure 4.1), and the links are labeled lines (e.g., "studied by" in Figure 4.1). When choosing a concept mapping or semantic networking computer program, educators should make sure the program supports the labeling of links, as the creation of descriptive link labels is a critical part of the creation of maps.

The map in Figure 4.1 was created using Semantica (www.semanticresearch.com). Note that the map is but one screen in a semantic network consisting of more than 100 screens describing different dinosaurs and their relationships. Semantica supports the feature of being able to view one portion of a map at a time simply by double-clicking on a node; the selected node becomes the central node in a new page. This ability to focus on one node as being central while not

Table 4.1 Sample Concept Mapping Software Tools

AXON idea processor	http://web.singnet.com.sg/~axon2000/index.htm Potentially powerful tool, but does not appear to be applied in K–12 settings.
Semantica	http://www.semanticresearch.com/
Inspiration/ Kidspiration	http://www.inspiration.com Popular tool that runs on both Macs and PCs. Kidspiration is the tool version for younger learners. The tool is visually appealing but does not offer the same learning functionality as Semantica. For instance, all maps must be created on a single page. Also, learners may focus too much on choosing pictorial icons instead of on organizing and creating meaningful links between nodes.
Mindjet	http://www.mindjet.com Offers free trial download; runs on PCs and Macs.

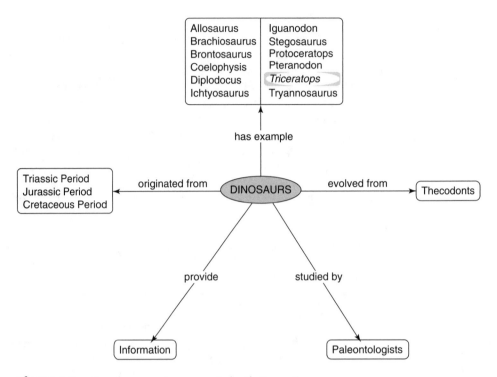

Figure 4.1   Sample concept map created with Semantica.

having to see the entire map allows the creation of more complex maps and more complex knowledge organizations.

For the writing process, semantic networks are an effective intentional planning and analysis tools. When students are planning a paper or a speech, they can create semantic networks to both generate and organize their ideas. Anderson-Inman and Horney (1996) describe steps for using a concept mapping activity for brainstorming as a precursor to organization and actual writing. Note that the activity is designed to be completed by students working collaboratively and that the use of a computer projector enhances students' ability to see the map progress and thus aids in collaboration.

1. Students generate ideas quickly and without evaluation of them. One student is designated as a "recorder" and generates associated nodes and links within the concept mapping software (see Figure 4.2a). Tools such as Semantica and Inspiration offer quick keyboard sequences for creating many nodes quickly.

2. Students arrange the existing ideas into clusters. Nodes are dragged around the screen into clusters (see Figure 4.2b).

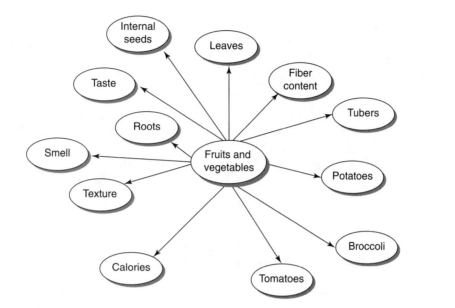

Figure 4.2a

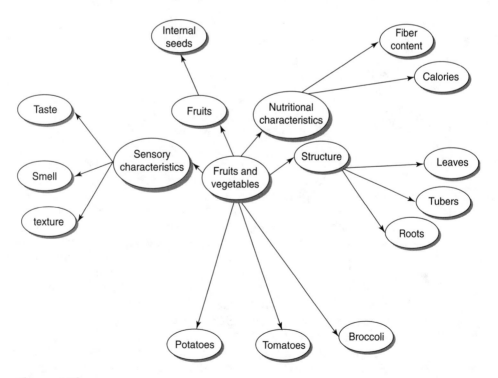

Figure 4.2b

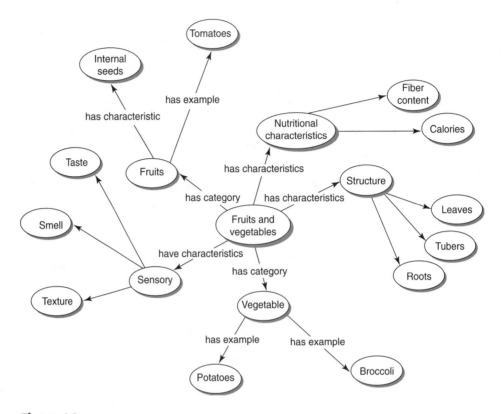

Figure 4.2c

3. Students elaborate the newly organized map so that it is more functional in the process of writing a paper or a report or constructing a presentation. Such elaboration may include editing duplicate ideas, adding more links to create a more well connected map (and eliminating isolated or nearly isolated nodes), or refining link descriptions (see Figure 4.2c).

Concept maps can also be used as an initial support or template for structuring different types of writing activities. Figure 4.3 is a map template that students could start with for constructing a persuasive argument. Similar templates are available with many concept mapping packages for writing activities such as developing a research topic, organizing a presentation, or writing a bibliography. We caution teachers that such map templates must be used carefully, as our experience indicates that students may limit their own maps to a simple replacement strategy of the nodes in the templates. If templates are used, students should see how a template is transformed into a completely developed map for the type of writing in question.

To summarize, the power of using concept mapping as a precursor to writing is that the process requires students to actively evaluate and organize their ideas as

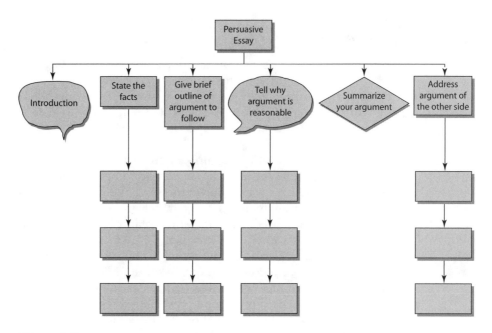

Figure 4.3

they are generating them. To create concept maps, students need to first identify important concepts and represent them in the software along with the relationships between the concepts. That means they must sythesize sources of information to identify the ideas that are important to the goal of their writing. Rather than defining these concepts, students need to describe how they relate to the other ideas that they have identified. They need to decide how clear and how descriptive those relationships are. These relationships will then be described in their written product. This process can be enhanced by collaboration with other students. We also note that the organization task supported by creating concept maps can be applied to any of the type of writing (e.g., research reports, prose, or poetry). Finally, and from a more practical standpoint, the visual nature of the mapping tools helps students keep track of what they have created so far and further allows easy "editing" or changing of the organization before it is turned into prose.

Note that the power of this tool is achieved only when students generate their own maps. Teachers may initially help students learn the software and provide sample maps and provide ongoing feedback on student-generated maps, but unless students generate their own maps (either individually or collaboratively), they will not actively need to organize and evaluate their ideas. Our experience has shown that because teachers show students how to construct them, student semantic nets tend to look the same. It is important to allow student groups to construct their own nets. Prompt them or ask them questions about the underlying semantic relationships that they are trying to convey. They will need the greatest amount of coaching in describing clear and concise relationships.

Supporting Presentation Writing

Although writing presentations is not as text "dense" as writing a research paper or other more traditional prose, it is still considered an important learning outcome. Aside from being addressed in standards, being able to develop (and deliver) an effective presentation is a skill that is required not only in the latter years of a K–12 education but also in many aspects of our everyday and work lives.

Presentation writing requires many of the same skills that other types of writing require: prewriting tasks such as deciding on goals and organization and sequencing of ideas, composition of message, and editing. Microsoft's PowerPoint offers several built-in tools that can facilitate this process. We briefly describe how this product can be used to facilitate presentation writing and also discuss some of the potential downsides of the product.

Mentioning Microsoft PowerPoint to educators can quickly produce glazed-over eyes and a barrage of commentary about the last hundred slide presentations we have most recently been subjected to. Certainly teachers have legitimate reasons to create and use PowerPoint presentations, but the teacher's use of this software won't help students learn how to create their own presentations. However, just as with many of the other technology tools described in this book, when we put the tool into the hands of students and ask them to create presentations, they can learn valuable skills.

PowerPoint offers several features that can help students create effective presentations:

- *"AutoContent" wizard.* PowerPoint offers sets of "canned" slides each for a different type of presentation (e.g., persuasive, reporting status, and educational). Each set is structured with an outline of the content that should be included in a presentation with the general goal of the presentation type selected (e.g., reporting status).
- *Outlining.* The software offers an outline view that shows only the text and its hierarchical organization. Text can be either viewed or edited in this mode. This mode facilitates thinking about and representing presentation content in an organized hierarchy. The easily viewed outline offers teachers a quick way to see the organization of a student's presentation and provide feedback.
- *Hierarchical organization of text.* In addition to the outline view, one can easily show hierarchical relationships between text content through the use of bulleted and sub-bulleted text (text indented under the initial bullet) or numbered lists that, again, can include lists within lists. This feature provides support for presentation writers to consider the relationships between concepts on individual slides.
- *Linking.* PowerPoint supports the insertion of different types of links to other applications. Users can insert labeled links to Internet addresses or to specific locations within a Microsoft Word, an Excel, or another

PowerPoint document. When in presentation mode, users can jump directly from their presentation to the specified page. Given that information comes in many forms, the support of links in presentations allows learners to seamlessly bring in multiple information sources.

- *Notes.* Users can create detailed notes for each slide either to help in the oral delivery of the presentation or to help someone who is reading the presentation at a later time understand the slide. Teachers can draw attention to (and perhaps require the use of) this feature to emphasize the importance of creating presentation slides that contain only key points while placing any lengthy prose into the slide notes.

PowerPoint also offers features that can distract learners from creating an effective presentation. Most of these features are focused on the visual design, graphics, and animation that are part of the presentation. Although we recognize the value of text and slide design as learning outcomes, if the primary goal is to write an effective presentation, then some students may need to be cautioned against spending too much time on the visual design features. For instance, Oppenheimer (2004) recounts the story of a student who spent 17 hours on a PowerPoint presentation of which only 7 hours were spent on the actual writing. Here are just a few of the potential pitfalls:

- *"Font-itus".* This term is used to describe the usage of too many fonts (e.g., Ariel, Comic Sans Serif, or Times New Roman) and/or too many font styles (underline, bold, or italic), sizes, or colors.
- *Overzealous slide transitions.* PowerPoint offers the ability to have sides fade in using a checkerboard pattern, slide in from one direction or another, appear as if opening up Venetian blinds, and so on. Selecting one of these and using it consistently throughout a presentation may be appropriate. However, learners may be overly entranced with these effects to the point of becoming a distraction.
- *Incongruous slide templates.* PowerPoint offers many combinations of slide backgrounds and prescripted fonts, bullet types, and graphics all of which combine to make a "design template." Some templates are abstract (e.g., digital dots), while others denote a theme (e.g., a mountaintop). They also vary in terms of their visual simplicity or complexity. These templates are easy to use and provide learners with a ready-made set of fonts and colors that generally work together well. However, learners should be cautioned against choosing a template that uses graphics that don't fit with the information in the presentation or, alternatively, a template that includes background graphics that conflict with their own presentation images. Fortunately, it is easy to change from one design template to another at any point during the creation of the presentation.
- *Too many slides.* PowerPoint makes it easy to create slides; that can be both a good and a bad thing. Learners may find they create many slides where fewer, more carefully designed and worded slides would be more effective.

To counteract these, teachers can provide guidance in the form of presentation requirements. For instance, one might stipulate that presentations may use a maximum of three different fonts and some specified number of colors or animations. Alternatively, teachers could require a phased approach to presentation development. Perhaps students are required to write only the text of their presentation initially with placeholder slides that describe in words the graph, animation, picture, or other visual that will be inserted in a next draft. Teachers can then work with students on developing a clear set of presentation text before students begin to engage in the potentially distracting features of PowerPoint for inserting graphs or animations.

Teachers may also wish to have students engage in the evaluation of existing PowerPoint presentations as a learning activity for writing presentations. An Internet search will quickly provide teachers or students with a variety of presentations to study. This activity can help students, together with teachers, develop their own set of guidelines for how to use the features of PowerPoint to support their presentations and, as important, what to avoid.

Regardless of its potential drawbacks, putting PowerPoint into the hands of students for creating presentations is a popular activity for a wide range of grade levels. The following two examples illustrate how the tool can be applied. Both examples illustrate how the writing aspect of creating presentations can be used within the context of other disciplines (e.g., science or history).

A suburban first-grade teacher used PowerPoint presentations as part of a research project on animals (KITE, 2001a). Students used the Internet to find and download pictures of animals; they created word problems that included their animal, gathered scientific facts about the animal, and finally combined all their unit work into a PowerPoint presentation.

A library media specialist worked with a fourth-grade teacher to modify the teacher's traditional project on historical figures from Missouri (KITE, 2001b). Normally, the teacher had students research their figure, write a report, and do an oral presentation. The media specialist worked with the teacher to add student-created PowerPoint presentations as part of the project. The specialist commented, "This is not the ideal situation for the use of technology, as it was really just adding work to what the kids were already doing," but even so students learned to use the software and were able to organize their research in a new way.

Supporting Creative Writing With Technology

Even creative writing can be supported through specific uses of technology. The National Commission on Writing recommends that using technology tools can help motivate writers because often an aspect of technology-based writing is publishing the writing in some form (Anonymous, 2005). One project, titled *The Pigman—Chapter Sixteen,* developed by Eileen Skarecki of Columbia Middle School in New Jersey, seems to have this potential. In this project, students read the popular adolescent novel *The Pigman,* which, in Skarecki's words, "leaves the reader hanging." Her response? Have students write a final chapter and post the submissions on the Internet for others to read and respond to.

This simple activity of placing their work on the Internet for public access inspires many students to take their work more seriously and to engage in a level of reflection about their work that is otherwise rare. It will also cause them to write with a purpose, to think critically about what they write, to read what others have produced, and to compare their own work to the work of others. In addition to this new level of reflection inspired by Internet publishing, it is possible to design activities that cause students to be more reflective—to think about their work and the work of others in ways that lead to academic growth.

Kidscribe (http://www.kidscribe.org) is a simple Web site that was created to provide young writers with a forum for publishing personal writing in either English or Spanish. The creator of Kidscribe wanted to provide an outlet that would build the young author's sense of confidence and pride in his or her own work while also providing an opportunity for site users to see creative writing samples in two languages and without the presence of commercial advertisements. Although the site offers no writing supports per se, it is easy to use and could be effectively used with teacher instruction on writing, especially for teachers who have limited resources (e.g., server space) for doing their own Web publishing of student work.

Although certainly not an ad-free Web site, http://www.scholastic.com also offers a potential publication venue for poetry and other forms of writing.[1] But beyond simply providing a potential publication venue, the Scholastic site also offers guided grade level–specific lessons on various aspects of writing poetry, memoirs, or short fiction. For instance, the site offers "writing workshops" on topics such as writing transitions, forms of poetry, and writing oral histories. Lessons often include simple practice exercises for the topic along with feedback based on the learners' response. Lessons also contain examples and lists of appropriate words to help construct the rhetorical construct being taught (e.g., a list of words and phrases for writing transitions). Such lessons could easily be used for whole-class discussion and activities or for students working in small groups around a single computer. A variation on these workshops is the lessons offered in Scholastic's "Writing with Writers" section (Rowen, 2005). This offering features a set of online workshops that are designed by professional writers (e.g., news wirters and poets). Each workshop provides a suggested process for that particular type of writing, and each workshop ends with a mechanism for students to submit their own work for publication. Scholastic does not publish all submissions.

---

[1]At this writing, we found these resources by following the "Teachers" and then "Online Resources" links.

Poetry Forge (http://www.poetryforge.org) was developed by the University of Virginia's Center for Technology and Teacher Education (http://www.curry .edschool.virginia.edu/teacherlink) and is another online site that offers tools to support creative writing, in this case focused on poetry. Poetry Forge offers a set of open-source writing tools for the English classroom. Downloadable tools work on either a Windows or a Mac platform and include a metaphor generator, a tool for building new poems founded on existing poetry, and a tool that explores the characteristics of "poetic text." The tools are designed to challenge student understanding of simple parts of speech, complex phrases, and what happens both semantically and syntactically for language to effectively convey meaning in a poem. For instance, Figure 4.4 shows the PoetryForge online metaphor tool. Users enter their own adjectives, nouns, and prepositional phrases, and the tool combines them into "poetic" phrases. According to the Web site, Poetry Forge tools are designed to be used with teachers working alongside students, coaching them and challenging their thinking. The site offers a good explanation of the technical requirements for the downloadable tools as well as lesson plans and suggestions for teachers on how to use them in their classrooms.

Tools like Poetry Forge are not likely to create the next national poet laureate, but they do help learners engage in poetry writing and practicing the application of literary structures that are essential and commonly used in poetry writing. The Web site authors directly acknowledge that the poetry that results from using Poetry

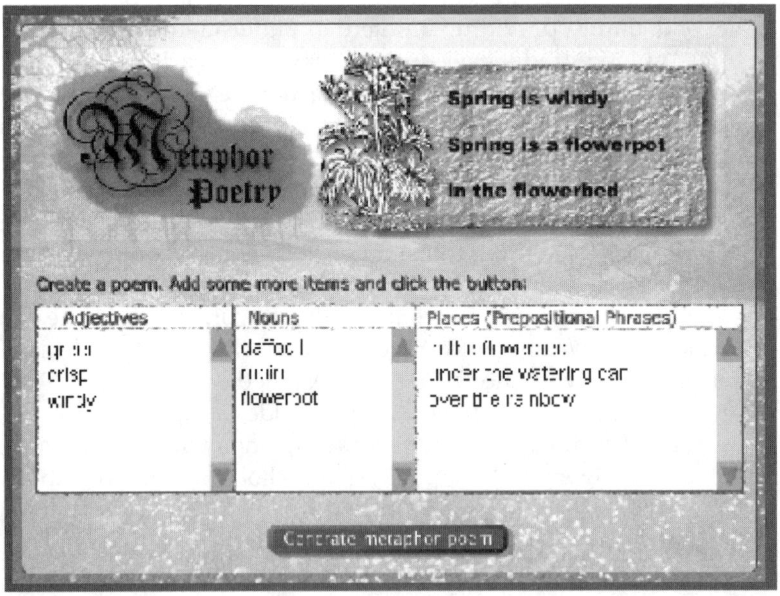

Figure 4.4

Forge tools will be "unpredictable" (http://www.poetryforge.org/about.htm). They do, however, posit that even such results will provide the basis for editing, adjustment, and evaluation—all of which are critical and commonly acknowledge parts of the writing process—and often parts that are overlooked by novices.

Supporting Collaborative Writing With Technology

Collaborative writing refers to activities where written works are created by multiple people together rather than individually. Ede and Lunsford (1986) described three general sets of collaborative writing activities: (a) intensive collaboration where authors create a text by working closely together, (b) significant writing that is done separately but on which writers work to a limited extent collaboratively, and (c) sequential group collaboration that occurs through a sequence of activities.

Just as in other collaborative processes, sometimes roles are assigned, such as editor, reporter, or leader. Ethnographers of writing who have studied these roles have described the complex interactions that can occur in collaborative reading and writing between "authors," "readers," and "texts" and posit that the roles are constantly being renegotiated during collaborative writing (e.g., Flower, Long, and Higgins, (as cited in Lunsford & Bruce, 2001). Potential benefits of having learners engage in collaborative writing include positive relationships between students, increased participation by students, opportunities for peer and self-assessment, more sources of input and ideas, varied points of view, and of course, when writing with persons from other cultures, cross-cultural fertilization (Hernandez et al., 2001).

Collaborative writing has been practiced for many years in business, educational, and personal settings; however, the advent of technology tools to support collaborative writing has increased its popularity (Lunsford & Bruce, 2001). Collaborative writing can occur in either synchronous (real time) or asynchronous (with a time delay) settings.

A synchronous setting may look as pictured in Figure 4.5. Individual or small groups of students are sitting at work stations running software that supports a collaborative writing space. The work stations may or may not be immediately proximate to one another. If they are not, then users would need to be in contact with one another, through the writing software itself, an instant messaging service, or e-mail to "dialogue". Learners could be engaged in the following activities:

- Brainstorming ideas
- Structuring the flow of their writing
- Generating text to be used in their written product
- Editing text
- Negotiating meaning of any of these tasks

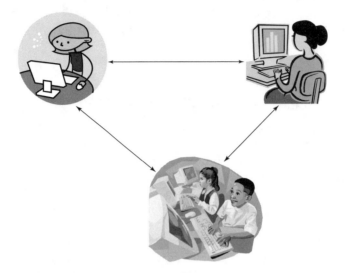

Figure 4.5 Students at different work stations writing collaboratively.

In an asynchronous setting, the activities could be similar; however, they would not necessarily occur in real time. Such a scenario and collaborative writing software make nationwide and even global collaborative writing feasible.

Many collaborative writing tools are available; readers can refer to the Wikipedia (http://www.wikipedia.com) entry on collaborative writing for a partial list. Although many tools and projects are focused on adult writers rather than K–12 learners, one tool that at this writing is free and also usable in K–12 environments is Writely (http://www.writely.com). Writely offers many features that can facilitate collaborative writing. Here are a few of the most important:

- *Importing documents.* Documents can be imported into Writely from Microsoft Word, HTML documents, text or image files, or anything from which you copy and paste. Writely documents exist in an HTML format, but you edit them in a WYSIWYG (what you see is what you get) method.
- *Sharing documents.* Once you create a document in Writely, you have the ability to immediately add up to 12 collaborators on that Writely document (see Figure 4.6). New collaborators are notified of their status through e-mail that you compose.
- *Revision history.* You can also view your document's revision history, compare versions, and roll back to any version.
- *Unlimited (at this writing) or generous storage space.* Documents can be up to 500K in size, and each document can be shared with up to 50 people.

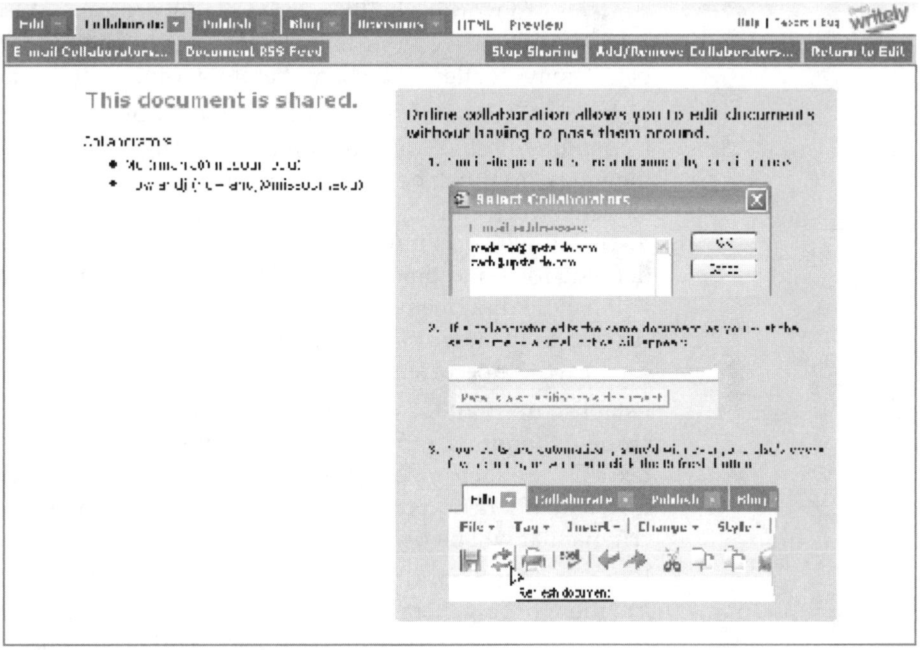

Figure 4.6   Document collaboration using Writely.

- *Levels of collaboration or sharing.* Writely allows you to specify that only specific users can also have editing and commenting privileges on your document. Other users can simply view the document. Writely calls this "publishing" the document.
- *Creating comments.* Any collaborator can insert comments.. Anyone who can edit the document can see the comments that are inserted. Persons with viewing-only privileges cannot.
- *Publishing documents.* Documents can be published for viewing (but not editing) by others through Writely simply by "publishing" it from the document window. Writely also offers publishing of documents to blogs.

Although word processing software offers some of these features (such as commenting), the sharing attributes of software like Writely is what makes it well suited for collaboration.

Even with the best software, we advise teachers to appropriately support not only the writing aspects but also the social aspects of the collaborative writing task. Students don't "just know" how to collaborate—they need help to be successful. The following guidelines can help students successfully engage in collaborative writing and other collaborative activities (Herandez et al., 2001):

1. Structure activities at the beginning of the project to build cohesion between the collaborators and to establish positive interpersonal relationships. If

students are working with other students at a distance, consider having them spend time engaging in Internet "chats" on nonacademic subjects (e.g., pets, family, or after-school jobs) before starting their writing projects.

2. Help the collaborators work out effective meeting or working procedures. Depending on the construction of the group and the task, synchronous meetings may not be how group members communicate, but even if students work entirely asynchronously, they will still benefit from having discussed who and how the writing process will work. This may involve defining roles and timelines. Additionally, help students discuss how they will handle disagreements or conflicts within groups. Having this discussion up front and/or setting up procedures for these inevitable situations can turn these occurrences into minor bumps rather than major roadblocks.

3. Establish up front the expectations for participation in the project. Are all students required to write approximately the same amount of original text? Or, are there roles where some students are writers, others are editors, and others lead or manage the team? Align these requirements to the criteria that will be used to evaluate the project or product.

4. Pay attention to students who are more susceptible to marginalization, isolation, or in general to being left out. Depending on the nature of the project and the group membership, the students in this category will vary. As a teacher, however, you should be aware of students who are not being allowed to actively and meaningfully participate in the project. This requires frequent monitoring by a teacher and can also be aided by periodic and preplanned team self-assessments.

5. Have students use the collaborative writing software for a "test" project before embarking on a major collaborative writing task. Packages such as Writely are fairly intuitive, but taking the "new software package anxiety" variable out of the collaborative writing equation can help ensure success.

Collaborative writing can be used meaningfully for a variety of tasks. Rogers and Horton (1992) suggest that teachers select topics for collaborative writing that encourage active participation, such as simulations of real-world job tasks, or that have the potential for "conflict" between writers that needs to be resolved. And as said previously, one advantage of collaborative writing is that it can support cross-disciplinary learning tasks. Here are some examples of current online collaborative projects that could easily include a writing task as well as potential cross-disciplinary collaborative writing tasks:

- Engage students in collaborative writing in the context of other Internet-based collaborative tasks. For instance, Telegarden (http://cwis.usc.edu/dept/garden/) allows students to collaboratively tend a living garden over the Internet. In Telegarden, users control a robot arm that can plant seeds, water plants, and monitor growth. This type of environment clearly supports science-learning outcomes; however, the activity could easily be combined with a collaborative writing task where students from a single class in one school or multiple classes in multiple locations could collaborate on the experiments as well as report writing.

- Have students partner with students at a distance to engage in collaboratively writing a newspaper article. Choose to partner with a school district that has access to data sources that are not available to your students. For instance, students in Columbia, Missouri, might co–write news articles with students in Baton Rouge, Louisiana, about the aftermath of Hurricane Katrina. Students in Columbia have access and can develop expertise with the Columbia-based Rescue One squad that did search-and-rescue operations after Katrina, while the Baton Rouge students can contribute the impact of Katrina on their community as refugees poured into the city and many now reside there permanently.

As teachers read these ideas, they may reasonably ask how they might find collaborative partners. The Global School House Network (http://www.globalschoolnet.org) is a registry service that allows teachers to submit calls for collaboration, search ongoing collaborative projects, or add a project of their own. A recent visit to the site showed they currently have more than 2,000 online projects registered; projects are organized by topic, grade, and project date, facilitating a variety of search strategies.

Supporting Peer Feedback on Writing

Writing instructors have come to realize the importance of multiple drafts in the writing process (Schriver, 1990). However, creating multiple drafts and the editing and reediting process is effective only when novice writers receive feedback. One reason writing instruction is difficult for teachers may be the time demands of providing the feedback necessary to help students both effectively revise their work and improve their writing in a next attempt. Teachers understandably have limited time to devote to such feedback, especially when they have many students and many subjects to teach. The result is often that students do not engage in many (if any) multiple-draft writing projects. Further, even when instructors provide feedback, it is often focused on accuracy of content and clarity of writing (both of which are extremely valuable forms of feedback) but may completely ignore writing style (Ziv, 1981).

Implementing student peer feedback on writing may offer a solution to some of these problems. While having fellow students provide feedback to their peers on writing has been implemented, more recent research has shown that student-to-student feedback may be more effective in helping students improve in their writing than the "expert" feedback they may receive from teachers (Cho, Schunn, & Charney, 2006; Schriver, 1990). In addition to helping to reduce the burden on instructors of providing writing feedback, reciprocal peer assessment may help students develop evaluation skills that can be applied in many settings, increase responsibility for their own learning, and improve writing skills.

SWoRD (Scaffolded Writing and Rewriting in the Discipline; Cho et al., 2006) is a Web-based reciprocal peer review system that is designed to facilitate peer review while providing mechanisms to ensure validity and the potential of student bias in providing feedback. SWoRD enables teachers and students to implement the peer review process by managing the distribution of papers to reviewers and reviews back to authors and addressing typical peer review concerns, such as author and reviewer confidentiality. It also includes evaluation mechanisms that structure the "reviewer" students' tasks and that help them take their reviewing task seriously. For instance, SWoRD includes an evaluation rubric that reviewers must complete and requires that reviewers include written comments in their feedback. Then, according to the draft, review, and revision schedule the instructor has defined, SWoRD automatically distributes the completed reviews to the authors. Figure 4.7 shows the "reviews and back-reviews" window an author would see for his or her draft.

SWoRD addresses another typically problematic part of high-quality writing: that of producing multiple drafts. To use SWoRD as an author, the student must submit first and revised drafts, and peers then evaluate both drafts. SWoRD is free to use for noncommercial purposes and is available at http://ladybug.lrdc .pitt.edu/sword. Note that to date, SWoRD has been used primarily in higher education.

Reviews and Back-Reviews on Your 1st Draft		
Flows ☆☆☆☆☆		
Reviewer	Comments	Back-Reviews
Reviewer 1 ★★★	Average (4) In order to certain writing can be regard as smooth flow, it is constructed locally and globally coherent. It means that each parts should written locally coherent, at the same time, they should be connected organizationally. For these connections, each paragraph has well associated with topic sentence or topic word, and subtitles also can play a role like that, I think. In this view point, if you present your writing procedure and revise each subtitle for global organization of paper, it will be definitely more coherent and flow smoothly.	☆★★★★ Although this was certainly needed, I think maybe some specific suggestions would have helped me out more.
Reviewer 2 ★★★★★★★	Average (4) Prose Flow Your review and summary of Schunn and Dunbar's (1996) work under the heading of background was well written. However, it is not clear where the literature review ends and your argument begins. What exactly is your position? If this is the case, perhaps the paper would flow more smoothly if you provide more detailed descriptions of the concepts you are addressing. For example, defining learning, base-level activation and chunking may perhaps allow you to make smoother transitions. Additional comments: The author did not following the instructions regarding doulble spacing, running head and page margins.	☆☆☆☆☆★★ I did not remember reading about instructions for spacing, running heads, and such, but after your comment I went back and saw that.

Figure 4.7

Conclusion

Even in today's technology-laden society, writing continues to be a skill critical to success in many in- and out-of-school endeavors. It also continues to be a task that is, at best, not pleasurable and, at worst, anxiety ridden for many—again both in and out of school. Like many other tasks, writing, depending on the type of writing activity one targets, can be broken down into subcomponent tasks, such as setting goals, planning, organizing ideas, composing text, and editing.

In this chapter we have described several tools available for different parts of the writing process (e.g., concept maps for planning and organizing), tools for different types of writing (PowerPoint for presentations and Poetry Forge for poetry), and tools for supporting collaborative writing. The tools offer a variety of ways of making writing more fun for students (e.g., Poetry Forge's metaphor generator), experiencing the motivation of having their writing "published," and providing supports and structure for different writing activities. Additionally, tools that support collaborative writing offer teachers and students opportunities to engage in meaningful writing tasks in cross-disciplinary settings with collaborators in almost any location. In nearly all cases, however, writing remains a complex task that will require considerable supervision, encouragement, and, perhaps most of all, frequent and high-quality feedback from teachers.

Things to Think About

We suggest that you use the following questions to reflect on the ideas that we presented in this chapter.

1. What type or types of writing do your students struggle with the most? How can you use an understanding of the writing process to further diagnose students' writing difficulties?
2. What types of writing activities would make the best use of technology in your classrooms?
3. How can you increase the use of meaningful writing activities in cross-disciplinary projects? How can technology help with these cross-disciplinary writing tasks?
4. Would the act of "publishing" student's written work (on the Internet, for instance) be motivating to your students? How can you leverage this potential for motivation in your classroom?
5. Writing is an activity that benefits from multiple revisions and high-quality feedback. Recognizing that your teaching time is limited, how can

you have students help each other during writing? How can you use technology tools to support peer feedback?

6. Collaborative activities have many potential benefits, but students don't automatically know how to collaborate successfully. What strategies can you or have you put in place to make collaborative teams effective in terms of both completing the intended task and helping students learn to be good collaborators?

References

Anderson-Inman, L., & Horney, M. (1996). Computer-based concept mapping: Enhancing literary with tools for visual thinking. *Journal of Adolescent and Adult Literacy, 40*(4), 302. Retrieved August 17, 2006, from the Academic Search Premier database.

Anonymous. (2005). Reading and writing tools. *T.H.E. Journal, 31*(5), 19.

Cho, K., Schunn, C., & Charney, D. (2006). Commenting on writing: Typology and perceived helpfulness of comments from novice peer reviewers and subject matter experts. *Written Communication, 23*(3), 260–294.

Ede, L. S., & Lunsford, A. A. (1986). Why write . . . together. A Research Update. *Rhetoric Review 5*(1), 71–81.

Flower, L. S., Schriver, K. A., Carey, L., Haas, C., & Hayes, J. R. (1989). *Planning in writing: The cognition of a constructive process* (Technical Report). Berkeley: University of California, Center for the Study of Writing.

Hernandez, N., Hoeksema, A., Kelm, H., Jefferies, J., Lawrence, K., Lee, S., et al. (2001). *Collaborative writing in the classroom: A method to produce quality work*. Retrieved August 24, 2006, from http://scholar.google.com/scholar?hl=en&lr=&q=cache:QvZksOWKIGsJ:www.edb.utexas.edu/resta/itesm2001/topicpapers/s2paper.pdf+k-12+technology+OR+software+%22collaborative+writing%22

KITE. (2001a). Case 8235–1. Kite Case Library. Retrieved August 22, 2006, from http://kite.missouri.edu

KITE (2001b). Case 9301-1. Kite Case Library. Retrieved August 22, 2006, from http://kite.missouri.edu

Lunsford, K. J., & Bruce, B. C. (2001). Collaboratories: Working together on the Web. *Journal of Adolescent and Adult Literacy, 45*(1). Available from http://www.readingonline.org/electronic/elec_index.asp?HREF=/electronic/jaal/9-01_Column/index.html

Oppenheimer, T. (2004). *The flickering mind: The false promise of technology in the classroom and how learning can be saved*. New York: Random House.

National Council of Teachers of English. (1996). *Standards for the English language arts*. Retrieved August 22, 2006, from http://cnets.iste.org/currstands/cstands-ela.html

Rogers, P. S., & Horton, M. S. (1992). Exploring the value of face-to-face collaborative writing. In J. Forman (Ed.), *New visions of collaborative writing* (pp. 120–146). Portsmouth, NH: Boynton/Cook.

Rowen, D. (2005). The write motivation. *Learning and Leading with Technology, 32*(5), 22.

Schriver, K. A. (1990). *Evaluating text quality: The continuum from text-focused to reader-focused methods* (*Technical Report No. 41*). Berkeley, CA: National Center for the Study of Writing and Literacy.

Ziv, Y. (1981, January). *On some discourse uses of existentials in English, or, getting more mileage out of existentials in English*. Paper presented at the annual meeting of the Linguistic Society of America, New York.

Modeling With Technologies

Learning by Building Models

Traditionally, technologies have been used in schools to "teach" students, much the same as teachers "teach" students. When technologies teach, information is stored in the technology, which is presented to the students, who try to understand and remember the information. Sometimes the technology asks students questions to find out if the students understood or remembered the information. The students reply to the technology, often by selecting and pressing a key. The technology then judges the students' responses and determines how well the students understood or remembered. The technology is "teaching" the students. Technologies have been developed by instructional designers and marketed to educators as *learner-proof* and *teacher-proof*, removing any meaningful control of the learning process by the learners or the teachers.

We argue that this method of using technologies to teach does not exploit the capabilities of the technologies or the students. It requires the technology, for instance, to do things that learners do better and the learners to do things that technologies do better. For example, using computers to teach requires computers to present information, judge answers, diagnose student understanding, and adapt the way they are teaching to meet the needs of the student. Artificial intelligence projects have spent millions of dollars in efforts to imbue the computer with enough intelligence to do these things. However, a good teacher can do them all far better than any computer. When computers teach students, students are required to memorize and recall information. Computers do that much better than humans. They are high-speed storage devices with much greater memories than humans. So, when working with technologies, why not ask learners to do what they do best (or at least what we hope they will do best), that is, conceptualize, organize, and solve problems, and technologies to do what they do best, that is, memorize and retrieve? That way, you'll realize a synergy from the student using the computer.

One way to realize this synergy is for students to use computer-based technologies as tools for teaching the computer what they know. When students teach the computer, they represent their internal, mental models in different ways using different programs. Why should computers be used to enable model building by learners? Because humans are natural model builders. From a very early age, we construct mental models of everything that we encounter in the world. For example, toddlers construct theories about their environments, what they can get away with, and what they better not do. These models make up our personal theories about the world that enable us to reason about the things that we encounter. There are models in the mind (mental models), and computers can support the construction of external models that represent the models in the mind. The relationship between internal and external models is not well understood; however, we believe there is a dynamic and reciprocal relationship between learners' internal mental models and the external models they construct. Mental models provide the basis for computer models. Building the computer models helps learners construct better mental models.

Students may externalize their internal mental models using a variety of computer-based Mindtools (Jonassen, 2006), including databases, concept mapping, spreadsheets, microworlds, systems modeling tools, expert systems, hypermedia construction tools, constraint-based discussion boards, and visualization tools, for constructing models of things that students are studying. Each tool requires that learners think in a different way about what they are studying. When using Mindtools to model phenomena, students are teaching the computer rather than vice versa. Mindtools can function as intellectual partners that share the cognitive burden of carrying out tasks (Salomon, 1993). Mindtools do not necessarily make learning easier. They are not "fingertip" tools (Perkins, 1993) that learners use naturally and effortlessly. In fact, learning *with* Mindtools requires learners to think harder about the subject-matter domain being studied than they would have to think without the Mindtool. Students cannot use Mindtools without thinking deeply about the content they are learning, and if they choose to use these tools to help them learn, the tools will facilitate the learning and meaning-making processes. The primary purpose of student modeling is the construction and revision of the learner's conceptual understanding, a process known as conceptual change and one that is sometimes difficult.

In addition to using different Mindtools to engage different kinds of thinking, they can also be used to build models of different phenomena. Mindtools can be used to model domain knowledge, or the content that students are supposed to learn in schools. Building models of that content will help students better comprehend and remember what they are learning. Mindtools may also be used to build models of systems, and this requires students to understand how domain knowledge is tied together. Systems are organizations of dynamic, interdependent parts that are oriented by a common purpose and controlled by feedback. Requiring learners to organize what they are learning into relevant systems that interact with each other provides learners with a much more integrated view of the world. Mindtools may also be used to build models of problems. To solve virtually any kind of problem, students must mentally construct a problem space that models the specific relations of the problem. Using modeling tools to create models externalizes learners' mental problem space. Some Mindtools, especially databases, can be used to collect, analyze, and organize stories of people's experiences. Stories are the oldest and most natural form of meaning making. Finally, Mindtools can also be used model thinking processes. Rather than modeling content or systems, learners model the kind of thinking that they need to perform to solve a problem, make a decision, or complete some other task. Each different phenomenon (content, systems, problems, stories, and reflective thinking) represents a different kind of knowledge. This is important because the more ways that learners can represent their conceptual understanding, the better they will understand. In the remainder of this chapter, we illustrate how some of the modeling tools have been used by students to construct models of different kinds of knowledge.

Modeling Knowledge With Concept Maps

Concept maps are spatial representations of concepts and their interrelationships that simulate the knowledge structures that humans store in their minds (Jonassen, Beissner, & Yacci, 1993). These knowledge structures are also known as cognitive structures, conceptual knowledge, structural knowledge, and semantic networks. The semantic networks in memory (conceptual model in the mind) and the maps that represent them are composed of nodes (concepts or ideas) that are connected by links (statements of relationships). In computer-based semantic networks, nodes are represented as information blocks, and the links are labeled lines. Figure 5.1 illustrates one screen of a complex concept map of domain knowledge related to the Shakespearean tragedy *Othello* produced with Semantica (http://www.semanticresearch.com). Double-clicking on any concept on the map puts that concept in the middle of the screen and shows all the other concepts that are associated with it. Most semantic networking programs also provide the capability of adding text and pictures to each node to elaborate that concept.

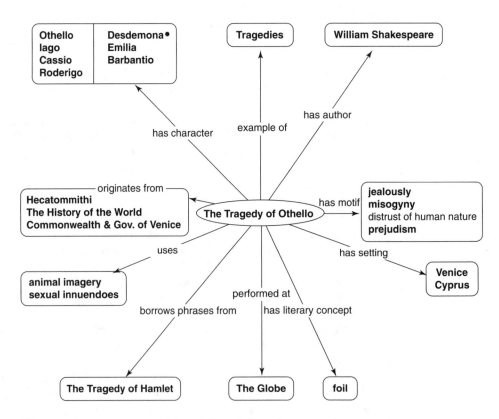

Figure 5.1   Concept map of domain knowledge using Semantica.

Figure 5.2 illustrates a concept map of chemistry content. This map describes all the major concepts and their relationships in molar conversions in chemistry. Understanding those relationships is essential to being able to meaningfully calculate molar conversions. Too often, teachers present formulas used to calculate without teaching the process conceptually. That is why concept mapping is so useful. The map in Figure 5.2 was produced with Inspiration, which, unlike Semantica, presents concepts on a single map. Users can use a special key sequence to create a submap under any concept. Unfortunately, the concepts wth submaps are not noted in the current version. The most important software requirement, we believe, is the ability to describe or type the links between concepts. Many concept mapping programs do not support this feature. We believe they are not worth using in classrooms. Linking is challenging, but it is absolutely necessary for constructing anything similar to an internal semantic network.

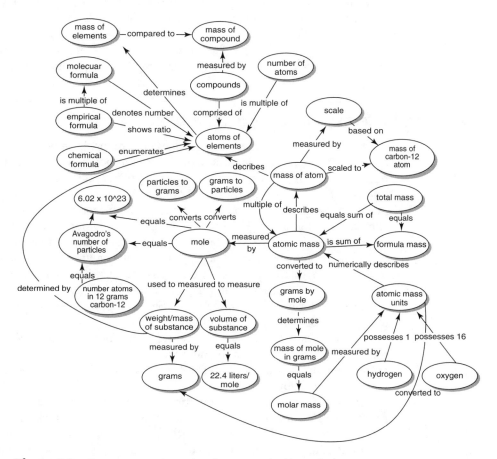

Figure 5.2 Concept map about chemistry created with Inspiration.

Concept maps provide learners with a tool for representing the semantic structure of domain knowledge. Concept mapping is a process of identifying important concepts, arranging those concepts spatially, identifying relationships among those concepts, and labeling the nature of the relationships among those concepts. Concept maps can be drawn by hand using simple artifacts such as cards and string and sticky notes. However, a variety of computer-based semantic networking software enables much easier (and arguably more powerful) production of concept maps. Concept mapping tools are also effectively used to model the semantic organization of systems, problems, stories, or thinking processes of students.

The most effective use of concept mapping tools for representing domain knowledge is for students to spend the entire year constructing a concept map that models content from textbooks, lectures, or other information sources. Such a map may include a few thousand concepts, helping students better comprehend the domain rather than trying to memorize their notes. As with all other tools, comparing your semantic network with others often results in conceptual change as students see how other models represent and structure the same ideas. We should also note that concept mapping is useful for modeling systems, problems, and stories (as evidenced by the map of *Othello*) but probably not as effective for modeling thinking processes. A recent analysis of research literature clearly shows that students learn more from constructing their own maps than by studying teacher-produced maps.

Modeling Systems With Systems Dynamics Tools

Modeling systems illustrates the causal interrelationships among the components of a system. Systems are dynamic when their components are related to changes in other system components; that is, components of a systems affect other components, which in turn affect the original components. The components of systems can be modeled using computer-based systems modeling tools for constructing dynamic simulations of systems. The students construct dynamic models that qualitatively and quantitatively represent relationships among system components. These models conceptually represent the changing nature of system phenomena in a form that resembles the real thing. These simulations are only abstractions, or models of reality. They are not faithful, actual simulations of things.

Computer-based tools, including Stella, VenSim, and PowerSim, help learners build these dynamic simulation models of systems. These tools use accumulations and flows as the primary modeling tools. For example, the systems model of the sun in Figure 5.3 was built using Stella and represents the factors that regulate the sun. Stella uses a simple set of building block icons to construct a map of a process: stocks, flows, converters, and connectors (see Figure 5.3). Stocks illustrate the accumulation or level of some thing in the simulation. In Figure 5.3, *total mass, energy capacitor, luminosity, radius,* and others blocks are stocks. Flows control the inflow or outflow of material to stocks. *Converting releasing energy, emitting light,* and others are flows. Flows often counterbalance each other, like the increasing and decreasing flows related to temperature in Figure 5.3. Converters convert inputs

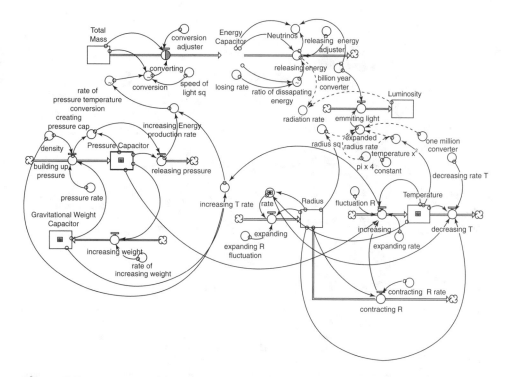

Figure 5.3 Systems model of the sun.

into outputs. They are factors or ratios that influence flows. *Releasing energy adjuster* and *ratio of dissipating energy* are converters that control the flow, *releasing energy*. Converters are used to add complexity to the models to better represent the complexity in the real world. Finally, connectors are the lines that show the directional effect of factors on each other by the use of arrows. Students generate equations in the stocks and flows for numerically representing relationships between the variables identified on the map.

A cautionary note is needed here. Systems modeling with Stella probably cannot be used effectively with elementary students. It requires formal operational reasoning skills, so to our knowledge it has not been used successfully with students younger than junior high school. However, a tool named Model-It (http://www.goknow.com) was developed to support systems modeling for middle school students. It may be useful for some elementary students. Figure 5.4 shows a model of the human circulatory systems and its relationships to other systems. The students who built this were definitely thinking systemically about the human body.

Once a model has been built, Stella and Model-It enable learners to run the model they have created and observe the output in graphs, tables, or animations. That is, Stella enables students to create and test simulations of their models. The models use simple algebra to convey the strength of relationships between each

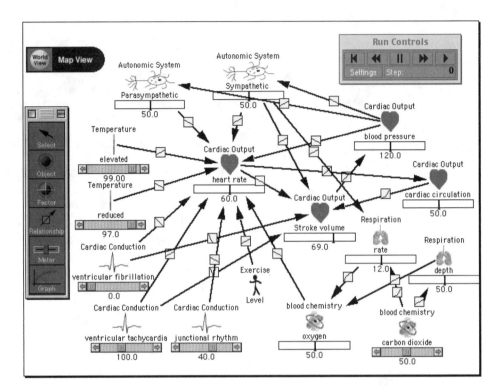

Figure 5.4 Systems model built with Model-It.

other. When the model is run, it becomes a simulation that is driven by an engine based on differential equations, emphasizing change over time. When running the simulation based on the model that students construct, students can change the variable values to test the effects of parts of a system on the other parts. If the results are inconsistent with expectations, students must examine their models to find the equations that are out of balance. Students may search the Internet for real-word statistics to use in their models, or they may use data from experiments they have conducted. The use of real-world data makes the modeling process all the more authentic and engaging. Finally, it is also important to note that systems modeling can also be used effectively to model complex problems and thinking processes (for examples, see Jonassen, 2006).

Modeling Problems With Spreadsheets

Spreadsheets are computerized record-keeping systems. They were originally designed to replace paper-based ledger systems. Essentially, a spreadsheet is a grid (or table or matrix) of empty cells, with columns identified by letters and rows identified by numbers. The information included in any cell may consist of text, numbers, formulas to manipulate the numeric contents of any other cells, or mathematical or logical functions to manipulate the contents of any other cells.

Spreadsheets have three primary functions: storing, calculating, and presenting information. First, information, usually numerical, can be stored in a particular cell from which it can be readily accessed and retrieved. Second—and most important—spreadsheets support calculation functions, such that the numerical contents of any combination of cells can be mathematically related in just about any way the user wishes. Finally, spreadsheets present information in a variety of graphs and charts as well as graphics.

Spreadsheets are an example of a Mindtool that amplifies and reorganizes mental functioning. Building spreadsheet models engages a variety of mental processes that require learners to use existing rules, generate new rules describing relationships, and organize information. The emphasis in a spreadsheet is on identifying relationships and describing those relationships in terms of higher-order rules (generally numerical), so it is probable that if users learn to develop spreadsheets to describe content domains, they will be thinking more deeply. Thus, spreadsheets are rule-using tools that require that users become rule makers (Vockell & Van Deusen, 1989). Defining the arithmetic operations that calculate values in a spreadsheet requires users to identify relationships and patterns among the data they want to represent in the spreadsheet. Next, those relationships must be modeled mathematically using rules to describe the relationships in the model. Building spreadsheets requires abstract reasoning by the user. Although spreadsheets have been used most consistently in schools as management tools for accounting, they are being used increasingly as Mindtools to support higher-order quantitative thinking. Spreadsheets have been used to model phenomena in at least four ways: computational reasoning tools for analyzing data, mathematics comprehension, visualization, and simulation modeling tools.

Spreadsheets may be used to construct simulations of problems that students are studying. For example, Figure 5.5 shows a simulation of a problem involving Ohm's law. The simulation presents a series of batteries and allows a user to manipulate the values of the impedence (ohms) or voltage. Simulating phenomena using spreadsheets provides a "direct and effective means of understanding the role of various parameters and of testing different means of optimizing their values" (Sundheim, 1992, p. 654). Having students construct simulations engages them more than simply using simulations that teachers develop.

In Figure 5.6, students have created a spreadsheet to illustrate the different chemicals that are inhaled when smoking cigarettes. This simple simulation allows a user to scroll the bar at the top to describe how many cigarettes are smoked. As the bar is scrolled, the bar graphs change. Understanding these relationships is important to understand the problems of smoking. When students see how many poisonous chemicals are inhaled, the problem becomes more acute.

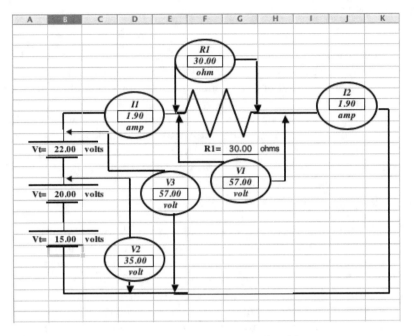

Figure 5.5 Spreadsheet simulation of an electrical problem.

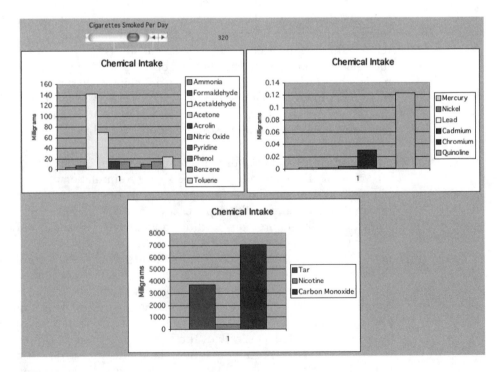

Figure 5.6 Spreadsheet depiction of the chemical effects of smoking.

Modeling Thinking With Expert Systems

Expert systems are computer programs designed to simulate expert reasoning to facilitate decision making for all sorts of problems. The first expert system, MYCIN, was developed to help physicians diagnose unfamiliar bacterial infections. Physicians consulted the expert system, which asked them questions about the patient's symptoms and then provided a diagnosis. Expert systems have also been developed to help geologists decide where to drill for oil, firefighters decide how to extinguish different kinds of fires, computer sales technicians configure computer systems, bankers decide on loan applications, and employees decide among a large number of company benefits alternatives. Problems whose solutions include decisions or predictions based on a variety of factors are good candidates for expert systems.

Expert systems consist primarily of a knowledge base of facts about objects and rules about the relationships among those objects that represent knowledge structures used by a human expert to reach a decision. Facts simply state given conditions, and rules consist of conditions and decisions. Rules state that *if* a set of conditions exists, *then* some decision is reached. Conditions can be combined in a number of ways into sets. Sets of *if* conditions can be combined using conjunctions (condition 1 *and* condition 2 must exist), disjunctions (condition 1 *or* condition 2 must exist), and negations (condition 1 but *not* condition 2 must exist) for a decision to be reached or another rule executed. A decision may be an action, or it may state another condition, which is then combined with other conditions to reach another decision.

An expert system, then, is a computer program that attempts to simulate the way human experts solve problems—an artificial decision maker. For instance, when you consult an expert (e.g., doctor, lawyer, or teacher) about a problem, the expert asks for current information about your condition, searches his or her knowledge base (memory) for existing knowledge to which elements of the current situation can be related, processes the information (thinks), arrives at a decision, and presents a decision or solution. Like a human expert, an expert system is approached by an individual (novice) with a problem. The system queries the individual about the current status of the problem, searches its knowledge base (which contains previously stored expert knowledge) for pertinent facts and rules, processes the information, arrives at a decision, and reports the solution to the user. When using expert systems as Mindtools, it is the student who attempts to represent the expertise needed to solve a problem. Whenever students try to learn something well enough to be an expert, they necessarily engage in deeper-level thinking.

When expert systems are used as Mindtools, it is most effective to use an expert system shell to construct a knowledge base. An expert system shell is an editor in which students construct a rule and an inference engine that evaluates and executes the rule. Expert system shells allow users who are not programmers to create expert systems. Our favorite is a simple shell, Win EXP, which comes bundled with a wonderful book titled *How to Model It: Problem Solving for the Computer Age* (Starfield, Smith, & Bleloch, 1993).

Context 'This knowledge base is intended to simulate the processes of calculating molar conversions.

D1:   You know the mass of one mole of sample.'

D2:   'You need to determine molar (formula) mass.'

D3:   'Divide sample mass by molar mass.'

D4:   'Multiply number of moles by molar mass.'

D5:   'You know atomic mass units.'

D6:   'You know molar mass.'

D7:   'Divide mass of sample by molar mass and multiply by Avogadro's number.'

D8:   'Divide number of particles by Avogadro's number'

D9:   'Convert number of particles to moles, then convert moles to mass'

D10: 'Convert mass to moles using molar mass, and then convert moles to molecules using Avogadro's number.'

D11: 'Convert from volume to moles (divide volume by volume/mole), and then convert moles to moles by multiplying by Avogadro's number.'

Q1: 'Do you know the number of molecules?'	A 1 'yes'	2 'no'
Q2: 'Do you know the mass of the sample in grams?'	A 1 'yes'	2 'no'
Q3: 'Do you know the molar mass of the element or compound?'	A 1 'yes'	2 'no'
Q4: 'Do you know the number of moles of the sample?'	A 1 'yes'	2 'no'
Q5: 'Do you want to know the number of molecules?'	A 1 'yes'	2 'no'
Q6: 'Do you want to know the mass of the sample in grams?'	A 1 'yes'	2 'no'
Q7: 'Do you want to know the molar mass of the compound?'	A 1 'yes'	2 'no'
Q8: 'Do you want to know the number of moles of the sample?'	A 1 'yes'	2 'no'
Q9: 'Do you know atomic mass units?'	A 1 'yes'	2 'no'
Q10: 'Do you know the volume of a gas?'	A 1 'yes'	2 'no'

Rule1:   IF q2a1 AND q8a1 THEN D2

Rule2:   IF (d1 OR q3a1) AND q2a1 AND q8a1 THEN D3

Rule3:   IF q4a1 AND q3a1 AND q6a1 THEN D4

Rule4:   IF q3a1 THEN D1

Rule5:   IF q3a1 THEN D5

Rule6:   IF q9a1 THEN D6

Rule7:   IF qq3a1 AND q2a1 AND q5a1 THEN D7

Rule8:   IF q1a1 AND q8a1 THEN D8

Rule9:   IF q1a1 AND q6a1 THEN D9

Rule10: IF q2a1 AND q5a1 THEN d10

Rule11: IF q10a1 AND q1a1 THEN d11

Figure 5.7   Excerpt from an expert system rule base on stoichiometry.

Expert systems, among other Mindtools (systems modeling tools are great for this purpose), can be used by students to reflect on and model their own thinking processes. We call these models of thinking processes cognitive simulations. "Cognitive simulations are runnable computer programs that represent models of human cognitive activities" (Roth, Woods, & People, 1992, p. 1163). They attempt to model mental structures and human cognitive processes. "The computer program contains explicit representations of proposed mental processes and knowledge structures" (Kieras, 1990, pp. 51–52). Thus, the models of cognition that you learn to build are cognitive simulations. Having students represent thinking processes is a form of metacognition, or thinking about thinking. Figure 5.7 illustrates the advice, factors, and rules for an expert system knowledge base on how to solve molar conversion problems in chemistry. Rather than solving the problem, students are building a model of how to think about solving the problem. Reflecting on the problem solution process helped the learners better solve other examples of this kind of problem. We should also note that expert systems are effective for modeling problems (described earlier).

Modeling Experiences With Databases

Database management systems (DBMSs) are computerized record-keeping systems. They were originally designed to replace paper-based information retrieval systems (such as patient medical records). DBMSs are, in effect, electronic filing cabinets that allow users to store information in an organized filing system and later retrieve that information just as a secretary stores documents in organized filing drawers. Database management systems store, retrieve, and manipulate information in databases. Databases consists of one or more files, each of which contains information in the form of collections of records that are related to a content domain, event, or set of objects (e.g., an individual's account information). Each record in the database is divided into fields that describe the class or type of information contained therein. The same type of information for each record is stored in each field. These records are systematically broken down into fields (subunits of each record) that define a common pattern of information. The content and arrangement of each field are standardized within the records, enabling the computer to locate a particular kind of information more quickly.

Databases are everywhere in our society. Records containing information about each of us are maintained by schools, utilities, doctors and dentist offices, libraries, merchandising companies, and so on. Whenever we check out a book, buy something online, pay our bills, or just about any other activity, someone looks up our record or creates a new one in a database.

When students model phenomena with database management systems, they are required to integrate and interrelate content ideas into one or more matrices. Matrices are an effective way to represent information that supports comparison–contrast reasoning. Rather than comparing and contrasting ideas, students may also build databases that collect, compare, and contrast stories of people's experiences.

Although educational institutions do not regard stories highly, stories are a primary means for negotiating meanings (Bruner, 1990), and they assist us in understanding human action, intentionality, and temporality. Stories can function as a substitute for direct experience. For instance, we have included "stories" of how other teachers use technology in their classrooms throughout this book to increase the relevance of the content. If, as most people do, we assume that we learn more from our experiences, then we should also be able to learn from stories of other people's experiences. Many of our decisions are based on the experiences of other people. Rather than study content, students might analyze the stories and experiences of others for what they have to teach us. If you replay and analyze most any conversation, it is probably made up of a series of stories. One person tells a story to make a point, which reminds other conversants of related events, so they tell stories that they were reminded of, which in turn reminds other conversants of stories they were reminded of, and so on. Why do we use stories to support conversation? Because we remember so much of what we know in the form of stories. Stories are rich, powerful formalisms for storing and describing memories. Thus, one way of understanding what people know is to analyze their stories. Databases are the primary tool for doing that.

Students can engage conceptual change by modeling people's experiences, which is a form of ethnography. That is accomplished by collecting stories about their experiences, indexing them, and storing them. Having collected stories, we must decide what the stories teach us. We tell stories with some point in mind, so the indexing process tries to elucidate what that point is, given a situation. Schank (1990) believes that indexes should include the experience and the themes, goals, plans, results, and lessons from the story. Themes are the subjects that people talk about. Goals motivated the experience. Plans are personal approaches to accomplishing those goals. Results describe the outcome of the experience. The lesson is the moral of the story—the principle that we should take away from the case. Indexing is an engaging analytical process, the primary goal of which is to make the stories accessible. While indexing, we must continually ask ourselves under what situations we would be reminded of this story.

Having determined the indexes for the stories, students next find excerpts in the stories that represent each index and include those excerpts in records, the fields of which represent the themes, goals, plans, results, and lessons or whatever indexes the students believe are appropriate. The database in Figure 5.8 recounts one of many stories collected by students studying the conflict in Northern Ireland. The database contains many stories that have been indexed by topic, theme, context, goal, reasoning, religion and so on. When students analyze stories in order to understand the issues, they better understand the underlying complexity of any phenomenon in terms of the diverse social, cultural, political, and personal perspectives reflected in the stories.

You may also be interested in a case library of technology integration stories that we created, Knowledge Innovation for Technology in Education (http://kite.missouri.edu), which was funded by a PT3 (Preparing Tomorrow's Teachers to Use Technology) grant from the U.S. Department of Education (Jonassen, Wang, Strobel, & Cernusca, 2003). We interviewed over 1,000 teachers, asking them to share with us a story about a successful use of technology in their classroom. After each story was submitted, we had to decide what the stories

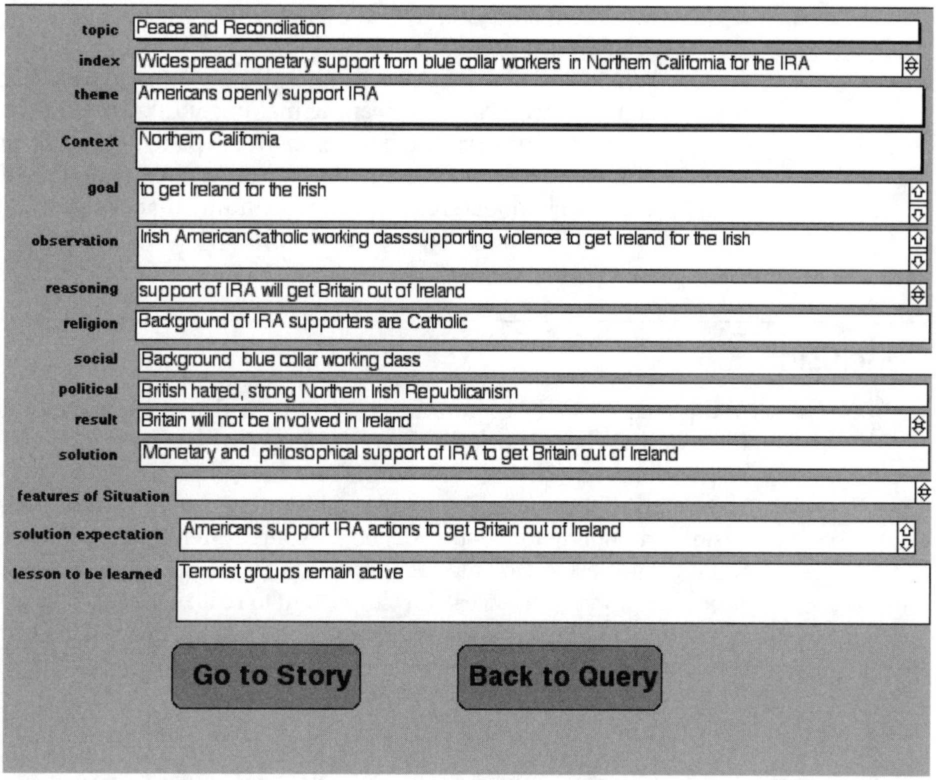

topic	Peace and Reconciliation
index	Widespread monetary support from blue collar workers in Northern California for the IRA
theme	Americans openly support IRA
Context	Northern California
goal	to get Ireland for the Irish
observation	Irish American Catholic working class supporting violence to get Ireland for the Irish
reasoning	support of IRA will get Britain out of Ireland
religion	Background of IRA supporters are Catholic
social	Background blue collar working class
political	British hatred, strong Northern Irish Republicanism
result	Britain will not be involved in Ireland
solution	Monetary and philosophical support of IRA to get Britain out of Ireland
features of Situation	
solution expectation	Americans support IRA actions to get Britain out of Ireland
lesson to be learned	Terrorist groups remain active

Go to Story   **Back to Query**

Figure 5.8   Record from a database of stories about Northern Ireland.

taught us, so the stories were indexed. These indexes became the fields in an Oracle database. You may retrieve relevant stories about how to use technologies in the classroom by searching the database on the basis of characteristics that are defined by the fields. Although this was not a student-constructed database, it provides an additional example of how databases may be used to collect and retrieve stories.

Why Build Models With Mindtools?

Constructing technology-mediated models of phenomena is among the most conceptually engaging tasks that students can undertake. Here are a few reasons why:

- Model building is a natural cognitive phenomenon. When encountering unknown phenomena, humans naturally begin to construct personal theories about those phenomena that are represented as models.
- Modeling is essentially constructivist—constructing personal representations of experienced phenomena.

- Modeling supports hypothesis testing, conjecturing, inferring, and a host of other important cognitive skills.
- When students construct models, they own the knowledge. Student ownership is important to meaning making and knowledge construction.
- Modeling supports the development of epistemic beliefs, or what motivates our efforts to make sense of the world. As already described, comparing and evaluating models requires understanding that alternative models are possible and that the activity of modeling can be used for testing rival models.

Conclusion

In this chapter we have introduced you to the idea of using computers as Mindtools for building models of meaning. We hope that you will give your students some responsibility for their own learning and meaning making. In this chapter we have shown you only a single example of how five different Mindtools (concept maps, systems modeling tools, spreadsheets, expert systems, and databases) can be used to build a single kind of model (domain knowledge, systems, problems, thinking processes, and experiences). It is important to realize that each kind of Mindtool may be used to build many different kinds of models. Jonassen (2006) illustrates how different tools can be used by students to build many different kinds of models.

Things to Think About

If you would like to reflect on the ideas that we presented in this chapter, then articulate your responses to the following questions and compare them with others' responses.

1. Can you as a teacher really teach students what you know? Is it possible for them to know ideas in the same way that you know them?
2. Do carpenters learn *from* their hammers, saws, levels, and other tools? Can they learn anything about them without using them? Do they learn about carpentry *with* their tools?
3. If mindful thinking is active, constructive, intentional, authentic, and cooperative (as we have claimed), then what is mindless thinking? Can you describe what students do if they are mindless? Is mindless thinking even possible?
4. Recall the first time that you had to teach a new topic or skill. How well did you *know* the topic before you taught it? Did you *know* it better after you taught it? Should learners become teachers without using technology? Recall that we have argued that learners should be teaching the technology.
5. Can a tool be intelligent? What is the smartest tool that you know of? What makes it smart?

6. We claim that the goal of Mindtools is to help students build external models of their internal, mental models. How can you know that the models that students build are their own and not what you taught them?

7. We argue that language and software applications like databases are formalisms for representing what you know. Can you think of other formalisms for representing what you know? How is the syntax of that formalism different from language?

8. Databases and semantic networks focus on the semantics of a knowledge domain. That is, they engage learners in describing the organization of meanings in a domain. Can you think of any other semantic formalisms?

9. Semantic networks are like the frame and foundation of a house. If that is the case, how would you describe the rest of the house (plumbing, trim, decorations, walls, and so on)?

10. We have claimed that building models with Mindtools reflects the learner's internal mental models. Is there knowledge in the external models? Does knowledge reside only in the head, or can it reside in the world as well?

11. Psychologists argue that *if–then* statements, like expert systems, are the best way to represent procedural knowledge (knowledge of how to do things). If that is the case, which of the Mindtools best support the learning of declarative knowledge (knowing that things exist)?

12. Dynamic modeling tools, like Stella, enable you to represent mental models. We argued that mental models consist of many different kinds of knowledge. Pick a small topic (like your car) and write down everything that you know about it: how it works, how to drive it, what it does in different conditions, and so on. See if you can separate that knowledge into different groups. What are those groups?

13. We argue in the conclusion that Mindtools represent an intellectual toolbox that can help students learn. We do not believe that these are the only kinds of intellectual tools that students should have. What other nontechnological intellectual tools should students have or develop to help them learn?

References

Bruner, J. (1990). *Acts of meaning*. Cambridges, MA: Harvard University Press.

Jonassen, D. H. (2006). *Modeling with technology: Mindtools for conceptual change*. Columbus, OH: Merrill/Prentice Hall.

Jonassen, D. H., Beissner, K., & Yacci, M. A. (1993). *Structural knowledge: Techniques for representing, conveying, and acquiring structural knowledge*. Hillsdale, NJ: Lawrence Erlbaum Associates.

Jonassen, D. H., Wang, F. K., Strobel, J., & Cernusca, D. (2003). Application of a case library of technology integration stories for teachers. *Journal of Technology and Teacher Education, 11*(4), 547–566.

Kieras, D. (1990). The role of cognitive simulation models in the development of advanced training and testing systems. In N. Frederickson, R. Glaser, A. Lesgold, & M. G. Shafto (Eds.), *Diagnostic monitoring of skill and knowledge acquisition*. Hillsdale, NJ: Lawrence Erlbaum Associates.

Perkins, D. N. (1993). Person-plus: A distributed view of thinking and learning. In G. Salomon

(Ed.), *Distributed cognitions: Psychological and edu-cational considerations* (pp. 88–110). Cambridge: Cambridge University Press.

Roth, E. M., Woods, D. D., & People, H. E. (1992). Cognitive simulation as a tools for cognitive task analysis. *Ergonomics, 35*(10), 1163–1198.

Salomon, G. (1993). On the nature of pedagogic computer tools: The case of the writing partner. In S. P. LaJoie & S. J. Derry (Eds.), *Computers as cognitive tools* (pp. 179–196). Hillsdale, NJ: Lawrence Erlbaum Associates.

Schank, R. C. (1990). *Tell me a story: Narrative and intelligence.* Evanston, IL: Northwestern University Press.

Starfield, A. M., Smith, K. A., & Bleloch, A. L. (1993). *How to model it: Problem solving for the computer age.* New York: McGraw-Hill.

Sundheim, B. R. (1992). Modelling a thermostatted water bath with a spreadsheet. *Journal of Chemical Education, 69*(8), 650–654.

Vockell, E., & Van Deusen, R. M. (1989). *The computer and higher-order thinking skills.* Watsonville, CA: Mitchell Publishing.

Community Building
With Technologies

Margaret Riel once told a story about a mother explaining to her 4-year-old about the e-mail message she had sent.

> The mother explained that the words on the computer screen "go on the telephone lines just like someone talking, and a computer on the other hand is going to get them. Then that computer will send them to other computers. So my message will be sent all over the world!"
>
> The child looked up from her coloring and said, "Oh, like a talking drum."
>
> The mother, dumbfounded, finally asked, "A talking drum?"
>
> "You know, like a talking drum." The mother thought some more, and then she remembered that not long ago, an African storyteller had visited her daughter's preschool and shown the class an African drum. When villagers wanted to get a message out to neighbors about a festival or a market, they would use the drum, and the message would be sent from village to village.

Throughout history, people have always found ways to communicate with each other to support community goals and activities; they have overcome obstacles and used considerable ingenuity in doing so. From preliterate cultures to today's media-saturated society, individuals have invented and utilized technologies to support that communication. Ong (1977, 1982) introduced the term "secondary orality" in his theory of transformative technologies. In contrast to "primary orality," in which cultures have no knowledge of print or writing, secondary orality describes the capacity of electronic communication technologies to bridge and convey aspects of both oral and print cultures. Today, people are able to connect with one another in ways that, until recently, were unimaginable.

The notion of community is used in a variety of ways. Increasingly, our notion of community is expanding to become a more global concept. Ong was writing of the technologies prevalent at the time—radio, television, and landline telephones—technologies that support one-way transmission of information or limited communication between individuals, as with a phone call. The ability of today's technologies to truly transform our concept of community offers great potential. The Internet enables communities to move beyond geographical boundaries and provides a vehicle for people around the world to interact and learn together. Messages once sent from village to village by drum can now be instantly sent and received from across the world. Advanced computer technologies have greatly increased our connections with one another. The one-way communication that allowed idea sharing has expanded, with new tools, such as wikis, blogs, desktop videoconferencing, and Internet radio, enabling broader learning communities.

Kenneth Boulding, an economist, educator, and social scientist, once said, "We make our tools, and then they shape us" (2006; see also Boyd, 2003; Roper, 2006). This phenomenon is evident, for example, when we consider how radically our behavior and mores regarding private conversations have changed since the wide adoption of cell phones. However, as new tools enabling diverse communities to form and maintain relationships are developed, the way in which they are used may shift from the original purpose. This shifting is often shaped by users, as technologies are revised and refined to better meet user needs. The increased sophistication and affordance of Web applications has greatly enabled this user shaping.

Many of the tools that are being created represent the philosophy behind the term "Web 2.0." What is Web 2.0? There is a lively debate on the Internet as to its meaning. It's the same Internet we've been using, but the "2.0" nomenclature is meant to signify changes. Web 2.0 is not a piece of software or anything physical; rather, it is more like a concept that points to where the Web is headed. At Web 2.0's core is a set of principles and practices intended to connect the collective intelligence of its users (O'Reilley, 2005).

Social software, emerging as a major component of Web 2.0, enables people to unite or collaborate through computer-mediated communication and to form online communities. Growing from earlier technologies such as listservs, discussion software, and Usenet groups, the current crop of social software includes blogs, podcasting, wikis, and social networking spaces like Facebook and MySpace (Alexander, 2006). Social software, like Web 2.0, means different things to different people. At its heart, however, is the capacity to bring people together and support sharing online communities through the use of technology.

One of Web 2.0's major advocates considers continuous improvement to be a fundamental characteristic of the Web 2.0 development (O'Reilley, 2005). This fluidity and common goal of improvement by a community of users is, as we shall see, also the vision of researchers and developers engaged in knowledge-building environments.

Knowledge Building With Knowledge Forum

Among the significant trends in technology found by the research-oriented Horizon Project report (NMC, 2005) was a shifting locus both of the process of constructing and sharing knowledge and of knowledge itself. Learners are willing to participate in knowledge construction and, in fact, are beginning to expect to do so. Technologies enabling social networks and knowledge webs offer a means of constructing knowledge by facilitating collaboration and teamwork. Scardamalia and Bereiter (2005) question whether this knowledge-building capacity might call for a new educational science, with the unique characteristic of treating ideas as things that emerge from a sociocognitive process and that are real and can be improved. This concept of improvable ideas parallels O'Reilley's (2005) view of Web 2.0 as fluid space, continually being improved by its user community.

Scardamalia and Bereiter (1996) argue that schools inhibit rather than support knowledge building by focusing on individual students' abilities and learning; requiring only demonstrable knowledge, activities, and skills as evidence of learning; and teacher-hoarding wisdom and expertise. Students' knowledge tends to be devalued or ignored, except as evidence of their understanding of the curriculum. What students know and believe is unimportant. Or is it? Should student knowledge not be the focus of schools, and should not schools support student knowledge building? The goal of knowledge-building communities is to support students to "actively and strategically pursue learning as a goal"—that is, intentional learning (Scardamalia, Bereiter, & Lamon, 1994, p. 201). Learning, especially intentional learning by students, is a by-product of schoolwork. To support intentional learning among students, Scardamalia and Bereiter have developed environments where students produce their own knowledge databases in their own knowledge-building community (Computer-Supported Intentional Learning Environments [CSILEs] and Knowledge Forum). Thus, student knowledge can be "objectified, represented in an overt form so that it [can] be evaluated, examined for gaps and inadequacies, added to, revised, and reformulated" (Scardamalia & Bereiter, 1996; p. 201).

Knowledge Forum 4, based on the philosophy that shared knowledge leads to innovation and growth, is based on over 15 years of research at the University of Toronto's Department of Cognitive Science. It is a knowledge-building environment that supports collaboration as users create and continue to improve ideas rather than simply complete tasks.

Knowledge Forum evolved from the original system, CSILE. Knowledge Forum is an electronic group workspace designed to support the process of knowledge building. To meet this goal, Knowledge Forum allows users to create a knowledge-building community. True knowledge-building environments enable learning that focuses on ideas and builds deeper levels of understanding. Knowledge Forum is a collaborative database that supports a shared process of knowledge building by defining problems, hypothesizing, researching, collecting information, collaborating, and analyzing. Research on knowledge-building environments suggests that the sustained inquiry in these environments results in improved scores in conceptual development as well as basic skills and a degree of student interaction that occurs regardless of ability. Gains in student confidence and the quality of student inquiry were also reported. The Knowledge Forum system has two important features:

- A special computer program for developing a common information base, installed on a local area network or on a remote server accessible through the Internet
- A systematic model of inquiry based on the scientific method and informed by current research in cognitive psychology

Using Knowledge Forum, a user community creates a database where notes are stored, ideas are connected, and knowledge is produced. Users may contribute ideas in the form of text, graphics, movies, or attachments. These ideas, which are central to the knowledge-building process, become connected, expanded, and refined as the individuals in the community question, add to, reference, and annotate each other's thoughts.

A key component of Knowledge Forum is "Rise-above" notes, which play a critical role in idea improvement. The idea of "Rise-above" is based on the philosophical concept of *dialectic*, recognizing that "the most constructive way of dealing with divergent or opposing ideas is not to decide on a winner or a compromise position but rather to create a new idea that preserves the value of the competing ideas while 'rising above' their incompatibilities" (Scardamalia, 2004, p. 7).

The design of Knowledge Forum's structured environment facilitates these idea- and knowledge-building processes. Users of Knowledge Forum 3 connect to their databases either through the Knowledge Forum Client, an application stored on their computer, or through a Web browser using the Internet. Knowledge Forum 4 is Web based. Students' process of knowledge building is scaffolded through the supports that are built into the Knowledge Forum system.

In Figures 6.1 and 6.2, a group of young students is considering the problem question, "Are people machines?" Figure 6.1 shows Marta's belief that people are machines based on her reasoning that both people and machines move.

In Figure 6.2, M.M. challenges that belief ("i don't agree"); the opened note shows her rationale. Marta's simplistic conclusion that because people move, as do machines, this means that "people are machines" is refuted, as M.M. states differences between people and machines.

In Knowledge Forum, students are expected to be contributors. The knowledge-building process requires them to formulate questions, define their

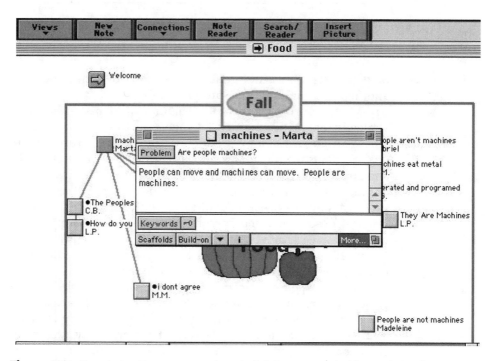

Figure 6.1   Knowledge Forum note stating a belief. *Source:* Used with permission from Knowledge Forum, www.knowledgeforum.com

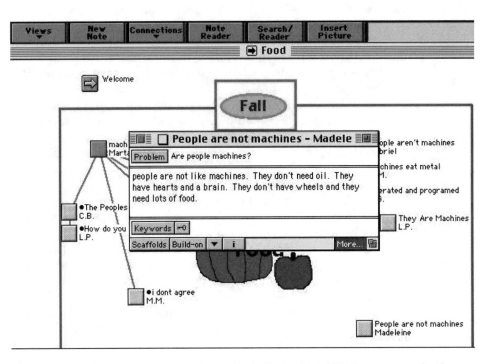

Figure 6.2 Knowledge Forum note disagreeing with another's belief. *Source:* Used with permission from Knowledge Forum, www.knowledgeforum.com

own learning goals, acquire and build a knowledge base, and collaborate with one another. Throughout this process, information sharing occurs because of Knowledge Forum's inherent structure. Students are cued to the thinking strategies that "expert learners" demonstrate through built-in scaffolds.

Learning is not a by-product of Knowledge Forum activities; it is a direct goal. Students are encouraged to make school more meaningful by being mindful and goal directed in their pursuit of learning objectives. Like scientists, Knowledge Forum participants approach a problem, develop hypotheses or theories about the problem, and then seek to confirm, modify, or discard their theories through research, observation, and interpretation. Also like scientists, participants collaborate, review each other's work, and publish their confirmed results. Knowledge Forum supports users in approaching information from multiple perspectives, building new connections from the knowledge.

Knowledge Forum can be applied to various subjects. Unlike many online projects that resemble electronic field trips or online databases, Knowledge Forum is a comprehensive model for inquiry designed to help students conceptualize and research a problem area. As such, it is more easily adopted within contained classrooms (relying less on outside Web access) and more demanding (requiring students to follow strict rules of reasoning and inquiry). Also in contrast to many online projects, considerable research has been conducted on CSILE and Knowledge

Forum, consistently demonstrating positive effects on learning (Scardamalia et al., 1994).

Knowledge Forum provides an explicit structure for engaging in thoughtful, reasoned, written discourse. Students need to practice thinking and reasoning. Written papers require reasoning, but they tend to be one-way monologues without opportunities to respond to questions from an audience. In-class oral discussions also provide reasoning opportunities, but studies show that bright students tend to dominate class discussions, leaving many students in passive roles as observers. Programs like Knowledge Forum seek to combine the best elements of writing assignments and live discussions. The communication medium is the written word, but the interactivity is similar to class discussions. Yet the programs provide more scaffolding and support for systematic reasoning than either writing assignments or class discussions: their imposed structure directs students to provide support for claims, to consider competing evidence or hypotheses, and to carefully respond to counterarguments or queries from classmates. The structured discourse that results can help students learn the norms and rules of systematic reasoning, and this in turn becomes valuable in other, less structured settings.

When students rather than the teacher or the textbook own the knowledge, they become committed to building knowledge rather than merely receiving and reprocessing it. Knowledge building becomes a social activity, not a solitary one of retention and regurgitation. Technology plays a key role in knowledge-building communities by providing a medium for storing, organizing, and reformulating the ideas that are contributed by each community member. Although these knowledge-building technology environments treat knowledge as a commodity, to the community of students it represents the synthesis of their thinking, something they own and for which they can be proud. In this sense, we believe, the goal of schools should be to foster knowledge-building communities.

Co-constructing Knowledge With Wikis

Like Knowledge Forum, wikis offer an environment for students to join together in a knowledge-building community. The wiki technology was created in 1995 by Ward Cunningham, with *wiki-wiki* meaning "quickly." A wiki is a type of Web site that allows users to add, remove, or edit and change available content. The fundamental wiki characteristic is an "edit" link allowing access to the source document. While some wikis require registration to manipulate content, others are entirely open and do not. Wikis use a very minimal form of HTML tags; this simplicity makes wikis a user-friendly, effective collaborative tool for constructing knowledge with others. Lamb (2004) notes that while wikis were originally envisioned as fluid, open, and simple, they have evolved to include more structured environments. This range of wiki tools offers users a wide choice of work environments, depending on one's needs and preferences.

A wiki Web site typically includes a "sandbox" feature that allows new users to experiment with editing wiki pages. The interactive, collaborative nature of wikis is evident in the associated discussion pages that encourage ongoing dialogue between wiki writers about wiki content, tasks that need to be completed, and other issues that arise as participants work together.

A major criticism of wikis is that because anyone can create and edit wiki pages, the content may not be accurate (Winkler, 2005). Wiki contributions are not subject to review before additions or modifications are accepted. This, however, is true of all Web pages and underscores the importance of making sure that students are educated in information literacy and have the skills to evaluate media. Ironically, the open-source nature of wikis may make them less susceptible to lingering inaccuracies, as there are opportunities for constant peer review of content, with users continually able to identify and correct content themselves. Wiki features, such as tabs associated with each wiki page's text, allow users to edit pages, discuss the page with other editors, and view the history and past versions of previously edited pages. Therefore, documentation of changes is freely available.

Wikipedia, the multilingual general encyclopedia wiki, strives to inform users about possible mispresentations or biases in material posted on its pages. One may find a note on Wikipedia pages announcing that the neutrality of the section being viewed is disputed. The Talk Page then allows discussion regarding accuracy, unbiased information, and so on.

Wikipedia is part of the Wikimedia Foundation Inc., a nonprofit educational corporation whose goal is to develop and maintain free, open-content, wiki-based projects. An emerging trend in technology is finding new ways of distributing content and software, including open-source software, with flexible copyright licensing (NMC, 2005). The nonprofit Creative Commons organization (http://creativecommons.org/) allows users to share their creations and to use online text and multimedia that are identified with the Creative Commons license. It is built within the current "all rights reserved" copyright law and offers a range of free, voluntary, "some rights reserved" licenses. Several Wikimedia Foundation projects utilize the options of Creative Commons licensing.

While the most widely known Wikimedia Foundation project is probably Wikipedia, the foundation also includes Wiktionary, a multilanguage dictionary and thesaurus, and Wikiquote, an encyclopedia of quotations. Wikisource is an online library of free content publications and source texts in any language. For example, one can find Jack London's *The Call of the Wild*, H. G. Wells's *War of the Worlds*, and Kate Chopin's *The Story of an Hour*. Users are invited to add new primary source texts or complete current ones; however, original texts should not be changed.

Contributing to Wikimedia Pages

While Wikisource exists primarily to house original texts, Wikibooks is expected to be significantly changed by participants. Wikibooks is a collection of e-book texts for students (e.g., textbooks and annotated public domain books). Wikiversity, whose beginnings were at Wikibooks, has evolved beyond e-books to become a space for a variety of learning materials as well as an environment for users to develop collaborative learning projects and a research community.

Wikijunior is a branch of Wikibooks that is developing a set of books targeted to children ages 8 to 11. This project will include a Web site and three series of magazines: *The Natural World*, a biology/geography series; *Our World of People*, a culture/ history/life/society series; and *A World of Discovery and Innovation*, a mathematics/ science/technology series. Issues are currently being developed for each series. For example, the Wikijunior South America project proposes articles on individual countries; some are begun and can be further developed, while others have no content.

A December 2005 version of the "Big Cats" issue of *The Natural World* series is available. While over a dozen authors are listed, it's not apparent whether all of them are adults. There are clearly opportunities to involve students in contributing to these series. In fact, some of the "Big Cats" discussion among the community developing this issue included questions about reading level, suitability of the image selected for the front cover, appropriateness of the title ("Big Cats" vs. "Wild Cats"), and structure of the book's contents—all questions that would appropriately be asked of the intended audience.

Including the audience for whom these series are intended as part of the collaborating community is a logical and needed step. It is also a viable step, needing only innovative teachers to offer opportunities for it to happen. Wikis offer collaborative environments for students not only to develop writing skills but also to engage in design work. The complex thinking required for designing a publication such as "Big Cats" is amplified when students work together to make decisions about content and structure.

Sites such as Wikitravel (http://wikitravel.org/en/Main_Page) and World66.com offer rich opportunities for students to contribute to existing wikis. Wikitravel, a user-created wiki travel guide, has over 10,000 destination guides and articles from "wikitravelers." Teachers often design the typical student project of researching locations and developing a travel guide. While Wikitravel could be used as an information source, a more authentic activity might involve students adding to Wikitravel, based on places they have visited. Creating entries for their own location would ensure that less traveled students could also contribute. Students might examine commercial travel guides such as *Fodor's* or *Lonely Planet* to compare accuracy with Wikitravel entries.

Interestingly, the collaborative nature of wikis is reflected in entire wiki sites, with Wikitravel and World66.com working together as sister sites. WikiIndex (http://www.wikiindex.com/) attempts to catalog all wikis available on the Web in an effort to bring the Internet wiki community together.

Hybrid sites such as Bloki combine Web hosting, blogs, forums, and online collaboration. Users can create Web pages and blogs, host online discussions, collaborate on shared documents, and annotate group Web pages.

Wikis offer environments for students to engage in collaborative, coauthored work that can continually evolve and improve. Because of the high degree of sharing and revision that wikis support, there is also a high degree of critical analysis possible, as students evaluate the ideas being coconstructed, make decisions regarding their accuracy or validity, and participate in a knowledge-building community.

Holocaust Wiki Project

Dan McDowell, a high school history teacher in California, developed the Holocaust Wiki Project for his students. First, the students create a family from an assigned country that was affected by the Holocaust. Dan describes the project on his Web site (http://www.ahistoryteacher.com/) like this:

> Basically they are creating a branching simulation (think choose your own adventure) about a family in the Holocaust. They have to come up with realistic decision points, describe the pros and cons, address the consequences of each decision, and fill it in with a narrative that reflects their research on the Holocaust. Now that in itself is pretty neat, but the REALLY cool part is that they are all (about 30 different groups), putting their branching simulations into a Wiki. Using a Wiki allows them easily create Web pages (ever try to teach Dreamweaver and academic content), edit each others work, and easily link the pages together.

Mediawiki was used for this project during the 2005–2006 school year. Figure 6.3 illustrates the introductory page and the Mediawiki interface.

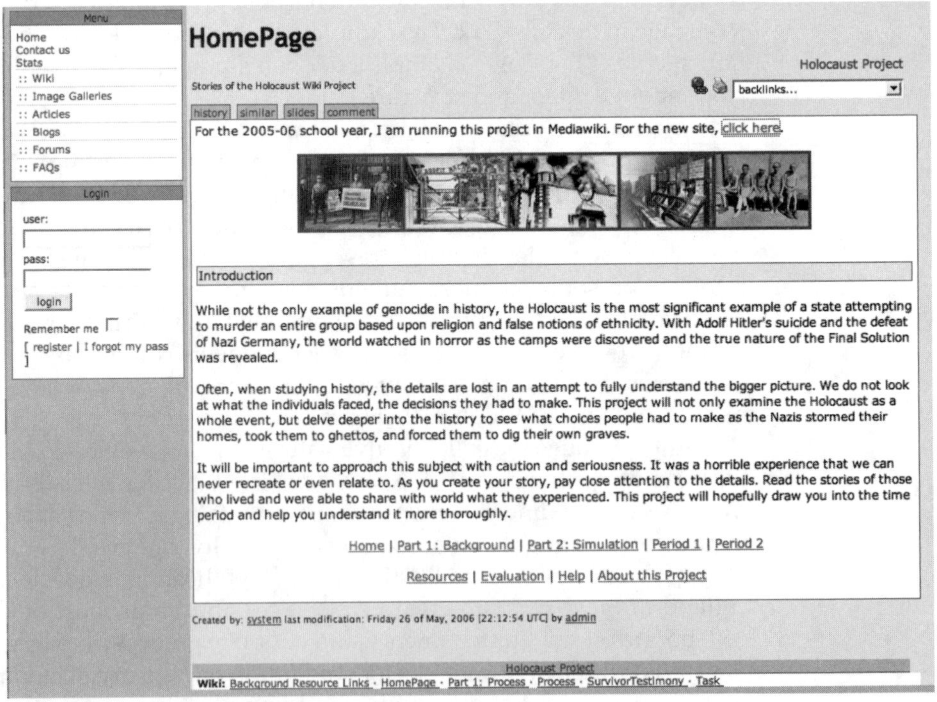

Figure 6.3   Holocaust Wiki Project in Mediawiki. *Source:* Used with permission from Dan McDowell.

An important aspect of this wiki project is the decision-point component (see Figure 6.4) in McDowell's project design. Students are faced with complex choices whose outcomes could potentially have grave consequences on the families they have created. Students are required to analyze the results of their choices and combine that critical thinking with a demonstration of the knowledge they have gained through researching the Holocaust. This kind of deep, reflective thinking is of much greater value to students than learning activities that are designed simply to meet content standards.

Students are given the freedom to go in many different directions within the structure of McDowell's project design. This autonomy engenders creative thinking, while the wiki technology supports a classroom community where students work together in small learning groups. Figure 6.5 shows one group's wiki page as they consider a decision point and its pros and cons. Wikis are simple to use not only for text editing but also for easily uploading media to the Web page. A graphic of the star emblem adds a supporting element to this decision-point page and represents some of the learning achieved by this student group.

More Uses and Suggestions for Wikis

McDowell also uses a wiki to support his students in advanced placement (AP) World History. To help students prepare for the end-of-year AP test, he designed a wiki project that involves students developing their own version of Wikipedia,

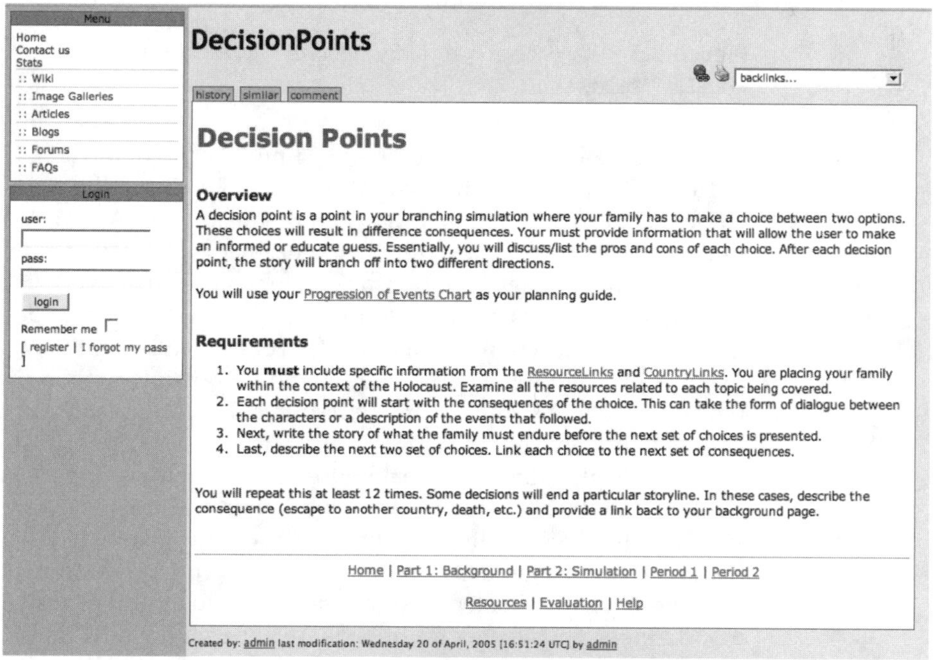

Figure 6.4 Decision Points screen of the Holocaust Wiki Project. *Source:* Used with permission from Dan McDowell.

Figure 6.5 Wiki page from a student group's Decision Point. *Source:* Used with permission from Dan McDowell.

based on the knowledge they have gained throughout their year in AP World History. Figure 6.6 portrays the Web page explaining the wiki-building task to students. It is probably safe to say that the majority of AP World History students in classrooms across the country experience exam reviews that are primarily question and answer. Use of a wiki offers a constructive, authentic, enjoyable method for students not only to review material but also to design the environment in which it will be displayed. By working collaboratively, students are able to cover much more material than would be possible with individual work, and the end result is a rich study guide resource that all students can use as they strive to pass the AP exam.

Although wikis are probably used most often to support writing in the curriculum (Lamb, 2004), the use of wikis can go well past simple writing tasks. For example, JuggleWiki (http://jugglingdb.com/jugglewiki/) is an extensive wiki dedicated to the juggling community (or those interested in it). JuggleWiki offers juggling advice, animated tutorials, and links to all things related to this activity. The difference between a traditional Web site on juggling and JuggleWiki is that the wiki pages are not static and controlled only by the Web site owner or developer. Rather than a one-way offering of juggling resources, this is a fluid, growing Web site offered and controlled by the community and developers. Users are

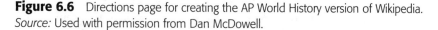

Figure 6.6 Directions page for creating the AP World History version of Wikipedia.
Source: Used with permission from Dan McDowell.

invited to post and compare their own juggling records, tell about their favorite juggling games, and tell about their way of practicing. Links such as "Learn JugglingJargon" and "Find JugglingVendors" are not simply information pages to be used but are open for others to add additional resources. (Notice the lack of spacing between words in wiki page titles. This is a common feature of wiki pages.)

For beginning wiki writers, trying out the sandbox feature is a good way to experience the environment. Other suggestions are the following:

- Start with simple tasks
- Create a list or collection of links
- Use as an informal bulletin board
- Make an online sketch pad
- Brainstorm
- Use for planning and/or note taking

While wikis can be a valuable learning tool for collaborating, designing, co-constructing, and representing knowledge, their basic form is open ended with little built-in structure to direct students' contributions. This freedom can encourage creativity but may also result in unfocused, unproductive time spent by students unless teachers provide an overall framework for their work. The guidance and direction that McDowell provided students in the Holocaust and AP World History wiki assignments is an excellent example of effectively incorporating wikis into the curriculum.

Finding Colleagues With Interactive Blogs

A central difference between a wiki and weblog (or blog) is that wikis were designed as a collaborative environment, whereas blogs were originally intended as personal diaries or journals for individuals to post their own thoughts and ideas. The purpose and function of blogs has evolved, however, with many being highly interactive spaces. Readers post responses to blog entries, creating opportunities for dialogue rather than a one-sided monologue. Blog writers can link to multiple Web sites, including links to other blogs that might substantiate or refute the opinions expressed in one's own blog. The structure of blogs is reverse chronology, with the most recent entry appearing at the top of the blog Web page. Common features of blogs include the ability to add permanent links allowing other Web sites to link directly to one's blog, archiving of posts, features that post a link from a currently browsed site directly to a user's blog, and the ability to add a search engine to a blog, making it possible for users to search blog content.

Technorati, a Web company that tracks and studies weblogs, estimates that 18 blog posts are being made every second. Technorati is currently tracking 51 million blogs as well as video blogs (vlogs), podcasts, and amateur movies and videos. This activity is monitored in real time and indexed. Technorati offers a search tool for blog content. It also collects and reports on top searches, top blog posts in various categories, and top tags (key words) that people are writing about.

David Sifry, Technorati's founder and chief executive officer, sees humans as fundamentally social who, if given tools to connect, will do so, and some people see blogging as the "signature item" of social computing (Alexander, 2006), given its influence. Educational blogging can be a transformational technology, creating the space for active exchanges of ideas and critiques. Blogs can be linked and crosslinked, forming dense learning communities. Group culture is enhanced, as blog interfaces are simple to use and conversation is easy to follow. The accumulated writing, responses, and links contributed by a community of bloggers sharing a common interest create an archived knowledge base that is easy to trace chronologically.

Educational Uses of Blogs

Blogs may be used for different purposes, each offering a set of different yet valuable outcomes. Expedition Web sites have provided rich learning opportunities for several years, with explorers often posting their observations and experiences as they travel and research. For example, National Geographic (http://www. national geographic.com/siteindex/adventure.html) offers several expedition opportunities. In "Kayaking Vietnam's Dragon Coast," explorer Jon Bowermaster called in dispatches from his 800-mile kayak journey down the northern Vietnam coast. This audio diary is archived online, as are the written dispatches from "Jannu: A Himalayan First Ascent," a chronicle of three climbers in the northeastern corner of Nepal who attempted to climb Kumbhakarna (Jannu), a 25,295-foot mountain face of rock and ice.

While these expedition chronicles are wonderful resources, the interactive nature of blogs creates a mechanism for students not only to read about explorers but also to comment on their postings, ask questions about the expedition, research, and add related links that enhance and support the explorer's mission. In so doing, students are creating a community of learners, the explorer being one member of that community.

Student participation in a blog created by another person is one use of this technology; a student defining a purpose for creating a blog of his or her own is another. In the following scenarios, we will look at examples of each.

Expert-Created Blogs Artic Ed's Travelog (http://arctic.concord.org/) chronicles a scientific journey to the North Atlantic. Ed, a former physics teacher and part of the Concord Consortium team developing innovative uses of technology for science teaching, used a blog to track his voyage as he sailed around the perimeter of Baffin Bay during the summer of 2006 on a 45-foot wooden sailboat. Along with Ed's observations are measurements taken from data loggers (see chapter 2) that enable teachers to tie real field measurements to discussions of global climate change.

One can navigate Ed's blog chronologically through a calendar or by location using the online map as well as view an extensive image gallery. During Ed's journey, the blog's interface supported an interactive experience as readers could comment on Ed's entries and engage in conversation about his trip. Ed's Journal Entry 37, depicted in Figure 6.7, discusses geology, biology, physics, astronomy, and tasty cuisine. In just a few entertaining paragraphs, this blog entry offers a variety of information, poses some probing questions, and ends with a hook to send kids off for some research on their own by saying, "We're right along the auroral oval here. Look that up!"

Ed's blog also offers coordinates taken from a GPS system (see chapter 9). When these links are clicked on, a Google map opens, showing the sailboat's location. In Figure 6.8, we see the title of the journal entry in the text bubble along with corresponding longitude and latitude information for that entry.

Using blogs as virtual field trips offers students the opportunity not only to read about the traveler's experiences but also to interact with scientists, researchers, and explorers in meaningful ways. Teachers may choose to develop blogs as instructional tools, as the next three examples illustrate.

Teacher-Created Blogs

Micah, a high school psychology teacher, used a blog with his students to allow them to explore information for which there was no time to cover in class and to increase students' understanding of the course content. He formatted the blog posts in such a way that the students had to do extra research on the Internet or apply some of the concepts they learned in class to the real world in order to participate. The other objective for Micah's class blog was to encourage students who wouldn't normally participate in class discussions. Some students had a fear of talking in public or felt time pressures in class to express their feelings and explore their thoughts regarding concepts and ideas from the course. Micah said,

Journal Entry 37: Blueberries and Nothern Lights on Nukasusutok Island

August 20 7AM

We anchored in a small bay with some protection from the strong winds after a wild and beautiful sail south from Nain among rocky islands that looked very much like the south coast of Greenland. No coincidence: they were once joined, before the continental plate split and spread to form the Labrador Sea. We set out early this morning, hoping to cover some distance today.

The islands here are hard and uniform rock (igneous anorthocite) that has been rounded and burnished by the ice but only reluctantly. They are bold like so many mountain tops, which they would be if the water dropped 100 m, which indeed it did at various times. Imagine sailing in and around the Presidential Range. The exposed areas have no trees, just dense tundra, covering every available square inch with low but luxuriant vegetation.

You would not expect to find a bumper blueberry crop in this setting, but there it was: fat juicy berries so ultra-lowbush that I sometimes couldn't get my fingers between the crop and the rocks against which the tiny branches were pressed. Nonetheless I picked enough for two hits of blueberry pancakes. It is also a great way to become intimate with the tundra. It's very beautiful ˆ so tight, interwoven, healthy. Like the polar bears, these plants are just fine here.

Last night was fresh scallops (onion, garlic, olive oil, and lemon juice) on pasta. Shortly it will be blueberry pancake time (second breakfast). Tonight it's fish chowder with arctic char and the remaining scallops. Nice. Just no fresh vegetables.

After dinner it was dark and clear, and the aurora borealis put on a real show: undulating wavy ribbons, brilliant vertical streaks, sheets of light over the whole dome of the sky. Barry Lopez has a vivid description in Arctic Dreams, including the involuntary awe and wonder that northern lights universally evoke. I was thrilled. This is what I came here to see: ions in their most spiritual manifestation. There was considerable discussion about the physics, which of course raised as many questions as it answered. Do the wild fluctuations correspond directly to variations in the solar wind? Does their appearance change over the course of the night with the changing relationship between the Sun and the magnetic pole? Are they visible every clear moonless night to a certain extent, since the solar wind certainly never ceases? We're right along the auroral oval here. Look that up!

Posted by Carolyn at 07:00 | Comment (1) | Trackbacks (0)

Figure 6.7 A blog entry from Artic Ed's Travelog. *Source:* Used with permission from Edmund Hazzard and Concord Consortium.

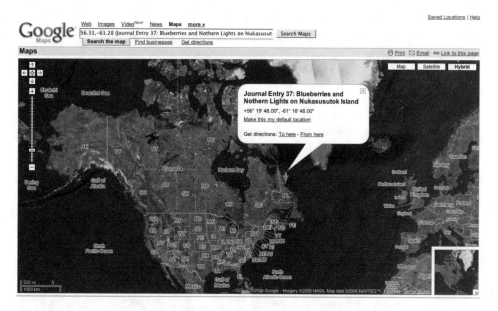

Figure 6.8 A blog entry's link reveals coordinates taken from a GPS system. *Source:* Used with permission from Edmund Hazzard and Concord Consortium.

"It allowed students who needed more processing time to respond to have as much as they needed to participate in the class's online discussion" (http://www.mhspsychology.blogspot.com).

Sherri, a high school librarian, created "Whatcha Reading?" to help students find books they might be interested in. Sherri's second purpose was for students to share their thoughts on these books and on other books they were reading or had read. Book discussions can connect young people with others who have similar interests, can foster friendships, and can provide the structure for bloggers and respondents to analyze issues, consider multiple perspectives, and relate significant issues to their own personal experiences (http://www.teenreads.blogspot.com).

This last example illustrates how a blog might reach beyond the classroom to educate and connect a community of users interested in special education issues. Lisa, a special education teacher, developed a blog to inform people about special education, how teachers work with students through instruction and learning activities, and the forms and records that special education teachers must maintain for each student. Her primary purpose was "to inform people that these kids are people too, with real feelings, dreams, and ideas who also deserve the chance to learn to the best of their ability." Lisa's blog offers the potential for parents and other special education teachers, among others, to join together in discussing critical issues, sharing problems and solutions, and offering resources (http://1cheese.blogspot.com/)

Student-Created Blogs Mrs. Watford, an English teacher, uses blogging as a means for students to share and build understanding of the topics discussed in class. Once a day, Mrs. Watford posts a journal topic; students select two journal topics each week and post their thoughts. Students must also respond to others' posts. Figure 6.9 illustrates some of the journal topics students may choose to write about, such as "I worry about . . . ," "If I could be famous for one day, I think I'd like to be . . . ," and "You may not be sure yet of what you want to be as an adult. But most students have a good idea what they don't want to be. What are you sure you don't want to be? Why?"

Questions such as these encourage students to think about who they are and what they value and to explain and justify why they think a certain way. In the sharing of their thoughts with one another, students are learning how they are similar to and different from others. They consider and evaluate new ideas, learning about themselves through reflection as part of a peer community.

Mrs. Watford addresses some of the issues that can make teachers hesitant about using blogs with students. In her "Note to Parents" link, she lets parents know that the class has discussed Internet safety and what is needed to protect them

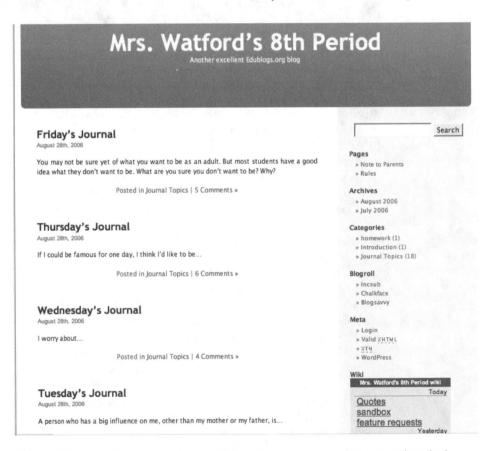

Figure 6.9 Journal topics in a classroom blog. *Source:* Courtesy of Mrs. Crystal Watford, Riverchase Middle School, Shelby County, Alabama.

on the Internet. Mrs. Watford reads student posts before they are entered on the blog to make sure they don't contain personal information that should be kept private.

Bob Sprankle, a third- and fourth-grade multiage teacher at Wells Elementary in Wells, Maine, is a 2005 Edublog Award winner. "Room 208," his class Web site, illustrates how a community of learners uses personal blogs to publish and share their ideas with each other as well anyone in the blogosphere. Individual student blogs are linked on the left side of the screen in Figure 6.10. This figure displays the "Elizabeth's Things" blog link, where Elizabeth has posted a picture of a dragon. The previous posting shared her story, "The Hamster and the Mouse."

Elizabeth has received eight comments about her "Dragons by Elizabeth" picture. In Figure 6.11, we see the screen that results from clicking the "Comments" link. The community of viewers who visited Elizabeth's blog have given her lots of

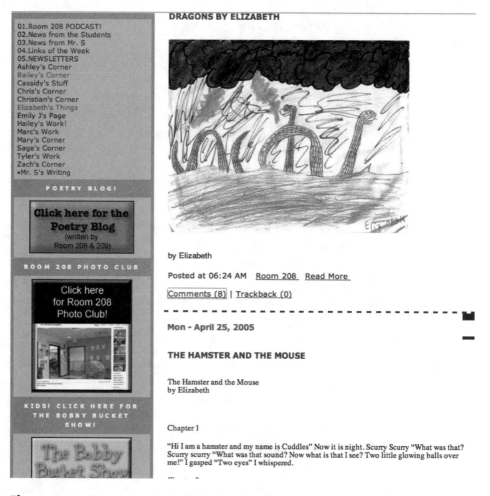

Figure 6.10 Blog entries of Elizabeth's picture and story.

Elizabeth,

I like your drawing of the storm. You can see the fear on the faces of the snakes. Maybe you could write a story about your drawing. You have a lot of talent. I like all the detail that you added.

Linda Cranmer | Homepage | 10.29.05 - 1:09 am | #

I love your dragons Elizabeth! I'm not sure I would want to meet them out in the ocean. I can't wait to read some of your writing this year.

Mrs. Onion | 10.30.05 - 9:05 pm | #

Your dragons look like they could be from Earagon.
Mrs. O

Mrs. O | Homepage | 10.31.05 - 7:03 am | #

Wow! Elizabeth!

I love the expression in your dragon picture! I always have loved your artwork!

I am impressed with your story, The Hamster and the Mouse. Nice!

Can't wait to see what you do next! Love, Charlene

charlene kohn | 02.03.06 - 1:18 pm | #

Elizabeth,

Your dragon picture is great! The artists for the movie "Sleeping Beauty" could not have done better!

Diana Locke | 02.13.06 - 10:27 am | #

Figure 6.11 Comments page on Elizabeth's blog.

Figure 6.12 Skates and Skis "Barrett Project Interaction"
What I Love About Winter Friday, February 17, 2006.

positive feedback. One reader commented on the way Elizabeth portrayed the emotion of fear and suggested that she might write a story about this drawing. This type of feedback can affirm young writers' concepts of themselves as conveyors of ideas, engage them in conversation with a purposeful community of other writers, and encourage learners to reflect on their work.

At Barrett Elementary School in Arlington, Virginia, students post blog entries not in the form of text entries but as video clips. The purpose of "Barrett Project Interaction" (http://barrettpi.blogspot.com/) is to allow students to express their creativity and ideas through the communication arts. Ms. Long's class shared what they like about winter through poetry. In a Friday, February 17, 2006, blog entry, the class recited a poem together listing many favorite winter things, as a series of their drawn pictures is displayed in a video. In Figures 6.12 and 6.13, we see the artwork and hear the children say, "Skates and skis, evergreen trees."

Other Barrett Elementary School podcasts include an animation about a runaway pizza created by a class of first graders, a music video produced by a fourth- and fifth-grade chorus who collaborated with special arts students, and a five-part "The Phantom of the Music Room," a Barrett musical production.

Why Blog, and What to Consider?

Blogs can provide the means to connect and communicate with others sharing the same interests. They can also open up new areas to explore and allow students to experience virtual travels and expeditions. Anne Davis, an elementary teacher whose fourth- and fifth-grade students wrote blogs that were read by high school students who mentored them, reported, "Having an outside audience really made a difference to them. They couldn't believe that someone else would care what they wrote" (Falloon, 2005).

Figure 6.13   Evergreen Trees "Barrett Project Interaction"
What I Love About Winter Friday, February 17, 2006.

While blogs can give students a wide audience for their writing, art, and other creative works, their unstructured format may result in postings that have little educational value for the students constructing them. To ensure that students are using blogs in ways that support significant learning, teachers need to clearly define their objectives and determine whether a blog is the best instructional tool for meeting those goals. Perhaps the objective is simply for students to engage in informal personal writing, but more likely, teachers will need to provide some guidance and structure to help students meet more complex objectives. Providing a scoring guide or other means for communicating expectations can help students use blogs more effectively.

Students' blog writing may be scaffolded by giving them choices as to the purpose of blog entries or by giving them starters such as Mrs. Watford's journal topics. Spammers and other unwanted visitors can be avoided by using blog programs that require a log-in. Teachers must provide guidelines and clearly communicate these, along with the reasons for security concerns. Student blog entries should be identified only by first names, pseudonyms, or other nonidentifiable labels. Previewing student blog entries before posting can also help teachers feel comfortable with the content and safety of blogging, especially if a public forum is used.

Building International Communities With iEARN Learning Circles, Global Schoolhouse, and KidLink

Recent world events underscore the need for all citizens to understand and respect other cultures and to be able to communicate with those who are culturally different. Internet communities supported through Web sites such as KidLink, the International

Education and Resource Network (iEARN), and Global Schoolhouse allow diverse students in different geographic areas to make connections with each other, helping to create understanding and appreciation between cultures and perspectives.

The National Council for the Social Studies (1992) includes the following culture and cultural diversity standard as one guide in social studies curriculum:

> In a democratic and culturally diverse society, students need to comprehend multiple perspectives. . . . These understandings allow them to . . . interact with people within their diverse society and throughout the world.

Global groups capitalize on cultural differences as a means of broadening students' perspectives and motivating learning. The new ideas and experiences that are encountered when students interact with peers in other countries and cultures can expand thinking and shape mental models that become more complex. Students may reflect on their experience as world citizens and broaden their understanding of how others live. Studies in language, geography, current events, and culture can be augmented through these groups.

iEARN Learning Circles

Learning Circles support constructive learning among a small number of schools located throughout the world through highly interactive, collaborative, project-based partnerships. Developed by Margaret Riel and a team of collaborators, Learning Circles are described generically as being "small diverse, democratic groups of people (generally 6–12) who meet regularly over a specified period of time to focus their different perspectives into a common understanding of an issue or problem. The discussion takes place in an atmosphere of mutual trust and understanding. The goal is deeper understanding by the participants and their efforts are often directed towards the construction of a final product or recommendation for a course of action" (Riel, 2005).

The circle has long been used as a way to structure the meeting of a group of people, encourage members' ownership of the group's purpose and work, and recognize and value the collective wisdom of the group. Many types of learning circles exist (e.g., wisdom circles, circle time, study circles, and quality circles) that are organized as face-to-face groups. In contrast, the Learning Circles described in this section are online structures that link students and teachers internationally, tapping into the diversity of the participants as a way to build respect and understanding.

Riel (1996) likens Learning Circles to local chapters of a larger organization, like scout troops affiliated with a larger council. Local troops "set their own goals and tasks but remain connected to those who work in other locations as part of a community with shared goals and values." She describes this cooperation between local and larger levels:

> In on-line Learning Circles, as in scout troops or in a Red Cross task force, the overall task and structure is clearly defined. There are enough examples for participants to use at every step. However, the members of the circle, troop or

task force know that they can take control and develop the ideas that arise from the participants. (Riel, 1996)

Learning Circles are often organized in support of a specific project or online activity, with theme-based project work that is integrated into classroom curricula. Like a task force, Learning Circles have a heavy work or activity orientation. Groups of classrooms, usually about eight, sign on to communicate and collaborate from a distance, following a time line to accomplish a defined task. The specific task may be any of a number of different activities, such as research, information sharing, compilation of a database, or publishing on a common subject. The outcome of the circle is a written document, a summary, or a collection of their collaboration.

Learning Circles are an integral part of iEARN, whose goal is to connect students and teachers around the world to build understanding as they collaborate on meaningful learning projects. Learning Circles incorporate significant, intentional work within a community striving not only to complete project work but also to gain social and cultural understanding of one another in the process.

One of the Learning Circles in place at iEARN is "Places and Perspectives," a project that integrates history, geography, culture, and government as students broaden their perspectives by sharing knowledge with one another. Students in a geography class might collaborate on producing a travel guide, an analysis of social patterns in relation to geographical locations, or a comparison of weather patterns. A collaborating history class's project might involve examination of local politics, historical landmarks, or stories from local natives. During 2006, students in Iran, Cyprus, the United States, Israel, Uzbekistan, Romania, and Egypt worked together to share information and create better understanding among themselves. A student from Iran, communicating about Iranian culture and traditions, said, "Iranian people are very friendly and hospitable. They love peace and friendship. Unfortunately because of some incorrect introduction and reflection of Iran from the media, most of the people in world do not know the real Iran and real cultures and traditions of Iran. Iran has an ancient civilization and rich culture. So, here I would like to introduce Iran in brief way, and I have attached some pictures of Iran. Hope all of you enjoy it."

A second Learning Circle, "Computer Chronicles," involves student reporters and editors from different locations working together to publish the Computer Chronicles Newspaper. This project connects students in journalism, computer publishing, English, and creative writing and has the potential to connect students in many content areas, with newspaper sections devoted to science reporting, lifestyle sections, and so on.

Learning Circles require high levels of collaboration and teamwork within participating classes and, to some extent, between classes. Much of the learning takes place as students participate in the virtual world of Internet resources. Other times, students complete off-line activities and report results to other members of their circle. The best Learning Circles have clear work activities specified that require planning, execution, and reporting of activities, followed by comparison and collaboration across sites.

Learning Circles often engage in more complex activities. Unlike forums where students are tasked with discussing issues or problems, Learning Circles often have a problem-solving purpose for their existence. That purpose may involve designing some artifact (a newspaper, Web site, or project). To complete any of these kinds of projects, decision-making problems almost always arise, so it is safe to speculate that Learning Circles, at the very least, engage students in decision making.

The best teacher within Learning Circles keeps the project going yet knows how to get out of the way when students are working well together. The teacher's critical role is one of attentive vigilance, with occasional support and intervention when obstacles threaten team progress. Teachers also need to maintain contact with other participating teachers, ensuring continuity and continuing attention to project goals.

Global Schoolhouse

Another major project supporting global learning communities is the Global SchoolNet Foundation (GSN). Among several GSN initiatives is the Global Schoolhouse project (see chapter 4). The purpose of GSN is to support students as they communicate, collaborate, and learn from one another and to provide a location for teachers to post collaborative project ideas and help them find meaningful collaborative partners for their students. Andres (1995) believes that the best collaborative projects require students to "measure, collect, evaluate, write, read, publish, simulate, hypothesize, compare, debate, examine, investigate, organize, share, and report." Why should classrooms join telecommunities? Andres (1995) argues that students

- enjoy writing more when they are able to write for a distant audience of their peers,
- enjoy communicating with schools from different geographical locations, and
- are given opportunities to understand different cultures and so begin to consider global issues in addition to local issues.

GSN's Project Registry is a clearinghouse for more than 2,000 online collaborative projects that are searchable by grade level, curricula area, type(s) of technology used, and types of collaboration. Over 1 million students in more than 100 countries participate in GSN projects. Among the projects beginning in 2006 are those described in the following summaries:

Most Prized Possession

Ages: 7 to 18

Project Level: Basic Project

Curriculum Areas: English as Foreign Language; Information Technology; International Relations; Language; Multicultural Studies; Social Studies;

Technology Types: Audio: files, clips, CDs, tapes; E-mail, Listserver; Graphics: photo, draw, paint; Live Text Conference: IRC, Chat, IM; Text: stories, essays, letters; Voice-over IP

Collaboration Types: Electronic Publishing; Information Exchange; Intercultural Exchange; Information Search; Peer Feedback; Virtual Meeting or Gathering

Project Summary

Goal of the Project: In sharing an image, audio recording, and personal sentiments, young people all over the world will have a better understanding of themselves and others. It is my hope that through this small gesture of sharing that my students will see the world differently . . . that maybe as they grow older and have a voice in the affairs of our world community, they will look outside of themselves, remember the connections they made, and act in the best interest of the world community.

Native American Tribes of North America

Ages: 8 to 12

Project Level: Basic Project

Curriculum Areas: Community Interest; History; Information Technology, Multicultural Studies; Social Studies; Technology

Technology Types: E-mail, Listserver; Desktop Document Sharing; Text: stories, essays, letters

Collaboration Types: Information Exchange; Information Search

Project Summary

Participating classes will help create a database of information on Native American tribes. This information will be posted on the Web in a user-friendly format for everyone to use. Contributing classes/students will provide basic information in a simple designated format. Each contributing student will be credited on the site right with their research along with the name of their teacher and school.

Elwood, the World's Most Traveled Doll

Ages: 6 to 11

Project Level: Basic Project

Curriculum Areas: Arts; Community Interest; Information Technology; Language; Mathematics; Science; Social Studies; Technology

Technology Types: E-mail, Listserver

Collaboration Types: Travel Buddy

Project Summary

Elwood is a life-size 2-year-old boy doll that has traveled to all 50 states, five continents, and 17 countries. He allows my class room to live a vicarious lifeline to their dreams and to their education. To the classes he meets he opens up their imaginations to discover their dreams.

To accomplish the active, collaborative learning envisioned by GSN, students engaged in the CyberFair initiative of GSN are encouraged to serve as "youth ambassadors" by working collaboratively with community members and using technology tools to publish a Web site that displays what they have learned.

Another aspect of GSN is "The Friendship Through Education" consortium, a coalition of several groups including the GSN Foundation, iEARN, ePALS, Schools Online, and World Wise Schools (part of the Peace Corps). The Friendship Through Education Consortium is committed to creating both on- and off-line interactions between youth to promote a culture of peace where all human rights and dignity are respected. The initial focus, in the aftermath of the September 11, 2001, terrorist attacks in the United States, was on creating links between schools in the United States and Islamic countries to "foster mutual respect and greater understanding of cultural differences." It continues to work to build strong and lasting relationships between children in the United States and in other countries and cultures (http://www.friendshiptheoucheducation.org/).

GSN sponsored a "Kids Share Hope" message board as part of the Friendship Through Education consortium. In the month following the terrorist attacks in the United States, over 100 messages of hope and support were posted from around the world (http://groups.yahoo.com/group/KidsShareHope/).

KidLink

KidLink is a grassroots project that is intended to interconnect as many children through the secondary school level as possible in a global dialogue. Most users are between the ages of 10 and 15. Since its inception in 1990, young people in 170 countries, from Antarctica to Finland, from Belarus to the Bahamas, have joined the conversation. The KidLink Web site is available in over 30 languages. Because of language constraints, KidLink provides several different dialogs. Some dialogues are individual, and some are between classrooms.

Before joining a dialogue, all new participants introduce themselves, answering the following questions (see Figure 6.14):

Question 1: Who am I? What is your full name? How old are you? Are you a boy or a girl? Where do you live (city, country)? What is the name of your school? What are some of your interests, your hobbies, your concerns? What else do you want others to know about yourself?

Question 2: What do I want to be when I grow up? Share your vision of what you want to be when you grow up in terms of work, education, and in general.

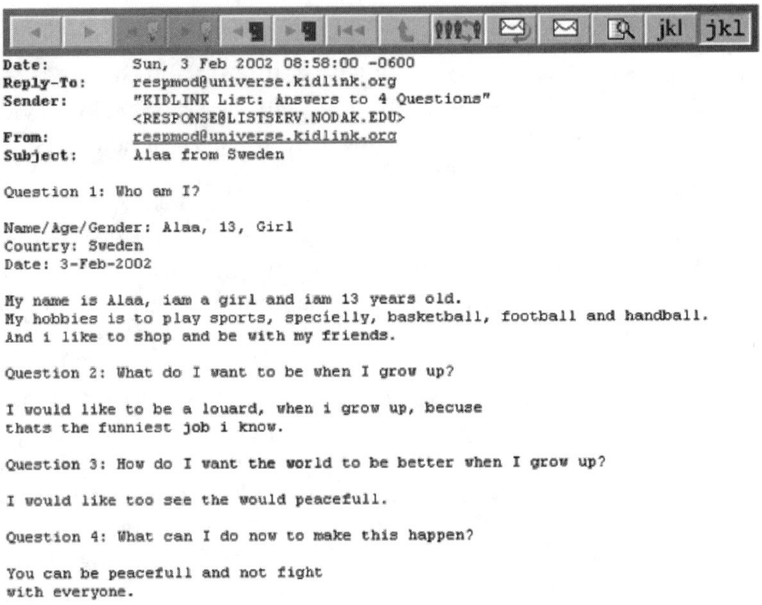

```
 ◄   ►              ◄▐  ▐►  ◄◄   ▐    ₪₪₪!  ✉   ✉   ◪  jkl  jkl
Date:         Sun, 3 Feb 2002 08:58:00 -0600
Reply-To:     respmod@universe.kidlink.org
Sender:       "KIDLINK List: Answers to 4 Questions"
              <RESPONSE@LISTSERV.NODAK.EDU>
From:         respmod@universe.kidlink.org
Subject:      Alaa from Sweden

Question 1: Who am I?

Name/Age/Gender: Alaa, 13, Girl
Country: Sweden
Date: 3-Feb-2002

My name is Alaa, iam a girl and iam 13 years old.
My hobbies is to play sports, specielly, basketball, football and handball.
And i like to shop and be with my friends.

Question 2: What do I want to be when I grow up?

I would like to be a louard, when i grow up, becuse
thats the funniest job i know.

Question 3: How do I want the world to be better when I grow up?

I would like too see the would peacefull.

Question 4: What can I do now to make this happen?

You can be peacefull and not fight
with everyone.
```

Figure 6.14   Response to the four KidLink questions.

> **Question 3: How do I want the world to be better when I grow up?** How would you like to improve the way we treat each other and the environment we share?

> **Question 4: What can I do now to make this happen?** What steps can you take now to realize your personal goals and your vision of the world?

Kidlink is in the process of gradually moving from the listserv to a new collaborative platform. The answers to the children's registrations are also being moved to a new platform, with public views such as http://www.kidlink.org./registration/index.php?action=publicViewRecord&responseNumber=17981.

Users will be able to update their answers, but the original answers will be kept to show how their dreams and views change over time.

In KidSpace, one component of KidLink, teachers and students can actively participate in collaborative projects. Dynamically generated links between activities, texts, and images make publishing within this space very simple. Students can interact with each other by inserting comments and annotations in the Web pages of the online materials with the approval of several moderators. A chat facility and online support are always available for teachers and students. The links at the bottom of Figure 6.15 illustrate the fluidity of KidSpace. As with wikis and other social software, users are able to actively engage in shaping and building resources within a community.

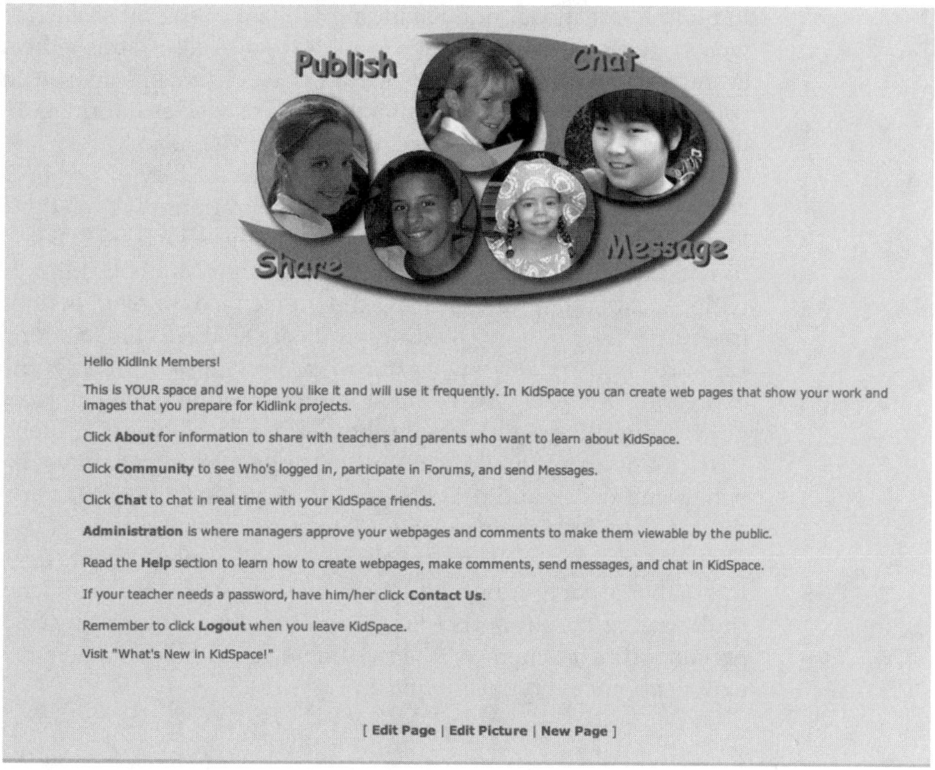

Figure 6.15 KidSpace, a section of KidLink.

KidLink supports different dialogues, such as KidCafe, KidProject, and KidLeader, each with several language choices. In each discussion group, a table of contents lists subject lines, and messages may be sorted by author or posting date. From the country codes in a recent list of messages, it is obvious that the dialogue that day was indeed global (Italy, Japan, the United Kingdom, and the United States) and covered a wide variety of topics. Some dialogues are constrained by topic and language. For that reason, there are volunteer translators who facilitate communication as well as language-specific conferences. Communicating with students from other countries in their native languages is one of the most constructive, authentic, and meaningful ways to study a second language that we can think of. Even if the students are communicating about their favorite stars or bands, they are still communicating, which is the purpose of learning a second language.

Participating in International Communities

Clearly, telecommunities open up vast new horizons to students, engendering a broader, more tolerant worldview for those involved. That should be an important goal of schools. Teachers wishing to begin using collaborative projects with students to build international understanding while meeting other curricular goals have a wealth of resources available through these well-established organizations. For example, GSN's Collaborative Learning Center contains links to collaboration tools such as blogs, chats, and instant messaging as well as information to support planning and implementing successful collaborative projects.

iEARN, GSN, and KidLink have a long history of promoting international connections among young people. The illustrations given in this chapter are but a few of the opportunities available through these Web sites. For example, in addition to Learning Circles, iEARN hosts Feeding Minds Feeding Hunger, an international classroom for exploring the problems of hunger, malnutrition, and food insecurity (http://www.feedingminds.org/). iEARN also sponsors the Laws of Life Project (http://www.iearn.org/projects/laws.html). Youth submit essays expressing what they value most in life, describing the principles and rules that govern their lives, and sharing how those ideals were influenced and formed. Participants respond to each other, engaging in meaningful dialogue about beliefs and values and providing multiple perspectives that can expand students' thinking and help them examine, compare, and solidify their own ideas.

Perhaps one of the most valuable resources for teachers beginning to explore international connections with their students are the teachers who have blazed the trail. Among the supports found in global community Web sites are mechanisms for connecting teachers as well as students to scaffold and enhance the community experience for everyone involved.

Building Professional Teacher Communities With Tapped In and TeacherTalk

Tapped In

Margaret Riel and Linda Polin (2004) say, "Sometimes a community is scattered and isolated. Unable to interact with each other or community cultural resources, members find it difficult to develop common practices or share values."

Teacher isolation has long been an obstacle to the exchange of ideas and information in the teaching profession. The current structure of our school system makes it difficult for in-depth interaction and collaboration to occur among teachers. With the rapid growth and potential of using technology as a learning tool, teachers are especially challenged. How do we avoid continually reinventing strategies for technology use? How do we share stories and resources among ourselves? By sharing ideas and experiences of technology successes and failures, we can break the barriers of isolated classrooms and develop a culture of collective knowledge.

In working with online communities intended for teachers' professional development, Riel (1990) found that "the community-building qualities of Learning Circles that bring K–12 students together are equally effective in supporting communities of teachers. The networking that led to cooperative learning experiences for students resulted in teachers acquiring knowledge and developing new instructional strategies. They experienced increased self-esteem and developed professional and personal relationships with their peers."

The time constraints and physical separation of teachers from one another can be mediated by using technology to bring together communities of practice:

> Learning communities share a way of knowing, a set of practices, and shared value of the knowledge that comes from these procedures. These learning communities, with expanded human and technological resources, bring together students, teachers, and community members in directing the course of education in new ways. (Fulton & Riel, 1999)

The Internet, while posing new challenges for teachers, may also be seen as a solution. Just as the Internet offers a vehicle to students for connecting with others and accessing information, it provides a means for teachers to continue their professional development. Teachers can become part of communities of discourse, of practice, of knowledge building, and of learners. Accessing experts, materials, and ideas to use for teaching and learning; staying current on events, issues, and trends in education and technology; and supporting each other as friends and professionals are all facilitated with Internet resources. Information abounds, and, like our students, we can learn not only by accessing that information but also by actively engaging with it—transforming, analyzing, evaluating, reflecting, and collaborating—all the processes we want our students to experience. The following examples are offered to open the doors to the vast community of educators around the world who are networking to support and improve their practice for learners.

One innovative community that combines these elements of learning and collegiality is Tapped In. Tapped In describes itself as "the online workplace of an international community of education professionals. K–12 teachers and librarians, professional development staff, teacher education faculty and students, and researchers engage in professional development programs and informal collaborative activities with colleagues."

Tapped In uses Java to create an updated version of a MOO (multiuser object oriented) environment. The Tapped In campus, depicted in Figure 6.16, consists of several buildings that house a variety of specific communities. Here, one can find buildings linking to universities that have created online spaces and to the Teachers for a New Era (TNE) community of professional educators. One of the purposes of TNE, funded by the Carnegie Corporation, the Ford Foundation, and the Annenberg Foundation, is the continued support of novice educators as they begin teaching. The campus map also links to a K–12 Student Campus where students can form their own communities of interest. The reception room, a public conference area, contained this message from a student in Liuzhou, China:

> Hi, there!
>
> I am the very first one from Yaodong large EFL classes coming all the way from China. I am new to TI and I hope to get acquainted with this environment.

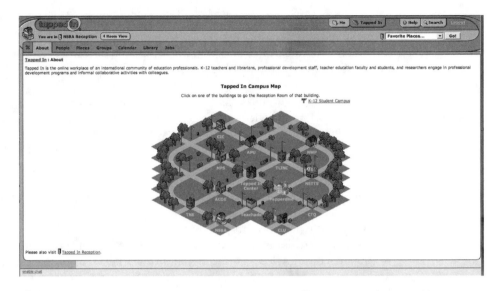

Figure 6.16   The Tapped In campus. *Source:* Tapped in ® is owned and operated by SRI International.

> Hope to meet my fellow-students here soon. More important, I wish I could meet American students on TI, too.
>   Thanks for your attention.

Teachers may also use the K–12 campus to connect their students with others and to collaborate and learn with other educators. For example, the reception room's whiteboard also displayed this posting:

> Hi, I'm from China. Are there any students who want to talk with my Chinese students. They are aged between 8–12. My students are eager to know the outside world.

After registering with Tapped In, users may elect to receive the Web site's monthly calendar by e-mail. This calendar lists online events such as orientations to the Tapped In community, synchronous discussions with experts, and sessions targeting specific software and/or methods for technology integration. An August 2006 online event featured Paul Bohac from the University of Western Florida hosting a special education group. The group met for an online discussion about how they used technology in their special education classrooms, to learn best practices in using technology in their particular environments, and to suggest topics for future discussions. Another group's purpose is to discuss national board certification and to support each other during the certification process.

Figure 6.17 represents a sampling of the 821 groups that are currently part of the Tapped In campus.

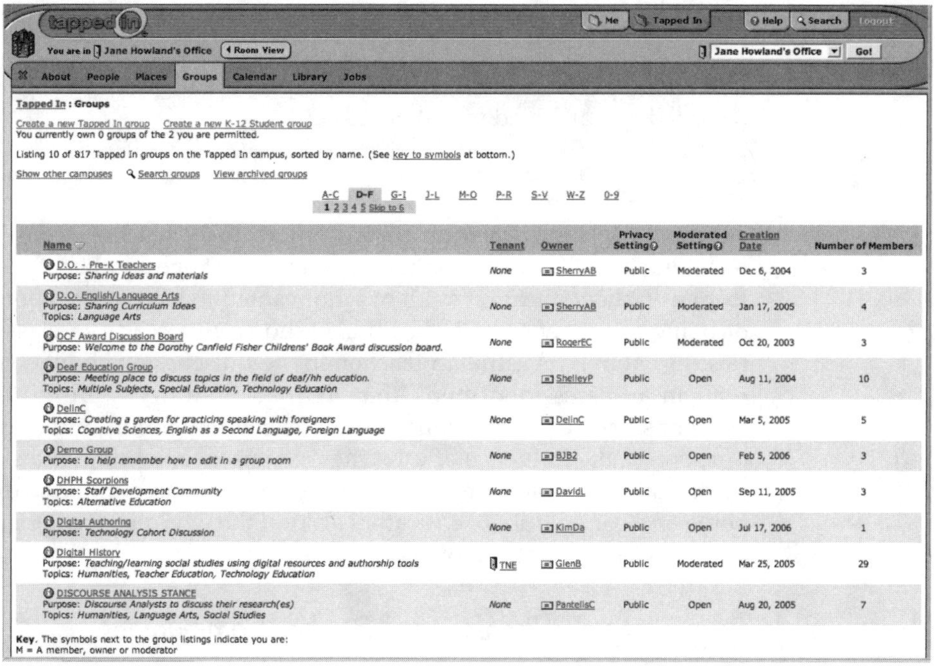

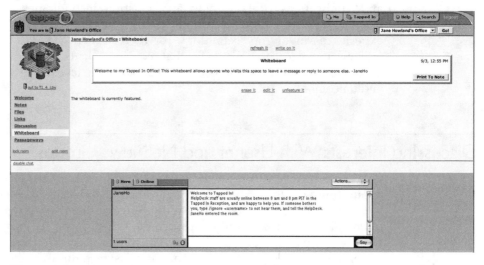

Figure 6.17 A few of the 821 Tapped In groups. *Source:* Tapped in ® is owned and operated by SRI International.

Figure 6.18 A Tapped In office. *Source:* Tapped in ® is owned and operated by SRI International.

Tapped In offers virtual offices (see Figure 6.18), which are private online spaces within the Web site where private conversations and meetings may be held. A unique feature is the capability of recording chats, with a transcript automatically e-mailed to the office's owner immediately after logging off.

Likewise, special events, such as the special education group's discussion, are recorded and archived for others to access.

TeacherTalk

TeacherTalk is a discussion forum where K–12 teachers can discuss teaching techniques, trade lesson plan ideas, and support one another. A recent posting was from a teacher education student who wanted to learn more about the experience of being a teacher from individuals who were already in classrooms. Another posting, from an Australian teacher, invited discussion about a statement he had read in an assessment book that defined grading as an indication of both a student's level of performance and a teacher's valuing of that performance. He questioned the influence of a teacher's subjective valuing of a student's work in determining a grade. The potential for sharing, debate, and rich exchange of ideas between a community of educators around the world is strengthened by availability of discussion board tools.

Participating in Professional Teacher Communities

Porter (2003) says that we are better able to manage the exponential growth of information by sharing expertise among ourselves in learning communities. Clearly, it is important that teachers are active, ongoing learners in the use and applications of both new and existing technologies. Knowledgeable teachers who are confident in their use of technology will plan more learning experiences involving technology for their students, and those experiences will encourage learning processes that require students to be active, constructive participants who engage in cooperative, authentic tasks with intentional goals and outcomes.

Discussing Interests With Usenet and NetNews Groups

People are social creatures who like to talk with each other. Generally, they talk about common interests—sports, gardening, and cars, dancing, and video games—whatever objects and activities engage them. When they can, people often talk face-to-face about their interests. When they must reach beyond their neighborhood to find others who share their interests or to expand their discourse community, people talk to each other at a distance through newsletters, magazines, and television shows. If you examine the magazine counter in your supermarket, you will find discourse communities focused on everything from brides to monster trucks. Cable television supports discourse networks on sports, cooking, and shopping.

Computer networks have evolved to support discourse communities through different forms of computer conferences. For instance, thousands of bulletin boards, Usenet and NetNews services, and chat rooms support special-interest discussion groups oriented to a wide range of topics as diverse as baseball, poetry, cooking, abortion, gun control, and religion. The number of active and interactive discourse communities has expanded exponentially with the growth of telecommunications. These communities can now stay in constant contact about their interests.

Electronic bulletin boards, such as NetNews or Usenets, are similar in purpose to listservs. Instead of messages being sent to subscribers by e-mail, they are generally posted in a central location (on an electronic bulletin board) with a subject heading, date, time, and author's name. Users browse through the subject headings and read and perhaps respond to messages of interest. Most responses are sent by e-mail directly to the person who posted the message rather than being posted for all to see. It works sort of like a newspaper, in which you scan headlines, article titles, and classified ads, deciding whether to read them. If you respond, it may be to the paper itself (a letter to the editor), to an individual or an organization mentioned in the article, or to the author. The software you use to look at NetNews generally keeps track of which articles you have read, and you can usually delete articles from your copy of the list of postings.

It is difficult to name a potentially interesting topic for which there is not an established conversation. In 2001, Google acquired the Deja News database, and these Usenet groups can now be found as Google Groups (http://groups.google.com/). Similarly, Yahoo has purchased several lists and now operates Yahoo! Groups. In its "Schools and Education" category alone, there are over 20 subgroups, as shown in Figure 6.19. One subgroup, K–12, has over 25,000 groups within it. Users can continue to drill down through subgroups to find those that are most promising for providing the desired community focus of interest. One Yahoo group concentrates on science experiments, with a new experiment offered each week. While this particular group looks more like a blog in its appearance, other groups clearly offer high levels of interaction. In the science category, the Astronomy Youth Group is a serious community of young people who want to talk about telescopes, celestial objects, accessories, amateur telescope making, and more.

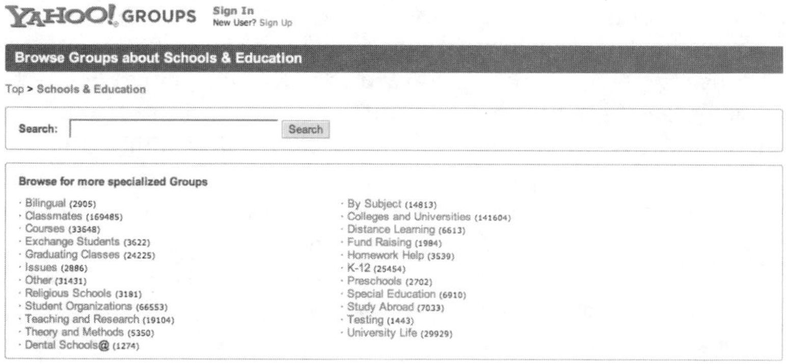

Figure 6.19 Yahoo! Groups: Schools & Education category. *Source:* (c) 2006 Yahoo! Inc, YAHOO! and the YAHOO! logo are trademarks of YAHOO! Inc.

Participating in Usenet and NewsNet Groups

Usenet was the initial Internet community, and although it is still in use today, it may become overshadowed by blogs, chat rooms, and other online social environments. As the number of users has grown, so have concerns regarding lack of standards and etiquette among users (see http://en.wikipedia.org/wiki/Eternal_September). Teachers should be aware of two things: first, many of the conversations are not suitable for students (many are not really suitable for adults, either), and, second, *flaming*, the practice of sending responses that are overly harsh, is relatively common. Students should be prepared for this before they encounter it. As with other Internet resources, wise teachers will take care to preview and evaluate the appropriateness of groups for student use.

Because of the storage demands created by thousands of conversations involving millions of people, Internet access providers make only a subset of the existing NetNews conversations available. If you or your students want to be involved in conversations on a particular topic but it does not appear available, ask your Internet provider to investigate and provide it to you.

Conclusion

Classrooms and schools can be communities of learners, although they often are not. Why? A community is a social organization of people who share knowledge, values, and goals. Classrooms typically are not communities because students are disconnected or are competing with one another. The students do not share common learning goals or interests. Within classrooms, there are social communities or cliques, but their purpose is not to learn together or from one another. Rather, those cliques seek to socially reinforce their own identities by excluding others. Learning communities emerge when students share common interests. Rather than forcing students to conform to prepackaged instructional requirements, emphasis should be placed on the social and cognitive contributions of a group of learners to each other, with students collaborating and supporting each other toward commonly accepted learning goals. Learning and knowledge-building communities depend heavily on both student and teacher buy-in, responsibility, and continuing motivation as well as a rich collection of information and learning resources to support them. We believe that learning communities can be an important vehicle for reforming schools.

While the tools we've discussed have great potential for enabling communities of learners to come together for meaningful work and interaction, the sophistication of the tools themselves is not enough for success. Schools must offer the type of curriculum that requires students to collaborate, problem-solve, work in teams, manage projects, and demonstrate leadership. Project-based learning that integrates subjects, that is complex and demanding, and that requires the skills that students will need to survive and flourish in a global economy is a curriculum that can challenge students with meaningful work while meeting necessary content standards (Pearlman, 2006).

Richardson (2006) says, "The current emphasis in our educational system is on accountability and formative, standardized testing, driven largely by federal legislation. As schools struggle to produce students whose test scores compare favorably with their international peers, some people criticize the tools emerging from Web 2.0 as detrimental to student achievement. However, these collaborative, constructionist tools have much to offer and their use does not preclude students' attaining necessary curriculum content and standards." Technologies that support community building offer great potential by providing the linkages to connect students in meaningful, collaborative learning relationships within the structure and requirements of the formal educational system. However, as with all technologies, the important consideration is not the technology itself but how well it supports and augments the learning process. Blogs and wikis are relatively new tools that can be used for instruction. Whether or not they and other technologies actually promote learning depends on how thoughtfully teachers plan and make use of them.

Are learning communities just another educational fad? We think not. Seen as complex systems, networks become the mechanism that allows adaptation and change, and adaptation and change equate to learning. Thus, while a business organization "learns" by adapting to its environment, teachers and students learn when they respond and adapt to each other and to information resources. As we see in a variety of settings, adaptive change goes hand in hand with a certain kind of structure—not hierarchical, static, or centrally controlled but rather decentralized, complex, dynamic, weblike networks of collaborating contributors. When classes or groups of students function together like that, they become more capable of learning.

Individual community members—students and teachers—work independently as well as collaboratively. In doing so, innovations, insights, and solutions to problems are developed that are shared with community at large. As students and teachers continue their work, the community takes on common attributes that shape its overall character and behavior.

By jointly pooling information through the collaborative efforts demonstrated in the projects presented in this chapter, students encounter a much greater body of knowledge than would be possible if they were working within a single classroom. Perhaps even more valuable is the insight they may gain by exposure to diversity. Seeing the world through another's lens expands each individual's worldview and lays the foundation for respectful, collaborative working relationships as students grow into the adult workers and leaders of tomorrow.

Things to Think About

1. What responsibilities do teacher and students share in cultivating a learning community in the classroom? How can technology serve the goals of a learning community, and how might technology get in the way?

2. With technology-supported learning communities, students learn different things at different speeds. How can a teacher keep track of students' various learning needs and make sure everyone is progressing well?

3. Every community has outliers—people on the margins who don't seem to fit or who struggle to participate fully. How can a teacher draw all students into the community circle? What steps can be taken to motivate students who may be reluctant to participate?

4. Do you believe that learning by conversing in learning communities can be more effective than traditional instruction? What evidence would we need to confirm (or reject) that belief?

5. With the advent of virtual reality and enhanced graphical interfaces, language may become less important in communication, especially among learners of different languages. What would a virtual language look like? How would students use it to communicate?

6. Some people think that the use of blogs or wikis in classrooms is frivolous and a waste of students' time. How would you respond?

7. What are some ways that you could use the technology ideas in this chapter to support your curriculum and student learners?

References

Alexander, B. (2006). A new wave of innovation for teaching and learning? *EDUCAUSE Review, 41*(2), 33–44.

Andres, Y. M. (1995). *Collaboration in the classroom and over the Internet.* Retrieved August 30, 2006, from http://www.gsn.org/gsn/teach/articles/collaboration.html

Boulding, K. (2006). *Kenneth E. Boulding.* Retrieved August 22, 2006, from http://en.wikipedia.org/wiki/Kenneth_Boulding#Quotations

Boyd, S. (2003). *Are you ready for social software?* Retrieved August 22, 2006, from http://www.darwinmag.com/read/050103/social.html

Falloon, S. (2005, February/March). All the world's a stage. *Edutopia,* pp. 16–18. Retrieved August 25, 2006, from http://edutopia.org/magazine/ed1article.php?id=Art_1223&issue=feb_05

Fulton, K., & Riel, M. (1999). *Professional development through learning communities.* Retrieved September 4, 2006, from http://www.edutopia.org/php/article.php?id=Art_481&key=238

Lamb, B. (2004). Wide open spaces: Wikis, ready or not. *EDUCAUSE Review, 39*(5), 36–48.

National Council for the Social Studies. (1992). *Curriculum standards.* Silver Spring, MD: Author. Retrieved September 30, 2002, from http://www.ncss.org/standards/foreword.html

NMC: The New Media Consortium and National Learning Infrastructure Initiative. (2005). *The Horizon Report.* Retrieved July 13, 2006, from http://www.educause.edu/LibraryDetailPage/666?ID=CSD3737

Ong, W. J. (1977). *Interfaces of the word.* Ithaca, NY: Cornell University Press.

Ong, W. J. (1982). *Orality and literacy.* New York: Routledge.

O'Reilly, T. (2005, September 30). *What is Web 2.0?* Retrieved August 15, 2006, from http://www.oreillynet.com/pub/a/oreilly/tim/news/2005/09/30/what-is-web-20.html

Pearlman, B. (2006, June). New skills for a new century. *Edutopia,,* pp. 51–53. Retrieved August 16, 2006, from http://edutopia.org/magazine/ed1article.php?id=art_1546&issue=jun_06#

Porter, B. (2003). Raising the bar for student performance and assessment. *Learning and Leading with Technology, 30*(8), 14–18.

Richardson, W. (2006). *Blogs, wikis, podcasts, and other powerful Web tools for classrooms.* Thousand Oaks, CA: Corwin.

Riel, M. (1990). Cooperative learning across classrooms in electronic Learning Circles. *Instructional Science, 19*(6), 445–466.

Riel, M. (1996, January). *The Internet: A land to settle rather than an ocean to surf and a new "place" for school reform through community development.* Retrieved September 5, 2006, from http://www.gsn.org/gsh/teach/articles/netasplace.html

Riel, M. (2005). *The teacher's guide to Learning Circles.* Retrieved August 29, 2006, from http://www.iearn.org/circles/lcguide/p.intro/a.intro.html

Riel, M., & Polin, L. (2004). Online learning communities: Common ground and critical differences in designing technical environments. In S. A. Barab, R. Kling, & J. Gray (Eds.), *Designing for virtual communities in the service of learning* (pp. 16–52). Cambridge, MA: Cambridge University Press.

Roper, D. (2006). *Quotes from Kenneth Ewert Boulding.* Retrieved August 22, 2006, from http://www.colorado.edu/econ/Kenneth. Boulding/quotes/q.body.html

Scardamalia, M. (2004). CSILE/Knowledge Forum®. In *Education and technology: An encyclopedia* (pp. 183–192). Santa Barbara, CA: ABC-CLIO.

Scardamalia, M., & Bereiter, C. (1996). Adaptation and understanding: A case for new cultures of schooling. In S. Vosniadou, E. De Corte, R. Glaser, & H. Mandl (Eds.), *International perspectives on the design of technology-supported learning environments* (pp. 149–163). Hillsdale, NJ: Lawrence Erlbaum Associates.

Scardamalia, M., & Bereiter, C. (2005). Does education for the knowledge age need a new science? *European Journal of School Psychology, 3*(1), 21–40.

Scardamalia, M., & Bereiter, C. (2007). Knowledge building: Theory, pedagogy, and technology. In K. Sawyer (Ed.), *Cambridge handbook of the learning sciences.* Cambridge, UK: Cambridge University Press.

Scardamalia, M., Bereiter, C., & Lamon, D. (1994). The CSILE Project: Trying to bring the classroom into World 3. In K. McGilly (Ed.), *Classroom lessons: Integrating cognitive theory and classroom practice* (pp. 201–228). Cambridge, MA: MIT Press.

Sifry, D. (2006, August 12). NPR Weekend Edition Saturday interview.

Winkler, C. (2005). Are wikis worth the time? *Learning and Leading with Technology, 33*(4), 6–7.

Communicating With Technologies

Today's students are, as a group, not only technologically sophisticated but also fundamentally different than previous generations in their approaches to, use of, and relationship with media. Whereas students once were admonished against the distraction of competing sensory input, today's kids are comfortably accustomed to interacting with multiple media inputs simultaneously.

The Kaiser Family Foundation reported that in 2005, young people spent an average of 6.5 hours per day with media and that, because of overlapping media use, they were actually exposed to the equivalent of 8.5 hours daily. While young people were spending almost the same amount of time on media in 2005 as they were 5 years ago, they increased the time spent with more than one medium simultaneously from 16% of the time to 26% of the time (Rideout, Roberts, & Foehr, 2005).

To illustrate, let's observe a 5-minute window in a typical teenager's life. Melissa is listening to music via MP3 player in front of a television set while instant messaging with a dozen friends on her computer. In the background, she's checking the price of the soccer shoes she wants to order online and downloading the lyrics and guitar tabs for a new song she's heard. An audio alert lets her know that she has a new text message from Ben on her cell phone, but before she can text back a reply, the phone rings. It's her best friend, calling to ask her opinion about the new dress she's found. Melissa doesn't want to go to the mall, so Katie takes a picture of the dress with her cell phone and sends it to Melissa. In the meantime, the DVD of pictures from Melissa's digital camera has finished burning, and Melissa remembers that she wants to post some of them to her MySpace account.

What does this media multitasking mean for educators? K–12 students are an information-inundated generation and are used to communication that is ubiquitous and instantaneous. These behaviors have strong implications for the way we should think about the structure of classrooms, curricula, and technology use in our schools. Although little research has yet been done regarding the effects of high exposure to media on learning processes, we cannot ignore the implications of learners' proclivity to this sensory input. Doing so risks losing the attention, motivation, and interest of a new generation of students.

Chapter 6 introduced you to several ways that technology devices and Internet resources can assist in the formation and collaborative work of communities. In this chapter, we review communication technologies and related activities and programs that allow sharing and exchange of ideas both individually and as groups. Most of the technology use introduced in this chapter also contributes to community building, which is such a critical element of meaningful learning as students engage in social negotiation and shared knowledge building.

The technological breakthrough that has afforded communication leading to learning communities is the Internet and related networking technologies. The Internet, particularly the World Wide Web, has become more than a source for retrieving archived information; it has become the communication medium that connects scattered people and resources together. Why? In many ways, the Internet's strength lies in its decentralized nature.

The Internet is the ultimate distributed network, linking users and institutions together, allowing interactions of all kinds to occur. The Internet can become the communications vehicle that both liberates and ties learners together, including students and teachers, into coherent learning communities. While some people have feared that telecommunications would replace face-to-face interactions, there is a growing realization that, instead, technology is facilitating the means for connecting us and increasing the opportunity for building relationships and social exchanges (NMC; 2005). The overwhelming growth in social networking spaces like Facebook (http://www.facebook.com) and MySpace (http://www.myspace.com) demonstrates the power of these online communities to capture and support the desire that humans have to bond. How online communication affects our off-line, face-to-face relationships may depend on how deeply one immerses oneself in the online world. A teenager who isolates him- or herself from concrete interactions with family and friends may lose important social ties. Is the increased social networking enabled by technology worth it if immediate relationships suffer? Or can online friendships provide an essential support that is difficult for some people to find in face-to-face interactions? Researchers will be investigating questions like these for some time. Rather than impose value judgments, we must critically assess the outcomes of online communication in an attempt to make the best use of new technologies.

The Internet can be part of the glue that keeps people connected—talking with each other, noticing and appreciating differences, working out divergent views, and serving as role models and audiences for one another. The education future portended by the Internet, therefore, is not isolated and targeted to individuals. Rather, it is a community-centered future in which persons are joined in working together through the power of telecommunication tools.

Exchanging Ideas Asynchronously With Discussion Boards

Communication in an online forum is different from and, in several important ways, better than face-to-face communication and other technology-based forms (e.g., telephone conversations and videoconferencing). It is true that an online discussion doesn't have the richness or, to use a computer metaphor, the *bandwidth* of a face-to-face conversation. We lose important communication cues, such as body language, tone of voice, accents, dialects, pace, pauses, and other important cues to meaning. Although this may be limiting, it may also be helpful, as authors must take more care to see that they are communicating clearly.

Paraphrasing a television commercial run by a major telecommunications vendor, on the Internet there is no race, no gender, no age, and no infirmities— only minds: people talking to people. This is certainly the case in text-based discussion boards.

Online communications are often *asynchronous* (not in real time), making them different in important ways. Howard Gardner (Gardner & Lazear, 1991; Gardner, 2000) has proposed a Theory of Multiple Intelligences, which suggests that intelligence is not a single capacity but rather a series of distinct capabilities.

He suggests that rather than asking, "How smart are you?" we should ask, "How are you smart?" Some people, Gardner believes, are high in *verbal intelligence*. They are often verbally deft and capable of carrying out stimulating conversations. They tend to do well in traditional school environments. This does not necessarily mean they are the best thinkers or communicators. Other people want more time to consider an idea and formulate their responses. Rather than speaking extemporaneously, they are often minimal contributors to real-time conversations—the conversation is off to other topics before they have developed their ideas and ways to share them.

When given a chance to think and then speak, as is the case in several forms of online conversation, these people experience a new freedom and level of participation. They can be heard clearly, and the power of their responses is often impressive. When combined with the removal of biases, as already described, it becomes easy to imagine why a number of strong friendships (some crossing international borders and generations) and even romances have begun on the Internet.

There are both advantages and disadvantages in computer conferencing, which is defined as group discussion in which messages are stored on computers rather than being sent real time, as with instant messaging services (Woolley, 1995). Some individuals prefer immediate response and feedback, which is not an attribute of asynchronous communication. Determining the message's content from a short subject line can be difficult, and reading discussion board postings is often quite time consuming. Threading, or the ability to respond to messages and have those responses clustered in sequence under the original posting, is an essential feature for conferencing, as it keeps messages organized and helps make the discussion relatively easy to follow. Wolley discusses several other attributes that are desirable in computer conferencing systems, including the following:

- Separate conferences for different topics, both for organization and individual interest
- Informative topic list that shows posting dates, number of responses, and titles of topics
- Search and filter tools allowing users to search messages by date, author, or key word

What advantages does computer conferencing have over a good old-fashioned discussion? Why not just converse face-to-face rather than talking through computers? There are several reasons one might want to participate in a computer-mediated conference. First, computer conferencing can support discussions, debates, and collaborative efforts among groups of people who are colocated or at a distance. Students do not have to be in the same place to converse and learn. Many classrooms are becoming virtual—communications and learning spaces located within a networked system connecting learners all over the country. Why it is necessary for students to share the same physical space with a teacher in order to listen to the teacher, ask questions, get assignments, or otherwise communicate with the teacher? The obvious answer is that computer conferencing supports long-distance collaboration among learners.

A second advantage is that computer conferencing enables learners to reflect on their ideas or responses before making them. In addition to providing opportunities to research topics and to develop arguments, conferences allow the students the opportunity to adequately present the group's position on the conference. That requires reflecting on your argument before carefully presenting it. Thinking about what you are going to say before saying it is fostered by computer conferences.

Third—and perhaps most important—different kinds of thinking can be scaffolded in computer conferences. Although in-class conversation is a powerful learning method, learners do not necessarily know how to constructively converse. Computer conferences can guide and scaffold students as they make comments, reminding them of needed support and development, and archiving past conversations for future use.

While the immediacy of real-time chats and instant messaging has much to offer, asynchronous communication can be a vehicle for promoting international connections and project work. The convenience of responding to others' postings at the time one chooses becomes virtually a necessity when students are communicating with others across time zones. While a live afternoon chat at 2:00 p.m. may work well for a student in Chicago, her team member in Bangkok could find himself quite sleepy from what would be a very early 2:00 a.m. conversation in Thailand.

Asynchronous discussion boards have the capacity to support classroom learning in a variety of ways. They can connect students with others beyond the immediate classroom, opening windows to new learning experiences by exposure to new ideas, cultural diversity, and unique partnerships. Asynchronous discussion boards can also serve a useful purpose within a contained classroom community by providing an outlet for extended conversations that enrich classroom activity. The 50-minute class periods so common in most secondary schools provide insufficient time for in-depth dialogue. In a typical scenario, just as students may be approaching some degree of meaningful conversation and reaching the point where significant thinking really begins, the bell signaling a change of classes sounds, abruptly halting the opportunity for learning. Collaborating and conversing on meaningful topics outside the regular school day gives students a chance to dig deeper and establishes a classroom community that exists beyond one class period. It may also connect students in separate sections of a course, broadening the range of ideas brought to the conversation.

Asynchronous discussion boards are also an excellent means for supporting second-language learning. Language students can converse with native speakers from another country on mutually interesting topics (e.g., music or fashion) or among themselves on relevant topics. In this way, students are learning to communicate in the language, not just to learn about conjugations and declensions. Asynchronous discussion boards are especially effective with nonnative speakers, as it provides them with time to consider and articulate their ideas, tasks that are difficult for them to accomplish extemporaneously.

In the following sections, some applications of asynchronous discussion boards are offered.

Discussion Boards in Purposeful Community Web Sites

When students and teachers engage in collaborative work through Web sites such as Global Schoolhouse or ePALS (see chapter 6), they have access to several integrated communication tools. Figure 7.1 illustrates the various ePALS discussion boards that are related to specific projects or are meant for more general, community dialogues.

Whereas the project-specific discussion boards can be an integral part of managing tasks and sharing ideas in collaborative project work, the Student Talk discussion board gives young people the means for exchanging their thoughts on just about anything that they care to talk about with one another. Conversation centered on project work is instrumental in building knowledge in the cognitive domain; informal conversation initiated by students and focused on students' lives and personal interests has great potential not only for cognitive learning outcomes but also for constructive outcomes in the affective domain. Increasing one's knowledge, understanding, tolerance, and valuing of other individuals' customs, opinions, and beliefs can have a positive effect on students' ability to work together in collaborative groups. Informal conversations can build a foundation for future interactions that may occur in our global economy.

As technology and the growing global economy dissolve the boundaries between countries, there is a critical need to become cognizant and well informed about one another. The Brazilian student who is curious about the social rules in other countries (Figure 7.2) is asking a question whose answers have important implications for cross-cultural interactions. It is not unreasonable to assume that international corporate business deals have been influenced by employees' sensitivity and knowledge of fundamental cultural expectations and rules. Figure 7.2 also illustrates the structure of the ePALS discussion board. Respondents to the original question have clearly identified their respective countries in the subject line of their responses, making it easy for readers to select replies they are most interested in reading. One of the unique features of ePALS is the built-in translator tool that allows users to convert messages to many languages, facilitating their usefulness to a wide audience.

Discussion Boards in Courseware

Teachers can utilize discussion through Web sites such as ePALS to extend and support a variety of curriculum requirements, but they may also wish to structure online conversations that take place only among members of their own classrooms. Many teachers are integrating the use of courseware into face-to-face classes, particularly at the secondary school level. One widely used application is the Blackboard system. This online environment provides built-in communication tools, including a discussion board. Figure 7.3 shows the functions of the Blackboard discussion board tool. Blackboard's threaded discussion board messages may be sorted by author, date, or subject and are searchable by key words. Messages can also be selected and "collected" or compiled on one page.

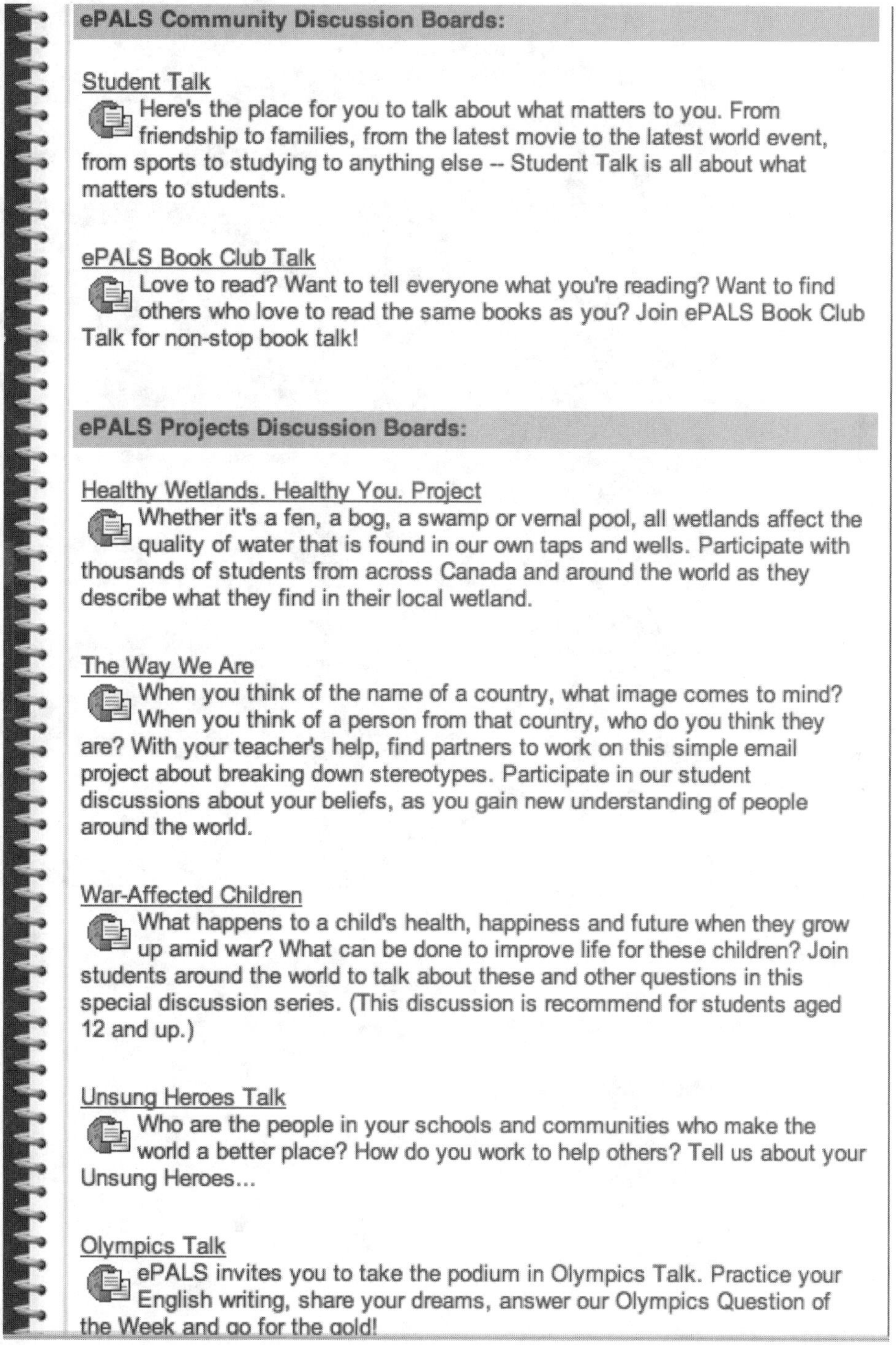

ePALS Community Discussion Boards:

Student Talk

Here's the place for you to talk about what matters to you. From friendship to families, from the latest movie to the latest world event, from sports to studying to anything else -- Student Talk is all about what matters to students.

ePALS Book Club Talk

Love to read? Want to tell everyone what you're reading? Want to find others who love to read the same books as you? Join ePALS Book Club Talk for non-stop book talk!

ePALS Projects Discussion Boards:

Healthy Wetlands. Healthy You. Project

Whether it's a fen, a bog, a swamp or vernal pool, all wetlands affect the quality of water that is found in our own taps and wells. Participate with thousands of students from across Canada and around the world as they describe what they find in their local wetland.

The Way We Are

When you think of the name of a country, what image comes to mind? When you think of a person from that country, who do you think they are? With your teacher's help, find partners to work on this simple email project about breaking down stereotypes. Participate in our student discussions about your beliefs, as you gain new understanding of people around the world.

War-Affected Children

What happens to a child's health, happiness and future when they grow up amid war? What can be done to improve life for these children? Join students around the world to talk about these and other questions in this special discussion series. (This discussion is recommend for students aged 12 and up.)

Unsung Heroes Talk

Who are the people in your schools and communities who make the world a better place? How do you work to help others? Tell us about your Unsung Heroes...

Olympics Talk

ePALS invites you to take the podium in Olympics Talk. Practice your English writing, share your dreams, answer our Olympics Question of the Week and go for the gold!

Figure 7.1 ePALS community and project discussion boards. *Source:* ePALs product screenshot(s) reprinted.

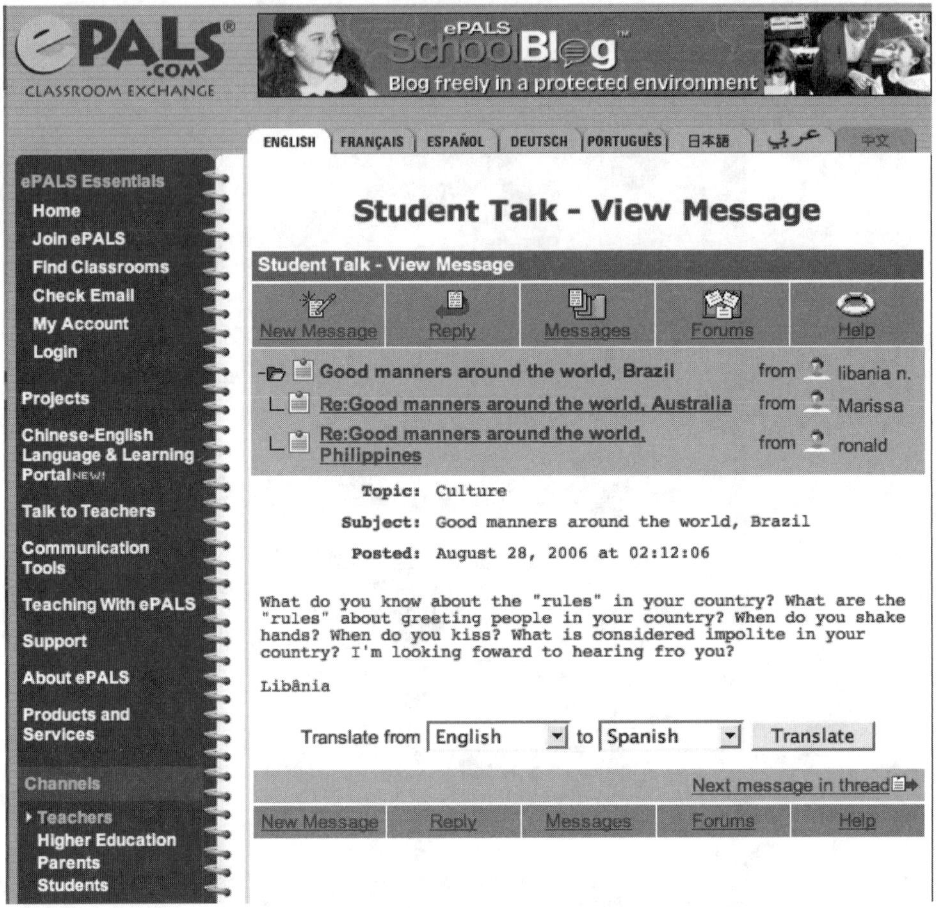

Figure 7.2 A message from the ePALS Student Talk discussion board. *Source:* ePALs product screenshot(s) reprinted.

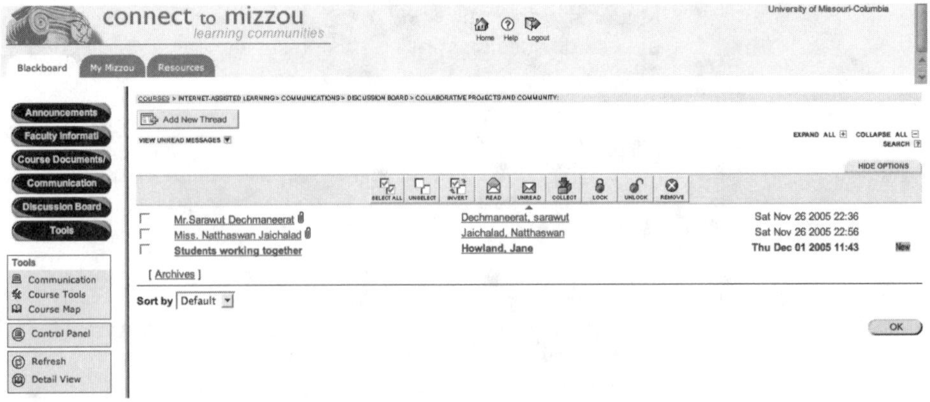

Figure 7.3 Discussion board tools in Blackboard courseware. *Source:* Used with permission from Blackboard.

Things to Consider

Online communication presumes that students can communicate—that is, that they can meaningfully participate in conversations. To do that, they must be able to interpret messages, consider appropriate responses, and construct coherent replies. Most teachers realize that not all students can engage in cogent and coherent discourse. Why can't they? For one thing, most students have rarely been asked to contribute substantive discussion in learning settings. They have been too busy memorizing what the teachers tell them. So it may be necessary to support students' attempts to converse. Environments such as Knowledge Forum (see chapter 6) offer the built-in structure to scaffold student discourse. When students use discussion boards that do not have these embedded supports, there are other methods teachers may use to assist students.

Salmon (2002) believes that motivated students and active, skilled moderators contribute to successful computer conferencing. Our goal is to encourage critical thinking within the discussion. Teachers must be on the lookout for conversation that remains shallow (e.g., "I agree" or "me too"), that is unfocused, or that demonstrates misconceptions, uncertainty, or imprecise thinking. There are strategies that teachers can employ to help students sharpen the focus and reach more depth in their dialogue (Collison, Elbaum, Haavind, & Tinker, 2000). To dig deeper into the ideas being generated, teachers can model use of analogies to help make connections, bring unexamined issues to the forefront, and encourage and respect multiple perspectives. Collison et al. (2000) offer the method of "full-spectrum questioning" to extract meaning from participants' conversation. The questions in Figure 7.4 demonstrate how a conferencing moderator can encourage meaningful dialogue among participants in an online discussion.

Facilitating Online Learning: Effective Strategies for Moderators

Discussion moderators can scaffold students' discussion capabilities by helping them concentrate on key points, identifying the most relevant ideas, and steering the direction of the conversation to maintain its purpose. Making students aware of these communication processes as the moderator helps shape and direct the discussion can result in higher-quality subsequent postings if students understand the characteristics that contribute to constructive online discussion. Providing general guidelines such as those in Figure 7.5 can give students some common understanding as to what contributes to effective online conversations.

Depending on the situation, teachers may want to provide a forum for general discussion that is not related to the specific topics in designated forums. This allows students the opportunity to discuss things that are interesting to them yet keeps the dialogue focused on the topic's purpose in other forums. Creating a "watercooler" or "break room" forum for discussions that are unrelated to other forums may result in conversations that become equally as valuable as those the teacher plans. Teachers may create new forums based on ideas that emerge from existing forums and may involve students in deciding on areas for discussion.

Questions that probe the "so what!" response	Questions that clarify meaning or conceptual vocabulary	Questions that explore assumptions, sources, and rationale	Questions that seek to identify causes and effects or outcomes	Questions that consider appropriate action
How Relevant or Important? To whom? To what constituency? Individuals or groups? What viewpoint would impart importance? Is that me/us/them? What audience is assumed? If we knew all about this, what good would it do? **How Urgent or Interesting?** Is immediate consideration needed? Or, is the detail best left for other times or forums? Is the issue compelling, or tangentially related to my or the group's task at hand? Is the issue of intellectual merit? **What Context?** Is the issue or question part of a larger view or strategy?	**Is There Ambiguity or Vagueness?** Are terms clear or meanings commonly shared? What alternative meanings might exist? Can quantifiers be made more explicit? How much? How long? How few? To what extent? Can implicit comparisons be made explicit? **Are Concepts Held in Common?** Are terms relying on professional or technical understandings? Does meaning shift from ordinary usage to technical sense? Is persuasion confused with definition? What might be a similar example in another area?	**What Qualities Are Assumed?** Is the claim or phenomena assumed to be: Real, unique, measurable, beneficial, harmful, neutral? Might the opposite assumption be equally valid? Are biases or preconceptions evident in gender, audience, categorization? What does the speaker assume about herself or himself or the audience? **Can One Be Sure?** What evidence supports the claim? How can it be confirmed? What are reasons for belief or disbelief or assigning value? What procedures or processes give evidence for certainty? What supports any analogies?	**Primary Vs. Secondary?** Is the claim/condition a root or secondary cause or effect? Is it a trigger for other mechanisms? What are they? **Internal/External vs. Systematic Interaction** Is the cause/effect mechanism internal or partly external to the system? What external factors affect interactions? Are reputed "causes" perhaps correlations? At what level might true causes operate? Are consequences long or short term? For whom? What limits or scenarios might apply? What are worst/best cases? What is most probable? Why? If cause/effects are connected systemically through feedback, what are the key feedback controls?	**Who Does What, How, When, with Whom, and Why?** Is there a quick fix or is a more considered view needed? Should I/we do something? Together, separately, as a group? Should it be done now? When? What is the commitment? Are those involved too close to act effectively? Are outsiders needed? Who can be engaged? What plans or strategies will be effective? What levels/conditions need addressing first? **What Comes Next?** How is effectiveness evaluated? What ongoing monitoring or re-evaluating of intervention is needed? Is there a backup plan? Who directs it? Under what conditions is operative?

Figure 7.4   Full-spectrum questioning from Collison et al. (2000). © 1999 The Concord Consortium. Adapted from Precision Questioning, Deniis Mathies (1991).

Many students find that the online environment enhances the dialogue among students. As we stated previously, the structure of schools often inhibits meaningful dialogue because of time constraints. Teachers who integrate asynchronous discussion boards into their curriculum provide a solution that gives students the chance to interact beyond the confines of four walls and too few minutes.

- The Discussion Board should be accessed at least twice weekly (one original posting and one response is required).
- Discussion board postings should begin early in the specified discussion time frame to allow maximum interaction.
- Make your subject lines informative and descriptive. When replying to someone, change the subject line to more closely reflect your topic. That will avoid the possible scenario of having 20 replies with something like "Re: My Idea" as the subject line.
- Postings should contribute something of value. Responses such as, "Thanks for the idea. This will help a lot" or "I know just what you mean" are not appropriate postings for the forum environment. Please email other students directly if a message is not important for the entire class to read.
- Messages posted should contribute to the group's overall understanding of the topic being discussed through one or more of the following:
  - examining a topic from a new or different perspective,
  - explaining issues more in-depth,
  - asking relevant and effective questions
  - elaborating meaningfully on the topic
  - responding to elaborate, contradict, modify, and/or explain the original message
- Remember that without the communication cues we get when conversing face-to-face, there is a greater chance for misinterpretation. Therefore, choose your words carefully and read what you've written before you submit your posting.

Figure 7.5 Guidelines for online discussions.

Exchanging Ideas Synchronously With Interactive Chats and Messaging

Asynchronous communication tools such as discussion boards provide the means for users to share ideas in a distributed environment, choosing when they will post messages to the board. As we showed in the previous section, there are benefits to this method of communicating; however, at times we may wish for students to communicate in a way that more closely resembles face-to-face interaction. Synchronous communication tools that use the Internet to transmit messages can provide that instant, real-time exchange of ideas.

Internet Relay Chat

Internet relay chat (IRC) is one form of real-time (synchronous) communication over the Internet. It is designed mainly for group (many-to-many) communication in discussion forums called channels but also allows one-to-one communication. IRC software allows anyone to post a statement to the group by typing into a field and then clicking a button to submit the statement. The software adds each comment to

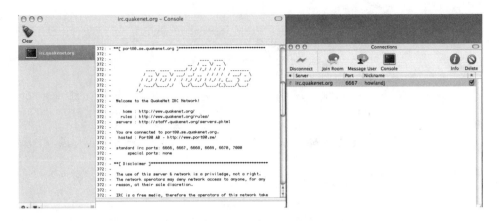

Figure 7.6   QuakeNet IRC network in Colloquy client software.

a scrolling list. The list is sent out to participants' screens periodically, say, every 20 seconds, keeping everyone informed about what has been said.

The conversations are often a bit confusing. It's rather like a cocktail party where there are several conversations going on at once. Chat exchanges among individuals are sometimes structured in a *virtual location*, set up perhaps as a house, with a lobby, library, kitchen, and dining room where people go to have private conversations. If the chat gets too busy, clusters of people can break off into another room to converse without the distraction of competing conversations. It is also possible to establish private chats, restricting entry to people who are registered to participate. Although some find this kind of communication confusing, others find it almost addictive.

Today there are several thousand running IRC networks in the world. The basic means of communication in an established IRC session is a channel. Users can join channels and then send messages to them that are subsequently relayed to all other users in the same channel. IRC client software such as Colloquy or mIRC is used for chat sessions. One can join servers by using the irc://irc.server.net:port/channel Web link; four of the largest IRC networks are EFnet, IRCnet, QuakeNet, and Undernet (Wikipedia). Figure 7.6 illustrates the QuakeNet network accessed through the Colloquy client software.

Instant Messaging

Instant messaging is a form of real-time communication between two people based on typed text that is transferred between computers connected over a network such as the Internet. Client programs that support instant messaging include ICQ (I Seek You), Yahoo! Messenger, Skype, Google Talk, AOL Instant Messenger, and MSN Messenger.

Messaging software such as ICQ, Yahoo! Messenger, and MSN Messenger typically give users control over those they talk with through the use of a presence information feature, or "buddy lists." Unless a user provides his or her personal information to a directory, he or she can receive instant messages only from individuals to whom he or she has provided his or her user screen name. Each one-on-one conversation in this type of chat environment is contained in a small, separate screen. While this allows several simultaneous private conversations, users must manage several windows and conversations at once. Based on one of the author's observations of two teenaged children, managing multiple conversations in an instant messaging environment is an easily learned skill. One may also invite users into a chat room, which enables shared conversation among a group of people.

Instant messaging typically increases communication and allows easy collaboration. The synchronous nature of instant messaging allows students to work together, immediately exchanging ideas with one or more individuals. Instant messaging and chats can serve as useful classroom tools for connecting students with others when real-time communication is desirable. The main consideration in choosing between instant messaging and a group chat session is whether one wishes to communicate one to one or with a group where several people are engaged in the same conversation. Because of the difficulty in monitoring conversations, teachers may need to carefully consider whether synchronous conversations are of benefit.

Informal use of instant messaging occurs outside the school day and reflects the normal activity of many young people. A vast number of kids spend time online during the evening, with instant messaging being an integral part of that activity. It is only natural that questions about homework are bandied about, with friends providing assistance to each other through instant messaging. Comparable questioning and assistance might be given among students working at a distance on collaborative projects.

Community-oriented Web sites such as Tapped In, ePALS, Global Schoolhouse, and iEARN (see chapter 6) offer several communication tools, and using chat and/or messaging services through these sites offers an element of safety that may not be present in many venues. Because teachers will want to identify a clear purpose for student use of chat rooms and instant messaging, they may find that these purposeful Web sites are, at least initially, the best source for them, as conversation is centered around project work or otherwise structured to some degree. Their parameters help ensure that student use of these tools is genuinely constructive and supports learning goals.

The bottom section of Figure 7.7 depicts the chat feature on the K–12 Student Campus of Tapped In. On the right side of the screen, the "Actions" menu has been opened to illustrate the various options available in this chat environment. For example, users may send a private message to someone with whom they are publicly conversing. They may also access user profiles to gain information about individuals in the chat room.

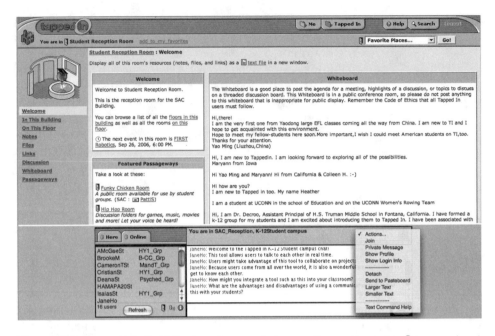

Figure 7.7   Tapped In's K–12 Student Campus chat room. *Source:* Tapped In ® is owned and operated by SRI International.

Safety Guidelines for Online Communication

- Use a pseudonym instead of your real name.
- Never give out personal information such as your last name, telephone number, home address, or parent's work address.
- Never share a password for an Internet chat room.
- Never agree to meet with someone you met in a chat room and tell your teacher if someone asks you to meet them.
- Notify your teacher if you receive an obscene or inappropriate message.
- Be aware that someone you talk with online might be pretending to be someone they aren't.
- If someone is rude or disagreeable, ignore them rather than engaging in conversation.

Figure 7.8   Guidelines for safety in online communication.

The ability to identify the individuals involved in a chat is an important factor in determining the safety of these online conversations. Teachers may want to share the list of guidelines in Figure 7.8 with students and parents to help build awareness of ways to take advantage of the positive aspects of online communication while maintaining one's privacy and security.

Making Connections Through Videoconferencing

Nearly 100 years ago, John Dewey commented on the dangers of a complex society that relies on schools and classrooms to convey essential knowledge and tools to its youth:

> As societies become more complex in structure and resources, the need for formal teaching and learning increases. As formal teaching and training grows, there's a danger of creating an undesirable split between the experience gained in direct association and what is acquired in school. This danger was never greater than at the present time on account of the rapid growth of the last few centuries, of knowledge and technical modes of skill. (Dewey, 1916, p. 11)

Reflecting on the state of formal education over the past several decades shows, unfortunately, that the danger Dewey warned against has, to a great extent, occurred. The schism between real-world experience and school learning is a serious concern. Technologies of various kinds can serve as bridges between schools and students' outside experiences—if they are used in the right way within a supportive context. Technologies can also link students with experts in real-life contexts through communication tools that support learning and interaction. Videoconferencing is a technology that allows two or more locations to interact simultaneously by two-way video and audio transmissions. In the following sections, some types of videoconferencing systems are discussed and ways to utilize videoconferencing to enhance learning offered.

Connecting With Experts

Interactive videoconferencing (IVC) is a technology that offers great potential for connecting students in live interactions with experts to whom they would otherwise have no access. Merrick (2005) acknowledges the hesitance many teachers may feel about adding a relatively unfamiliar new technology into their classrooms, especially when the current K–12 emphasis is so strongly slanted toward accountability through standardized testing. Would it not be more effective to directly teach the material on which students will be tested? We agree with Merrick that IVC can strengthen curriculum, bringing it a richness and depth that would not be possible without the expertise of professionals who are accessible through videoconferencing technology.

Teachers, particularly those in elementary classrooms who are expected to be knowledgeable in all content areas, may quickly recognize the value of the rich supplemental resources available through videoconferencing. Their curriculum can be enhanced by drawing on additional resources and on a novel approach to learning that can engage and motivate students.

Videoconferencing overcomes barriers of cost and distance since physically transporting a classroom of students to another location is often impossible.

Students not only benefit from the knowledge of experts in content areas but also can practice and gain important interpersonal skills through their interactions. Moreover, videoconferencing can result in bridging gaps between schools and the community, encouraging relationships that demonstrate to students the real-life application of classroom learning.

Technical Considerations

Inexpensive desktop videoconferencing is possible through use of desktop videocameras, also called webcams. These USB devices connect to a computer that uses the Internet to link users for conferencing. Early videoconferences often resulted in rather jerky video, as data transmission was limited to the speed of slow modems. High-speed (broadband) cable and digital subscriber line Internet connections have greatly improved the quality of desktop videoconferencing. By connecting an inexpensive webcam to your computer, you can videoconference with anyone who has similar tools. In addition to the webcam and Internet connections, users simply need some type of software that supports videoconferencing (often free), computer speakers, and a microphone. Although some webcams have a built-in microphone, users may be more satisfied with the ease and quality of using a headset that combines a microphone with speaker headphones.

Many computer programs are available for participating in desktop videoconferencing. Skype is a free telephony software program that supports one-to-one phone calls through the Internet and conference calls for up to four people who also have the Skype software. Skype uses Voice-over Internet Protocol technology that allows one to make telephone calls using a broadband Internet connection instead of a regular (or analog) phone line. With a webcam, Skype can also be used for desktop videoconferencing. Instant messaging programs such as AOL Instant Messenger and MSN Messenger also allow video messages. Applications like Microsoft NetMeeting support multipoint data conferencing, meaning that data collaboration is possible between several people at once. Users can communicate with audio and video and conference and work together using the Whiteboard or shared program features.

While these desktop applications may be adequate for one-to-one interactions, higher-end systems are typically needed to videoconference when at least one of the participating sites includes several people. For more robust conferencing that can connect multiple locations, dedicated systems are often used. These systems typically feature a console that uses a high-quality remote-controlled video camera. Dedicated systems integrate all the required components into this single piece of equipment, including the control computer, speakers, necessary software or hardware for converting compressed audio and video signals, and a monitor. Polycom is one widely use dedicated videoconferencing system. Multipoint systems can allow users to connect up to four separate sites simultaneously.

Videoconferencing Interactions With Astronomers at Dyer

Scott Merrick facilitated the "VIA Dyer" (Videoconferencing Interactions with Astronomers at Dyer) program, wherein students across the country engaged in weekly videoconference presentations with scholars at Vanderbilt Dyer Observatory. He described the experience this way:

> During this series I witnessed several repeat presentations on the same topic, and one excellent example is Bob O'Dell's "Astronomical Observatories"—a fascinating overview of extra-Earth telescopes including a discussion of why they are needed. In the ensuing question and answer sessions, I sometimes heard O'Dell receive the same or similar questions in subsequent sessions. While his answers would often be informed by his earlier ones, every time I heard him construct a new response, it was in some way different—and often more substantive, more interesting, or more age-appropriate—than the answers he had given before. Not only was he getting better at IVC, but he was also so obviously passionate and knowledgeable about his topic that he inspired genuine engagement among his audience. It was not a canned presentation; it was conversation.
>
> For example, in the course of his presentation, O'Dell often narrated a three minute computer-generated virtual fly-through of the Orion Nebula. While students could use Google to find and download this digital video from the Internet, with IVC they could see it and also simultaneously hear narration by the man who directed the 500-personhour team that actually constructed the animation. O'Dell's team constructed the animation out of mathematical models and images sent back to Earth by the Hubble Space Telescope, and O'Dell himself was project scientist for the first team that undertook the design of the Hubble telescope. IVC affords students a unique opportunity to interact with someone immediately involved in current research in a given discipline. (Merrick, 2005, pp. 1–2)

A second Vanderbilt University videoconferencing initiative aimed at improving K–12 science education involved weekly videoconferences between the students and Vanderbilt faculty research scientists, physicians, postdoctoral fellows, upper-level graduate students and medical students, as well as other science professionals (McCombs et al., 2004). Figure 7.9 shows the range of topics and presenters that were part of the series.

Videoconferencing Weekly Topic Series (Year 3)

While these examples are primarily science based, videoconferencing may be used in any content area. In Missouri, high school students gained important understanding of civics by interacting with two Missouri Supreme Court judges and a University of Missouri professor who is a constitutional expert (Heavin, 2006). During this live broadcast, in recognition of Constitution Day, panel members discussed topics chosen by the students, including the Constitution as it relates to the war on terrorism, religion in school, and drug testing and drug dogs

WEEKLY TOPIC	DATES	DAY 1	DAY 2	DAY 3	DAY 4	DAY 5
Science Careers I	11/4 – 11/8	Medical Doctor	Pathologist	Nutritionist	Nurse	Medical Student
Science in Current Events	11/18 – 11/22	Bioterrorism	Chemical Warfare	Mars Expedition	Global Warming	Advances in Technology
Neuroscience	12/2 – 12/6	Parkinson's Disease	Epilepsy	Mental Health Issues	Multiple Sclerosis	Alzheimer's Disease
Physics/Chemistry	1/6 – 1/10	Space – The Final Frontier	Near Earth Asteroids	Radiation	Big Bang Theory	Gravity
Earth/Environmental Science	1/13-1/17	Volcanoes	Earthquakes	Dinosaurs	Planetary Geology	Pollution
Genetics	1/27 – 2/3	Human Genome Project	Genetically Altered Food	Cloning	Genetic Diseases	Genetic Counseling
Bacterial Diseases	2/10 – 2/14	Epidemics	Tuberculosis	Anthrax	Bubonic Plague	Bacterial Meningitis
Viruses	2/24 – 2/28	Overview	West Nile Virus	HIV	Ebola	Vaccines
Cancer	3/24 – 3/28	Childhood Cancers	Breast Cancer	Lung Cancer	Cancer Treatments	Discussion with Cancer Survivors
Health and Wellness	3/10 – 3/14	STDs	Smoking	Binge Drinking	Recreational Drugs	Eating Disorders
Science Careers II	4/21 – 4/25	Engineer	Physicist	Science Writer	Computer Programmer	Geologist

Figure 7.9 Weekly topics and presenters in Vanderbilt University videoconferences.

in schools. During the broadcast, students had the opportunity to e-mail questions to the panel.

This program was provided by the Missouri Bar in cooperation with Education Solutions Global Network (ESGN), is an Internet-based, video broadcast distribution network offered by the Missouri School Boards Association for education and training. It supports the delivery of digital video and audio of live events and events that have been recorded and made available "on demand." Other ESGN videoconference programming is a nature series is called "Top Down: Predators and Prey," which explores the mysteries of great animal hunters and escape artists. This series originates from the Wonders of Wildlife Museum and Aquarium in Springfield, Missouri, and has connected up to 50 school districts, including ones in Alaska and Mexico.

Likewise, the Vanderbilt Virtual School connects many schools simultaneously. The school's director explains that by "using a 'bridge' at the University of Tennessee, we can connect with many schools at one time. That is very cool because students at each site can see and hear students at the other sites" (Jackson, 2005). She goes on to say,

> One of the most touching videoconferences we had was when we first ran our Holocaust Survivors series. Mira Kimmelman, a sweet and gentle woman in her late eighties, spoke with students in six schools about her experience in Auschwitz. Although Mira's story lasted almost an hour, those elementary and middle school students sat still and did not make a sound. Following her talk, the students took turns asking her questions about Nazis, the war, her family.

Figure 7.10 shows how AT&T's Knowledge Network Explorer (http://www.kn.att.com/wired/vidconf/ideas.html) implements videoconferencing not only to connect students with experts but also for peer connections, virtual field trips, and course offerings that aren't available at all schools.

The Pacific Bell program in California (Videoconferencing for Learning) has introduced the concept of student videoconferencing groups within partner schools and has shown that videoconferencing results in positive outcomes. Specifically, videoconferencing does the following:

- Increases motivation
- Improves communication and presentation skills
- Allows students to learn to ask better questions
- Increases communication with the outside world
- Lets students learn from a primary source rather than a textbook
- Increases the depth of understanding in subject area content (http://www.kn.pacbell.com/wired/vidconf/intro.html)

Mark Haddon, director of education at the Smithsonian Environmental Research Center (SERC), described the Smithsonian's ventures with video conferencing. SERC's research projects are comprised of a variety of outdoor studies, including shoreline and marine life research:

> We are, in essence, a content provider to schools that have invested in video conferencing technologies. It gives students from these schools the ability to visit the Smithsonian and learn all about different types of life forms found throughout our environment, without leaving their classrooms. The fact is that many school districts are looking for content providers with good equipment because it justifies usage and encourages more schools to get involved in video conferencing. Video conferencing has developed into an excellent way for schools to provide quality education for their students, regardless of where the subject matter is located (German, 2005).

Things to Consider

The cost of videoconferencing equipment and the needed infrastructure are certainly important considerations. While most systems are fairly easy to use, teachers will nevertheless need training before they begin scheduling videoconferences with others. Because time differences will always be a factor between distant locations, scheduling synchronous communications might tend to limit videoconferencing to partners in time zones that are not substantially different. Equipment should be checked before beginning the videoconference to ensure that everything is functioning well. During the session, mute any microphones that aren't in use to avoid distracting noise. Users should also consider basic elements such as lighting, acoustics, and the position of participants.

Beyond the technical aspects, there are several things that videoconference participants and planners can do to optimize the experience for all involved. Care should be taken to keep the technology in a support role and not to become

Courses and Tutoring

- Students take classes not offered at their school, such as advanced honors, foreign language, or music courses.
- Teachers team-teach with remote teachers, sharing subject matter expertise or a unique approach to a topic.
- Students meet with tutors for enrichment, remediation, or a helpful bit of personal attention. This is great way for businesses to support schools.
- A librarian offers an introduction to library services and library tour for local schools before they come to the library.

Virtual Field Trips

- Students organize and moderate a panel discussion with a dolphin trainer, fisherman, and animal rights activist as part of an ocean unit.
- A librarian using document sharing technology, auxiliary input, or a whiteboard answers questions about research and actually demonstrates search queries using the online catalog.
- Students connect with athletes at an Olympic Training Center for advice and feedback on sports, training, and health issues.
- Students watch a play performed at a remote site followed by interaction with the actors.
- A small group interviews the author of a book the class is studying.
- Students meet with university advisors for admission counseling or interviews.
- A remote teacher or student role-plays a historical or literary figure, sharing a special experience with a larger audience.
- A graphic arts student shares a document with a professional or client for feedback and evaluation.

School to school projects

- Teachers and students collaborate and exchange information with other schools in areas such as peer counseling, bilingualism, and student government.
- Students communicate with "video pals" to experience diverse cultures and ways of life, both economic and ethnic. Video pals also provide an excellent opportunity for foreign language practice.
- Schools known for outstanding programs or projects model those projects for other schools.
- Contests between schools—debates, spelling bees, or research conferences—take place via two-way video.
- Videoconferencing facilitates distributed cooperative learning, where groups at distant sites take on a learning task and teach remote peers.
- Distributed projects make use of videoconferencing technology for collaboration and communication.

Community Connections

- Town hall meetings, government hearings, school board meetings, court functions, and other government-related activities.
- Public health discussions
- Support of special interests or hobbies
- Adult education in areas such as English, literacy, job training, etc.
- Virtual author tours

Figure 7.10 Videoconferencing ideas and examples from AT&T Knowledge Network Explorer (n.d.). Copyright 2007 AT&T Knowledge Ventures. All rights reserved. Portions of this page have been copied and distributed with the permission of the copyright owner, AT&T Ventures. AT&T Ventures is not responsible for and assumes no liability for any loss, injury or damage which may be incurred by persons or entities using this page. Any person or entity using this page does so at its own risk.

enamored of the tool itself. As Arthur C. Clarke, British author and inventor, once said, "Before you become too entranced with gorgeous gadgets and mesmerizing video displays, let me remind you that information is not knowledge, knowledge is not wisdom, and wisdom is not foresight. Each grows out of the other, and we need them all" (Clarke, n.d.). As you plan, the essential focus should be the intended learning outcomes for your students. Think about the structure of the videoconference in relation to other learning activities. What can you do to prepare students? Is there background knowledge that will help them get the most from the videoconference and enable them to ask probing questions? Encourage students to generate questions before the videoconference. While they will undoubtedly think of questions during the session, it is advisable not to depend solely on those. Some prior thought and reflection may result in deeper inquiry than simply relying on on-the-fly questions. If possible, involve students in planning the entire session.

If students are new to this technology, they may need coaching on how to be respectful partners in the videoconferencing process. Although they see the presenter, they need to remember that they, too, are being observed. Plan for engaging interactions that go beyond the "talking head" model. There is little value in simply watching and listening to someone lecture, whereas there is significant learning potential in two-way interaction where all participants are involved in sharing information, questioning, demonstrating, and offering other activities that would otherwise be unlikely to occur.

Remember that learning doesn't end when the videoconference cameras are turned off. Plan follow-up activities that capitalize on the videoconference and involve students in analysis and constructive work that draws on and extends the videoconferencing experience.

Broadcasting With Podcasts and Internet Radio

Just as blogs now make online text publishing possible for anyone, podcasting is enabling all of us to produce the equivalent of online radio programs. Two types of Internet radio technology deliver audio files. The first, streaming audio, delivers content that the user listens to as it is delivered, much as one would listen to a radio or television. The second form of Internet radio, podcasting, provides audio in a form analogous to a tape recording or CD, where content is recorded and made available for future listening.

The delivery of audio files over the Internet took a giant leap with the invention of MPEG-1 Audio Layer 3 (MP3). In the mid-1990s, a compressed audio format called MP3 enabled digital streaming audio over the Internet. MP3 technology involves transforming an audio signal into a smaller digital file, allowing it to be transmitted over the Internet in a reasonable amount of time. Consider a song or recorded talk. Within the sound waves it contains, there are many more data than our ears require to make sense of the tune and words. MP3 technology samples the data and discards some of them—a trade-off between sound quality and size.

Luckily, our senses don't miss the data that are discarded (unless too much gets tossed), resulting in a compressed file that is a manageable size. A Codec program or device encodes (compresses) and decodes (decompresses) the audio stream, and a server stores the data.

In addition to streaming media, another type of Internet radio has emerged. The podcast, a term that blends "broadcasting" and "iPod" (a popular portable audio device), makes audio broadcasting much simpler, allowing almost anyone to create and offer podcasts. Because streaming audio demands more advanced technology than is available at most schools, the following section focuses on podcasting.

What Is Podcasting?

One of the most rapidly expanding technologies today is podcasting. In 2005, *USA Today* reported that in 6 months' time, a Google search for "podcasting" had increased from a few hundred hits to 687,000 hits (Acohido, 2005). These numbers continue to rise, as 1 year later a "podcasting" search returned 112,000,000 hits.

Podcasting enables anyone to become an independent producer and distributor of audio and/or video content that can be offered worldwide through the Internet. As with blogs, there is great latitude for all kinds of publishing with podcasts. Many Web sites include the RSS (Really Simple Syndication) language and podcast feeds, allowing you to request, or subscribe, to their content. For example, National Public Radio, at http://www.npr.org/, offers programming through RSS or podcasts. From *National Geographic* to news and media Web sites such as the *New York Times*, sports channels like ESPN, the Philadelphia Museum of Art, and the Culinary Podcast Network, there is audio (and often video) content available in just about every subject imaginable.

A podcast is an audio recording that is saved as an MP3 file and made available on the Internet through RSS. Audio podcasts have been joined by video programs, sometimes called a "vodcast." Users "subscribe to" or choose the audio or video content they wish to listen to.

Creating and Listening to Podcasts   Software that downloads podcasts will check the RSS feeds of the podcasts you subscribe to. When a new podcast is added, the feed is updated, and the software downloads the new audio file to your computer. You can play this file in a Mac or Windows application (such as iTunes) on your computer. You can also have iTunes automatically synchronize and transfer the audio files to a mobile device, such as an iPod that connects to your computer. While there are several podcasting applications, iTunes offers a nice setup. It has an organized directory of podcasts you can subscribe to and will automatically download the new editions of podcasts you've subscribed to when you open iTunes.

The Apple Web site (http://www.apple.com/podcasting/) provides the iTunes player as a free software download. Once iTunes has been installed, click on the "Podcasts link in the left pane's menu. On the lower portion of the main window, you'll see "Podcast Directory." That link accesses the iTunes music store, where you can select from "Top Podcasts" or go to the category listings on the left. Click on the "Subscribe" button next to the podcast you want. Most podcasts offer a "Subscribe" button, but a direct URL for a podcast you've located on a Web page can be entered using the "Advanced" menu in iTunes. Click on "Subscribe to Podcast" and enter the URL in the text box window. The "Settings" button in the lower right of the iTunes pane gives you options for managing your podcasts.

Many other programs besides iTunes are available for listening to podcasts, including iPodderX, Juice, Playpod, and Podspider. A search for "podcast software" returns thousands of hits; the Podcasting News Web site has a good collection categorized into software for publishing and client software for listening to podcasts (http://www.podcastingnews.com/topics/Podcasting_Software.html).

If you have an iPod, the downloaded podcasts will synch to it when it's connected to your computer with iTunes. Palm and Pocket PC handhelds with wireless Internet access can also be equipped with software that checks RSS feeds, downloads podcasts, and allows them to be played on the handheld with software such as Windows Media Player, RealOne Player, or Pocket Tunes.

The basic technique for creating a podcast involves recording audio using a computer, microphone, and software. Free audio software such as Audacity or Easypodcast can be used for recording and editing podcast content. For Macintosh users, Apple's GarageBand is an excellent solution. Programs like FeedBurner or Feeder can provide the necessary RSS feed, which is written in a language called XML. The MP3 and feed files are then uploaded to a Web server and a link to the podcast is listed on your Web page or blog.

Podcasting in the Classroom

While there is much to be gained by listening to others' podcasts, it is an even more valuable experience for students to create their own broadcasts. As with student-created WebQuests, the cognitive requirements for designing and developing a podcast are multidimensional. A class-created podcast offers opportunities for students to collaborate, with decision making in the forefront, as students determine the purpose and content for the podcast. Will others be involved, or will the taping consist solely of students? Are there opportunities for students to develop interview questions and bring in experts or community members to codevelop the podcast?

Student-created podcasts give students a chance to broadcast to an authentic audience and can motivate them to become experts in preparation for podcast development. Rather than regurgitating material, students should develop podcasts that contain original material or that analyze and deepen the understanding of existing material. Podcasting is a tool that supports meaningful curriculum integration, and the technical aspects of producing a podcast offer students a unique learning opportunity. Determining how to sequence material, finding or creating copyright-free music or other audio to transition between segments, practicing public speaking, and locating additional resources to extend the value of the podcast—all of these are valuable elements of podcast production.

Podcasts can also be an important component in collaborative work by enhancing the connections between students. In lieu of text-based communication, students might record personal messages to learn more about each other. Digital storytelling allows students to share experiences or create original works to record. International collaborations offer opportunities to practice second-language skills or to learn new language. Students might also create and share music or take a walking tour of their city, recording sounds on the street. Podcasts can be used to discuss plans and ongoing work during a collaborative project and are a vehicle for sharing project outcomes with a larger audience. They give students who may be more skilled in oral communication than in written words the chance to excel.

One technique for adding value to podcasts is by extending their content through other media. A common practice is combining one's blog with his or her podcast. Ideas can be expressed in writing with a blog that contains links to other Web sites and to a podcast related to the blog entry. Using multimedia combines the attributes of text, audio, and video, offering users the choice of engaging different modalities.

Podcast Bangladesh Podcast Bangladesh is produced by students and teachers at International School Dhaka. It aims to use emerging technologies to highlight educational activities at the school and to form global cross-cultural collaborations. Some of the Podcast Bangladesh tapings included discussion and interaction on global issues (e.g., the digital divide), online debate about local and global issues, discussion and reflection about digital story development, and teacher/student curriculum-based interviews.

Students at International School Dhaka also used podcasting and vodcasting tools to facilitate a debate with Presbyterian Ladies College in Melbourne, Australia. The debate topic was "School Students Can Use the Web to Change the World." Julie Lindsay (2006), head of technology at International School Dhaka, believes that podcasting has enhanced their school's global collaborations by enabling closer relationships with partners, providing alternatives to text-based communication.

Radio WillowWeb At Willowdale Elementary School in Omaha, Nebraska, technology specialist Tony Vincent facilitates the Radio WillowWeb podcast, an online radio program/podcast created for kids by kids. Radio WillowWeb was one of the first podcasts produced by elementary students and has been used as a guide for many other schools as they embark on this new technique of instructional technology use.

For one podcast, fifth-grade students created a show about sound and light that consisted of seven segments sharing students' knowledge (Figure 7.11). During the podcast, students explained how the ear works, how to protect hearing, and why color blindness occurs. Other students "interviewed" Helen Keller and reviewed "Reeko's Mad Scientist Lab," describing an experiment available there. Students shared poetry and described assistive devices for deaf and blind individuals. The

Willowcast #19

Posted April 26, 2006

Fifth graders in Ms. Sanborn's class have studied sound and light. Spencer host this show about these two important forms of energy. There are seven segments packed with interesting information:

- Ear-Regular Radio Show by Hannah
  - ○ Let's Hear It for the Ear!
- Interesting Interview by Mandy
  - ○ Helen Keller Photograph Collection
- Vocabulary Theater by Tyler
- Wonderful Website by Will
  - ○ Reeko's Mad Scientist Lab
- Did You Know? by Stephen
- Poetry Corner by Shelby
- Incredible Inventions by Jessie

MP3 | 10 minutes 36 seconds | 10.2 MB
If the show doesn't play automatically, click here.
XML

Spotlight on Sound & Light

Figure 7.11   A podcast from Radio WillowWeb.

"Vocabulary Theater" segment explained bioluminescence through a firefly example. Links on the podcast Web page take users to related information.

At the "Our City" podcast Web site (http://www.learninginhand.com/OurCity/), students from around the world are invited to submit a recording about the city they live in, with a teacher's assistance. The resulting Web site is a rich travelogue, with student podcasts describing their cities from California to Pennsylvania. The "Our City" podcasts give listeners an inside view on geographical locations across the country from a young person's perspective. Even more important, they are a means for the students constructing the podcasts to meet content and process standards while creating a product for an audience of peers. Student developers will need to critically evaluate and choose the information they include in the podcast, write a script, locate additional resources, and engage in a variety of technical tasks.

NASA's 21st Century Explorer Podcast Competition   As podcasts become increasingly common, knowing how to create them becomes an essential skill for today's students. In September 2006, NASA hosted the first 21st Century Explorer Podcast Competition. The competition is an education and public outreach project designed to inspire and motivate the next generation of explorers and to compete effectively for the minds, imaginations, and career ambitions of America's young people (http://www.explorationpodcast.com/about.php). To compete, students created and submitted podcasts that answer the question, "How will space exploration benefit your life in the future?"

NASA astronauts plan to return to the moon before the end of the next decade, staying to build outposts and pave the way for eventual journeys to Mars and beyond. Recognizing that today's students will be tomorrow's explorers, NASA encourages students to think seriously about the possibilities and impact of space exploration and how it might affect their lives, then share those thoughts through audio or video podcasts. Teachers who take advantage of initiatives such as the NASA competition create learning opportunities for students to use podcasting as a tool that supports meaningful learning. Considering the influence of space exploration on future life, exploring goals and careers, and contributing ideas to a larger pool are activities that can excite and motivate students while meeting any number of possible curriculum objectives and standards.

Getting Started With Podcasting

There are many Web sites with resources, suggestions, and educators' experiences in working with podcasting. In addition to podcasting instructions on the Apple Web site, one can find "How to Podcast" (http://www.how-to-podcast-tutorial.com/) and the Podcastnews tutorial (http://www.podcastingnews .com/articles/How-to-Podcast.html). Julie Lindsay offers "How to Podcast" at "Podcasting and All That Jazz," a wiki designed to support collaboration and resource sharing among individuals using podcasts in education (http://podcast-jazz.pbwiki.com/How%20to%20Podcast). The "Podcast Directory for Educators" (http://recap.ltd.uk/podcasting/index.php) has links to school podcasts, subject podcasts, and education news podcasts. It also offers tips and resources for those interested in podcasting technology.

We also suggest that readers refer to the chat transcript at http://www .learninginhand.com/articles/chat013006.html as an interesting example that demonstrates how the Tapped In Web site was used for a live chat about podcasting. Links within the chat transcript provide additional resources for teachers. Tony Vincent, mentioned previously, offered a chat for the monthly Tapped In technology event that is sponsored by the International Society for Technology in Education's Special Interest Group for Technology Coordinators. The chat, titled "SIGTC—Radio WillowWeb: Podcasting with Elementary Students," gave participants the opportunity to talk with a professional who has acquired much knowledge about podcasting through his experiences at Willowdale Elementary School.

Vincent, facilitator of the Radio WillowWeb podcasts, also offers the "Our City" podcast, described previously, as a way to help teachers experiment and get started with podcasting. To contribute to this Web site, teachers and students create the MP3 audio file and send it to Vincent at the address he provides. The RSS feed and posting is taken care of, making this a simple way for teachers to "test the waters" and explore how podcasts might be an effective addition to their curriculum. Vincent also offers downloadable examples, planning packets, and a discussion forum to help teachers' beginning podcasting efforts.

The purpose of the KidCast: Podcasting in the Classroom Web site (http://www.intelligenic.com/kidcast/index.html) is to explore podcasting applications in education. An August 2006 show encouraged teachers to think about how they can incorporate podcasts into their classrooms. The host suggested that students be asked about their experiences with podcasting. Are they consumers, producers, or both? A "quickcast" is recommended as a fast way to introduce short "bites" of podcasted material to students each day. Teachers might use this technique to become familiar with the podcasting process, but involving students as the podcast creators offers much more value than simply asking them to listen to teacher-created podcasts.

Conclusion

In this chapter, we have introduced you to several forms of communication that can enhance learning by exposing students to experiences they would otherwise not be afforded, by bringing the expertise and knowledge of professionals who are authorities in their fields into the classroom, and by allowing interactions between students and collaborating partners.

Online discussion boards, chats, blogs, and instant messaging are not meant to replace face-to-face interactions. While online communication presents opportunities for connecting people, it can also result in isolating and disconnecting us. Technologies that join us with those at a distance may interfere with our immediate relationships if they are used thoughtlessly. When a dinner partner ignores the friend sitting across from her in order to have a cell phone conversation with someone else, interaction suffers. When we ignore or neglect family members while maintaining online relationships with people at a distance, we negate the benefits of communication technologies. We have tried to show, however, that computer conferencing can support learners in unique ways as they engage in reasoned dialogue, collaborate with remote and diverse audiences, and learn to express themselves in writing.

Advances in technology, particularly in widespread broadband Internet access, have made it easy for users to be not only consumers of audio and video but also participants and creators of these media. We have offered reasons for integrating videoconferencing as a means of unique interactions that support learning and for podcasting, particularly when students are the creators of these broadcasts. We hope that you will reflect on the reality of media in the lives of today's young people and design creative ways that your curriculum can intersect with some of the technology ideas presented in this chapter. In the words of the futurist and author Alvin Toffler (n.d.), "The illiterate of the 21st century will not be those who cannot read and write, but those who cannot learn, unlearn and relearn."

Things to Think About

1. Are multitasking media consumers really able to process all the sensory data they are taking in, or is learning being compromised?
2. How far should educators go in matching the technology used in instruction and classroom activities to the technology their students use?
3. Are online chats and instant messaging of value in the classroom? Do they add to student learning, or do they distract from "real" instruction? What is "real" instruction?
4. How can you integrate videoconferencing in your classroom? Who might you partner with to bring expert knowledge, to collaborate, or to offer new perspectives to students?
5. Can the technologies presented in this chapter be a means of engaging and involving parents in their children's schools? In what ways?
6. Does videoconferencing benefit communication by allowing participants to see each other, or does it offer little more than "talking heads"? If videoconferencing is constructive, what is it about the visual element that enhances communication?
7. Are there benefits to asynchronous, text-based communication over synchronous, face-to-face communication? In what situations?
8. Does using podcasts with students really enhance learning, or is it simply a newer version of passively delivering information?
9. In many ways, audio podcasts are akin to listening to a radio broadcast. Are radio broadcasts typically used in classrooms? Why or why not? If not, why would using podcasts be of any greater value?
10. How should libraries approach information offered through podcasts? Print media are increasingly augmented with other types of media, but how are all of them managed and made available to users?

References

Acohido, B. (2005, February 9). Radio to the MP3 degree: Podcasting. *USA Today*. Retrieved August 25, 2006, from http://www.usatoday.com/money/media/2005-02-09-podcasting-usat-money-cover_x.htm

AT&T Knowledge Network Explorer (n.d.). *Videoconferencing for learning: Examples and ideas.* Retrieved July 15, 2006, from http://www.kn.pacbell.com/wired/vidconf/ideas.html

Clarke, A. (n.d.). Retrieved August 25, 2006, from http://www.linezine.com/7.3/themes/q2002.htm

Collison, G., Elbaum, B., Haavind, S., & Tinker, R. (2000). *Facilitating online learning: Effective strategies for moderators.* Madison, WI: Atwood Publishing.

Dewey, J. *Democracy and education: An introduction to the philosophy of education.* New York: Macmillan.

Gardner, H. (2000). *Intelligence reframed: Multiple intelligences for the 21st century.* New York: Basic Books.

Gardner, H., & Lazear, D. C. (1991). *Seven ways of knowing, teaching for multiple intelligencies: A handbook of the techniques for expanding intelligence.* Victoria, BC: Hawker Brownlow Education.

German, H. (2005). A museum on the go. *Converge Online*. Retrieved August 15, 2006, from http://www.convergemag.com/story.php?catid=231&storyid5100461

Heavin, J. (2006, August 16). School kids get chance to talk shop with judges. *Columbia Daily Tribune*. Retrieved August 25, 2006, from http://archive.columbiatribune.com/2006/aug/20060816news007.asp

Jackson, L. (2005, January 12). Videoconferencing deserves a second look! *Education World*. Retrieved August 25, 2006, from http://www.educationworld.com/a_issues/chat/chat127-2.shtml

Lindsay, J. (2006, July 5). *Podcast Bangladesh: Communicating globally with ubiquitous computing tools*. Paper presented at the National Educational Computing Conference.

Merrick, S. (2005). Videoconferencing K–12: The state of the art. *Innovate: Journal of Online Education*, 2(1). Retrieved July 15, 2006, from www.vanderbilt.edu/cso/download.php?dl=file&id=244

McCombs, G., Ufnar, J., Ray, K., Varma, K., Merrick, S., Kuner, S., et al., (2004). *Videoconferencing as a tool to connect scientists to the k–12 classroom*. Paper presented at the annual meeting of the American Educational Research Association, Montreal. Retrieved July 15, 2006, from www.vanderbilt.edu/cso/download.php? dl=file&id=62

NMC: The New Media Consortium and National Learning Infrastructure Initiative. (2005). *The Horizon Report*. Retrieved July 13, 2006, from http://www.educause.edu/LibraryDetailPage/666?ID=CSD3737

Rideout, V., Roberts, D., & Foehr, U. (2005). Generation M: Media in the lives of 8–18-year-olds. Retrieved July 15, 2006, from http://www.kff.org/entmedia/upload/Executive-Summary-Generation-M-Media-in-the-Lives-of-8-18-Year-olds.pdf

Salmon, G. (2002). *e-tivities: The key to active online learning*. London: Kogan Page.

Toffler, A. (n.d.). Retrieved August 25, 2006, from http://www.quotationspage.com/quotes/Alvi n_Toffler/

Woolley, D. (1995). *Conferencing on the web*. Retrieved August 15, 2006, from http://thinkofit.com/webconf/wcunleash.htm

Designing With Technologies

Learning by Designing In and Out of Schools

Design is a ubiquitous activity. In professional fields and personal lives, people design products, creations, processes, systems, activities, models, and a host of other outcomes. People everywhere are engaged in some form of design: writing software program; designing a building; designing a new car or any of its 10,000 components, composing music; writing a book, play, short story, article, or poem; creating a marketing campaign for a new product; creating a new food product; designing a storefront display; decorating a home's interior or exterior; or decorating a cake. These and thousands of other tasks engage designing.

Design problems are among the most complex and ill structured of all problems (Jonassen, 2004). Many see the strategies used in problem solving as similar to those in designing (McCormick, 1998, p. 231):

Problem Solving	**Designing**
Define the problem	Identify a need or opportunity
Develop alternative solutions	Generate a design
Select the solution	Plan and make a solution
Implement and evaluate the solution	Evaluate and reflect on solution

Despite the often-stated goal of finding an optimal solution that meets multiple criteria within determined constraints, real-world design problems usually have vaguely defined or unclear goals with unstated constraints. They possess multiple solutions rather than a single "right" answer, can't be verified as correct, and so lack "stop rules." A vexing aspect of design problems is that the way the problem is framed determines the set of solutions that solve it, making encoding the problem exceedingly difficult (Buchanon, 1995; Churchman, 1967). Design problems often require the designer to make judgments about the problem and defend them or express personal opinions or beliefs about the problem. Ultimately, the designer must please the client, whose own framing and criteria for an acceptable design can change, requiring that the whole process begin anew. Such ill-structured problems are uniquely human interpersonal activities.

In schools, you can find design challenges in courses where you would expect them—technology education, computer programming, and music and science classes—and sometimes in more esoteric venues, such as mathematics and media art. Design is also taking center stage in a growing number of informal education settings, notably design competitions, like the FIRST Robotics and Lego design competitions (http://www.usfirst.org), Science Olympiad (http://www.soinc.org), and the ASME's Student Design Competitions (http://www.asme.org). In all these settings, design competitions act as a key motivator for students to develop deeper understandings of concepts in memorable contexts, which is a basic formula for building meaningful learning in students of any age.

Recently, innovative technologies and software applications have been developed to support professional designers in doing their work. Most notable among these are computer-aided design systems. Low-cost or no-cost versions of these powerful programs have been making their way to the classroom and are now available for use by students and their teachers. Other learning technologies have been devised specifically to help students make better designs and design decisions in a wide range of design endeavors.

This chapter describes four such contexts where meaningful learning in traditional subject areas can be enhanced with the use of design activities that are made more effective through learning technologies. These cases of designing with technologies include the following:

- Drawing design ideas with computer-aided design software
- Testing designs and building mental models with simulation software
- Developing programming skills while designing in the media arts
- Designing music with composition software

Drawing Design Ideas With Computer-Aided Design Software

The picture most people have in mind when they think of the work designers do is of someone making pencil sketches on the back of an envelope or a group huddled around a whiteboard doing rapid-fire drawings of brainstormed ideas. Experts also claim the primacy of sketching and drawing as essential procedural skills that designers must be also to do (Ullman et al., 1990), although recently researchers and educators have been challenging this view (Bilda, Gero, & Purcell, 2006; Kimbell, 2004; Welsh & Lim, 1999).

One of the challenges of using design tasks in classrooms is that many students are not skilled at converting their conceptions into usable graphics that can then be examined and developed further. Until recently, designers needed to be skillful in producing what are called orthographic projection drawings—front-, side-, and top-view and isometric drawings of products or systems (Figure 8.1), with sizes of parts clearly noted. Manufacturers follow exactly the instructions contained in those drawings when making the device. However, a well-established technology tool, the computer-aided design (CAD) program, has been helping designers do that for some time.

CAD programs and systems were first developed in the early 1960s and involved early users wielding light pens as input devices, typing commands with their keyboards, and using oscilloscopes as screen displays to draw simple lines, circles, and curves and to manipulate these images on screen (Mann & Coons, 1965). A key feature of these groundbreaking yet rudimentary programs was that drawings could be stored and used later by any person with access to the appropriate time-shared computer system.

Since then, CAD systems have lived up to the promise of acting as a virtual drafting table to aid visualization. Designers use CAD programs during early phases of designing to examine their ideas and make changes in their design's

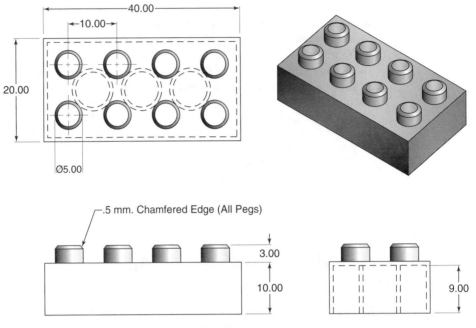

Figure 8.1 Orthographic projection drawings of a Lego piece.

structural features, color, or surface texture. The solid-modeled objects can be rotated on screen, zoomed in and out so that key details can be viewed without the need to fabricate materials or handle and use tools. CAD programs show their value even more strikingly during later design phases: they help produce final drawings from which physical prototypes of devices get made. Throughout the design process, high-quality rendered drawings, ones suitable for presentations, can be generated from these same files. All this is done using a pen that never runs out of ink, drawing lines that never waver, and writing text in the perfectly readable script that only those who put in years at the drafting table ever master.

Today's professional CAD systems, which are used throughout the design world, are available in educational "lite" versions that schools get to license for free. One such feature-limited yet powerful CAD program, *Pro/DESKTOP*, produced by Parametrics Technology Corporation, is based on their "industrial-grade" *Pro/ENGINEERING WildFire* program. Schools benefit from this arrangement by having Window-based *Pro/DESKTOP* available for students' use at no cost, while the software producer benefits when students, weaned on their products, hit the job market and as new employees show higher rates of productivity using the CAD program on which they cut their teeth.

In *Pro/DESKTOP*, students develop their ideas as virtual objects using the first of three "interface" views: the "Design" mode supports constructing solid-modeled objects, the "Drawing" interface works with flat, 2-D orthographic drawings, and the "Album" interface displays these ideas as high-quality rendered illustrations. The design interface screen (Figure 8.2) is surrounded by the three toolbars, has a browser area to the left to access particular elements and layers of the drawing, and has a menu bar that provides a host of menu commands.

An object like the Lego block shown in Figure 8.2 would be drawn from scratch by first making a 2-D rectangle on one of the three "workplanes" available to users in the design mode. Using the "extrude" command from the Feature menu bar, the flat rectangle gets extended vertically to make a rectangular box. Other Feature commands are used to create solid figures from 2-D shapes and include the "sweep" feature (used to make the bent wires in Figure 8.3, left), and the "revolve" feature (helpful in drawing the wheel rim in Figure 8.3, middle). These basic 3-D shapes can be filled with colors, hard edges rounded, and objects joined with other basic shapes (like a cylinder) to make more complex 3-D objects.

Pro/DESKTOP's interface provides clear feedback to students to guide them in creating 3-D shapes that don't violate constraints of the real world or the

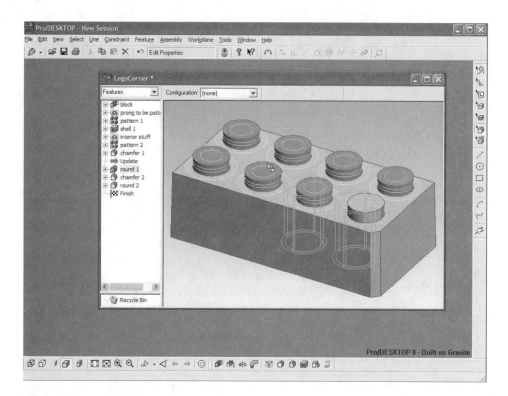

Figure 8.2 Students can design their own custom Lego-styled block using *Pro/DESKTOP*'s "pattern" feature, which replicates the block's cylindrical bumps, and the "assemble" command, which mates, aligns, and fixes items onto the block. *Source:* (c) PTC, all rights reserved. Used with permission.

Figure 8.3 Student from Gateway Regional High School in New Jersey used *Pro/DESKTOP* features to design a virtual reality glove ("sweep" feature), custom tire rim ("revolve" feature), and different USB memory storage devices ("extrude" feature).

conventions of engineering drawings. For instance, when one shape (cylinder) overlaps another (cube)—something that would be done to make a block with one round end—the view on screen of the object would suddenly lose its fill color. This is *Pro/DESKTOP*'s dramatic and arresting way to indicate that the drawing is no longer "valid" and that line segments that overlap the two shapes must be removed with the "delete line segment" tool. Once this is done, the composite shape's fill color returns, letting the user know that work on this object is once again valid and can continue. To review the many features contain in this CAD program, go to the PTC website (http://www.ptc.com) and search for information on *Pro/DESKTOP Student Edition*.

Chris Anderson and Chris Better, technology education teachers at Gateway Regional High School in Woodbury Heights, New Jersey, have their students use *Pro/DESKTOP* to do concept sketches as well as final drawings for long-term design projects. They introduce their students to the program by having them work through tutorials in *Designing with Pro/DESKTOP* (Hutchinson, 2005) and incorporate a design process model in both their Tech and Design courses to help structure students' work. Typical student projects (Figure 8.3) include designing a pushpin, a handheld calculator, sunglasses, a USB thumb drive, a convenience case for a specified teenage audience (e.g., makeup kit or iPod protective container), a dock station for a cell phone, and car accessories (e.g., wheel rim covers or exhaust pipe decoration). These teachers report that most of their students, by the end of their course, strongly prefer designing with CAD than with paper and pencil.

Related Programs and Technologies: Architectural Design With SketchUp

There are a number of specialty CAD programs: some focus on architectural design. *SketchUp* fits into this subclass of software that helps users build solid models of houses and their interiors from which blueprint-styled floor plans can be printed (Figure 8.4). Programs like *SketchUp* helps designers visualize the buildings or rooms they created "from the ground up," specifically by starting with basic 2-D shapes and then using the "push/pull" and other tools to make 3-D objects. Plans of buildings can be populated with trees and people. The house can be "moved" in different configurations until the designer sees a good fit between form and place. One of the real boons that architectural CAD systems like *SketchUp* provide is the capability for users to do a "walk-through" of the design (Figure 8.5). This allows them to travel through the designed space to see how the "built environment" will look before anything gets built.

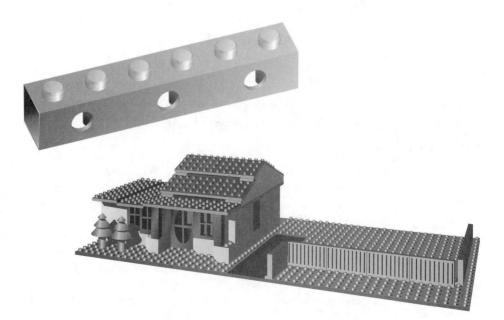

Figure 8.4   One CAD project at Gateway Regional High School involves designing a custom Lego piece and then using it to create a Lego model of a house.

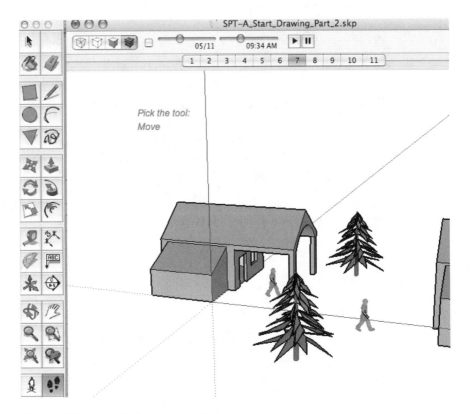

Figure 8.5 *SketchUp*'s walk-through tool.

Testing Designs and Building Mental Models With Simulation Software

A number of materials development projects funded by the National Science Foundation have used design activities as contexts for students to do investigations into key science and engineering ideas (e.g., see the *Design In The Classroom* Web site, http://ditc.missouri.edu). Teachers themselves need a deep understanding of relevant principles of science and engineering as well as the "device knowledge" (Johnson, 1988; McCormick, Murphy, & Davidson, 1994) of how the system being designed works for the potential that these activities possess to be realized (Vattam & Kolodner, 2006).

Using simulation software (see also chapter 3) to support design planning can help in these areas. Simulation programs have been used for years in science classrooms to help students build mental models of how the natural world works—whether it is the transmission of genetic traits to progeny (natural selection), behavior of electrons as current flow through electric circuits (Ohm's law), or movement of objects under the influence of net forces (Newtonian mechanics). Simulations operate by running complex mathematical calculations in the background that generate a user-friendly view of predictions of some rule-driven behavior in the real world. These programs can help students build causal links and explanations of how the system works and how elements within the system interact with one another. When simulations are well designed, they can act as "intermediate causal models" that bridge the real world with abstract theories and laws of nature while carrying the benefit of being understandable, learnable, transferable, and linkable (White, 1993) to students. Some simulation programs, like the one described next, can be adapted to provide designers with fast feedback on design ideas they have and to help reveal critical problems with planned devices, showing how some may perform better or more poorly than others.

Trebuchet Simulator

Near the end of the school year, science teacher Doug Steinoff and technology education teacher Craig Adams, both of Columbia, Missouri, have their Jefferson Junior High School students create a gravity-powered catapult (Gurstelle, 2004) called a trebuchet (pronounced TREB-yoo-shet). The machine that students design and build must hurl a tennis ball so that it hits a target placed between 3 and 49 meters from the device. This challenge appears at the end of their instructional unit on simple and complex machines and mechanical advantage. Students must create a trebuchet that can not only survive early testing trials but also perform accurately enough for the team to earn the most points during the final competition.

Iterative design is central to doing an effective design. For iterative design to work, students need to be able to propose ideas, build and test prototypes, diagnose and remedy problems with their interim designs, and then implement improvements quickly. A perennial problem with doing design challenges that involve lots of building—the trebuchet is made out of plywood and two-by-four lumber—is that too much project time gets consumed making and testing a single design plan, resulting in final projects that either fail outright or barely work.

A simulation program can help address this dilemma of design pedagogy, as Adams and Steinoff have found (Figure 8.6). The teachers divide students' trebuchet work into three parts: build and test a Lego model of a catapult, use a trebuchet simulator to produce early design plans, and construct and test a working prototype.

The Trebuchet Simulator program (http://www.algobeautytreb.com) enables students to run a simulation of the device throwing a projectile before they touch a saw, select a counterweight, or design a trigger for an actual prototype. The

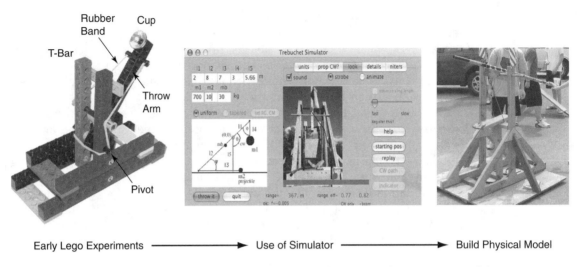

Early Lego Experiments ⟶ Use of Simulator ⟶ Build Physical Model

Figure 8.6 Sequence of design activities for creating a gravity-driven catapult: test a Lego model, use a trebuchet simulator, and make a working device.

interface is straightforward: users type in values for key variables in the trebuchet's design (center left of screen). Once the test configuration has been entered, users select either the "strobe" display view, which shows a multiframe shot of the simulated test throw (Figure 8.7, center), or an animated view of it. They then click on the "throw it" button and watch the counterweight and throw arm move, the angle at which the projectile gets released, and, most important, how far the ball travels ("range").

Students can use the simulator to run a large number of experiments in one or two class periods. Students can experiment with various masses for the projectile (M2) and the counterweight (M1), the length of the throw arm (L2), the counterweight arm (L1), as well as other parts of the trebuchet's design. Results of each test are collected and displayed in the bottom field of the simulator's screen. By watching the "animate" view, which shows a moving stick drawing of the device in operation, students can develop a qualitative sense of how this device works and the impact that key variables have on the catapult's performance.

Steinoff and Adams have their students use the Trebuchet Simulator to help them make informed design decisions based on evidence, not just gut feelings or random guessing. "We want them to recognize patterns to make them more successful. Their job is to manipulate those patterns to get the maximum efficiency." After conducting and reporting to one another about their tests, students possess a set of workable dimensions for their first physical prototypes. They then can build and refine their machines with greater confidence and in

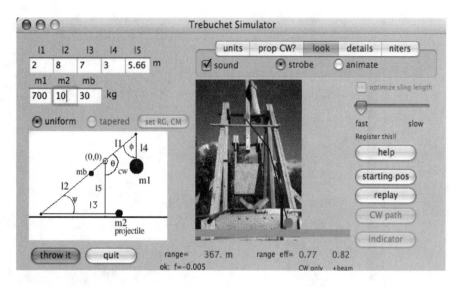

Figure 8.7   Results from tests on different designs appear at the bottom of the Trebuchet simulation program.

less time than if they did hands-on investigations exclusively in building and testing their ideas.

Related Programs and Technologies: Model Car Design

Setting the stage so that students can authentically use science, math, and engineering concepts and procedures in making their design is a daunting challenge. This is true in part because many designers don't do such things themselves. One concerted attempt to support students in doing science-integrated design work appears in the form of Georgia Tech's SIMCAR program, developed by Janet Kolodner, Swaroop Vattam, and others (Vattam & Kolodner, 2006), which accompanies the Vehicles In Motion (VIM) design challenge in their *Learning By Design*™ curriculum. The VIM challenge asks middle school students to design a simple model car that uses one or more propulsion systems (e.g., inflated balloons, rubber bands, or falling weights) to climb a hilly pathway and then travel as far as possible. The SIMCAR program use a design workbench metaphor linked to an animation-based simulation to show the impact of different design decisions on the model car's performance (Figure 8.8). The program provides students with the appropriate science concepts to help them understand why certain designs of model cars work better than others. For more information and a video on this task, go to (http://ditc.missouri.edu/designTasks/otherTasks/vehiclesMotion/index.html).

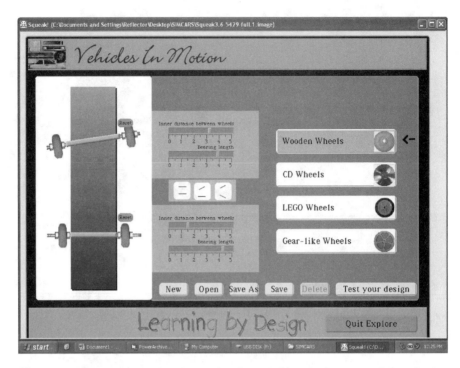

Figure 8.8   Using SIMCAR, Students adjust key variables in a "coaster car" (length of bearing, wheel separation, and tire angle) for the VIM task.

Developing Programming Skills While Designing in the Media Arts

Software design is a content area where researchers conducted some of the early studies on the use of learning technologies to create meaningful learning environments. In fact, Seymour Papert's (1980) Logo programming language was one of the first contexts in which constructionist pedagogy was ever enacted (Kafai, 2005). Students using Logo could type computer commands and control an "evocative object" (Turkle, 1995): an on-screen turtle that made drawings on-screen. By watching the turtle move and draw lines through these commands, children got the immediate feedback they needed to make debugging their programs more concrete and doable. This contrasted to kids programming with languages like BASIC, which allowed manipulation mainly of text or numbers. Studies in the 1980s showed not only that young children could learn to program in Logo but also that this work impacted their capacity to think reflectively, divergently, and metacognitively (Clement & Gullo, 1984). Later research suggested that these congnitive effects did not transfer to all situations but were bound to the contexts in which students did their original work (Pea, Kurland, & Hawkins, 1985).

A number of Logo-inspired products have been developed since then, including "microworlds" that gave students creative control over multiple characters on-screen, "construction kits" that enabled students to manipulate Lego bricks in the real world, and environments where students could design software for use by their peers (Kafai, 2005). This chapter describes the most recent manifestation of construtionism in action: a piece of software that empowers users to create object-based programs that manipulate digitized video and audio in an environment called *Scratch*.

Scratch has been studied primarily in Computer Clubhouses. These after-school programs support students' learning of basic computer literacy skills while they design games, animations, graphics, and music. The *Scratch* program, which runs on most computer platforms, gives students the capability to build programs that manipulate digital images using Photoshop-like tools, add and replay audio tracks and music, and work with video, all while learning fundamentals in computer programming. *Scratch*'s interface uses a Logo-styled building-block metaphor to represent programming moves. It replaces code writing with virtual programming blocks that users can insert, move and combine, and set values to variables through drop-down menus.

The insights that drove the design of *Scratch*'s interface and collection of features are impressive and powerful. Its creators at MIT, UCLA, and elsewhere (Mitchel Resnick, Yasmin Kafai, Natalie Rusk, John Maloney, and others) wanted a tool that students in informal education settings (a tough environment) would find cool, required little training to use, and could run without the frustrating work of writing of syntax-sensitive commands. It was targeted to appeal to preteens and teenagers from different cultures, support them in creating projects they could be proud of, and, when used over time, could lead to the development of more advanced programming skills. Observations in Computer Clubhouses revealed that students enjoyed doing image manipulations with Photoshop and liked producing and editing video and music. Creating a single platform that supported all these sought-after capabilities in an environment where students could also develop programs concepts and skills was a main mission of *Scratch*.

The main *Scratch* screen (Figure 8.9) has five main work areas. The "Blocks" palette to the left provides a collection of programming tools that manipulate imported digital images, sprites, and music through programming procedures ("control" commands are visible in Figure 8.9, left). In the middle-left "Scripts" area, users can drag blocks to construct sets of procedures, much as puzzle pieces can be fitted together. When procedures are not compatible, students encounter the graphical equivalent of a mismatch of puzzle parts. *Scratch* forces students to alter their program until they are in a form that can be implemented. Scripts manipulate "sprites," which are visible in the lower-right area. The full program is run by clicking on the green "go" flag at the right top, the results of which can be viewed in the "Stage" area.

The program's capacity to provide tools that Clubhouse members enjoy using and to give timely feedback helps these students "tinker" in productive ways and supports meaningful exposure and learning of modular programming.

Figure 8.9 *Scratch* has different sections with programming, graphics, and sound tools; a place to compose scripts; and a stage (right) where sprites get animated.

Simultaneously, these features allow students to produce interactive games, music videos, and other creative projects in the media arts. Work on this project is ongoing. The *Scratch* program will be available for free download at http://scratch.mit.edu in 2007.

Related Programs and Technologies: iStopMotion

The *iStopMotion* software, produced by Boinx (http://www.istopmotion.com), enables designers as young as elementary students to create their own animated movies and time-lapse recordings. Using a desktop or laptop Mac, digital camera, or direct-video input device like *iSight*, students can capture and then compose animations frame by frame with this easy-to-learn application. When its "onion skinning" feature is turned on (Figure 8.10), the program allows for the easy juxtaposition of contiguous frames when making a movie file. This helps users produce a coherent video sequence without jerky movements from its characters, helping to limit the need for reshooting or reediting. Claymation movies can be easily made with *iStopMotion*. Children are capable composing single-frame shots of the easy-to-manipulate clay figures whose evolving positions and changing shapes collectively tell a desired story.

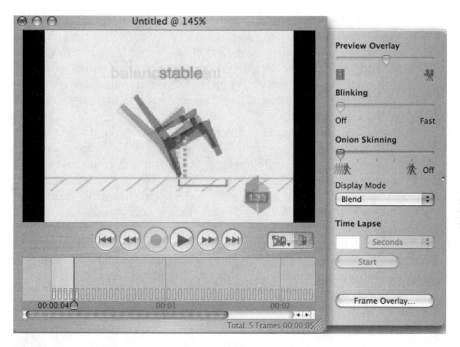

Figure 8.10 *iStopMotion*'s "onion skinning" helps ensure that contiguous frames have just the right amount of "jump" between each other to create seamless animations or pans.

George Rota, media specialist at Glen Lake Elementary School in Minnetonka, Minnesota, works with elementary teachers in his school to create animation and claymation movies. He introduces *iStopMotion* to all sixth graders at Glen Lake, who then use it to complete an extended animation project that is part of their social studies and language arts classes. Students work in groups of three or four, do research on their topics, and use index cards to create storyboards of major scenes when planning their movies. Their videos typically last from 20 to 60 seconds, not including titles and credits, which often double the total length of students' final movies.

Designing Music With Composition Software

Applications for developing songs and scores on the computer have been available since the days when microcomputing first started sporting plug-in sound cards and could produce the synthesized "voices" of various musical instruments. These programs—and their subsequent offspring like Apple's *GarageBand*—display a number of music tracks on which users can enter, edit, and replay the notes of their compositions. Current programs offer multiple means for inputting music that include doing direct recordings, connecting and playing a guitar controller or MIDI keyboard into the computer, or doing it the "old-fashioned way" of mouse clicking one note at a time onto a five-line staff. Applications such as these do for music composition what word processors do for writing—they work as eminently useful tools for users who start with a blank page and collect, revise, and review groups of notes while working toward a finished composition.

A pedagogically powerful, elegant, and free piece of software for designing music, called *Impromptu*, was created by MIT's professor of music and design researcher, Jeanne Bamberger. Her program gains inspiration from cognitive science notion of "chunking" (Miller, 1956), constructivist approaches to learning described by Vygotsky (1978), and the children's programming language, Logo. *Impromptu*'s work space (Figure 8.11) is composed of five areas and a menu bar that supports students in developing their own musical intuitions while constructing tunes from groups of musical notes called "Tuneblocks." The "Tuneblocks" area is the place where music chunks or motifs can be found and stored and where collections of prefabricated blocks, based on a previously transcribed musical pieces, can be loaded from the program's "catalog." Users can

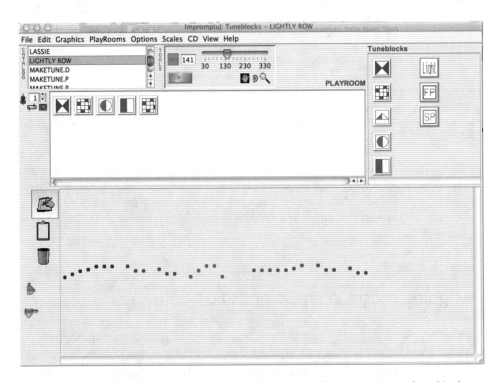

Figure 8.11 The *Impromptu* program has five work areas. Three cursor types found in the Tools area allow Tuneblocks to be moved, heard, and modified.

assign Tuneblocks a color and an abstract pattern to help them identify one from another. They then arrange them as they wish in the "Playroom" area of the program's main window.

The key to this program's approach, seen earlier in Logo and subsequently in *Scratch*, lies in how it has users—primary school aged or older—work with musical "chunks," or groups of musical sounds, rather than individual notes on a five-line score when constructing a musical piece. This enables users to grasp the composition more as a conceptual whole, as it contains far fewer parts, and each part has its own familiar sense and meaning. The immediate feedback that *Impromtu* gives to its users—an approach shared by many programs described in this chapter—helps users conduct experiments in musical meaning making. *Impromptu* provides multiple representations of the collected notes contained in a row of Tuneblocks in its "Graphics" area (bottom of main window), where the relative relationship of individual notes according to pitch, rhythm, or both can be seen. The use of multiple representations has been a favored approach to helping students building more flexible and transferable understandings since the 1980s.

Bamberger conducted studies on the use of *Impromptu* by her own MIT students—people with little or no musical background who used it in conjunction with the software's companion volume, *Developing Musical Intuitions* (Bamberger, 2001). Her students were asked to develop their own original compositions by *reconstructing* a tune using a small collection of Tuneblocks and *creating* an original melody *with a given collection of unfamiliar blocks* (Bamberger, 2003). Neither of these constrained design tasks asked students to face the more daunting "start-from-scratch" design challenge, where the designer faces a blank page with only a full palette of single notes from which to build a composition.

Students tinkered with music by arranging and rearranging the order of the blocks themselves and using the "Improvise a Melody" menu bar selection, changing the tones within a Tuneblock. Bamberger found that her subjects were able to identify key features within music, notice "when a piece sounds finished," and recognize that some Tuneblocks worked better at the beginning and others elsewhere in the piece. One subject reported, "To my ears, the sense of starting something is best portrayed with a block which seems to go in different directions—up and down." Such attention focuses not on individual notes but on the meaning and impact that groups of notes have. Functional descriptions or portraits of each musical chunk helped these users make strategic decisions about music composition on a level that was graspable and that made sense to them.

Impromptu also provides a Notepad so that users can keep a running log of their process of designing music. With it, they can more easily engage in what Don Schön (1983) calls "reflective practice"—where the designer frames a desired goal, creates "moves" and partial solutions that are seen as experimentat attempts to reach that goal, and then reviews the results. Such reflections can then lead to a modification of the designed artifact as well as the goal itself (Adams, Turns, & Atman, 2003). *Impromptu* is an environment where novice designers can have such a "conversation with materials" (Bamberger & Schön, 1991)—where they can develop, order, and make alterations to blocks of music based on intentions they had for the piece and how they heard them turn out on replay. With this tool, they are less likely to create compositions that they stumble into accidentally—something that is more likely with other music composition environments.

Related Programs and Technologies: Musical Sketch Pad

The "Musical Sketch Pad" (http://creatingmusic.com) is an online music composition environment that is designed for use by primary school children. It provides an engaging pallet of tools for kids to create musical pieces (Figure 8.12), where strings of notes are drawn with a pencil tool that in turn play a small number of instrument voices (trumpet, clarinet, piano, or drum). Overlapping lines of music, each voice represented with a different color, can be heard at one of three different playback speeds.

The clear advantage of Sketch Pad's music line-drawing tool is the speed with which children can enter lines of music into the program. Editing capability for individual notes, however, is limited. Children can highlight sections of their newly created score and either delete it with an eraser tool or alter it with the program's inverse, reverse, or parallel tracking tools. Once drawn, however, the separate voices appear as a single-layered representation rather than as separable

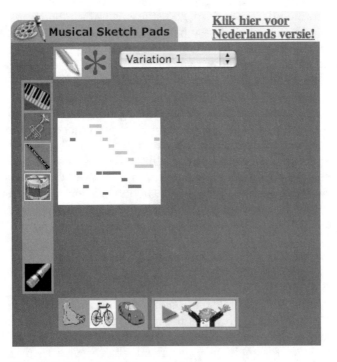

Figure 8.12 Musical Sketch Pad.

layers. Children may find it a challenge to create musical patterns that involve widely separated notes, a small trade-off considering this program's accessible interface and appeal to a younger audience.

Conclusion

Most educators agree that developing composition skills and writing literacy is a viable mission for all subject-matter areas taught in schools. With the right kinds of support, students can compose sensible science lab reports, provide written explanations for how they cracked a tough math problem, or defend their views of key historical events that led up to World War II. Such work can help them become better writers.

Many of the contexts described in this chapter show how design is being used to contextualize and motivate learners to explore and learn big ideas in science, mathematics, music, and computer programming. What may be on the horizon for education is the emergence of design as the new literacy for the 21st century. Developing a fluency in design will become a reality as more programs are created that support designing in a variety of contexts and as teachers see themselves as designers, learn about strategies that designers have developed and honed over the years, and become conversant in the pedagogies that can make the use of design challenges effective in the classroom.

Design is not the panacea to all of education's ills, but it is one additional tool for teachers that can give an added measure of meaning to work done in the classrooms. As design tasks get used in more informed ways and their use is enhanced by learning technologies such as those described in this chapter, teachers will get the most out of these tasks, which hold much promise for building transferable concepts and skills and a joy of learning and creating in their students.

Things to Think About

1. What makes for an engaging and effective design challenge? Do challenges with solutions that converge on a single "optimal" solution violate the spirit of exploring a meaningful design space?
2. What aspects of the design process could be emphasized and reinforced while students are doing learning technologies–enhanced design? (Candidate topics include doing "rapid prototyping" using simulation programs, using the Internet to do information searches that can help in making better design decisions, getting faster feedback that supports doing iterative design work, and using programs that help designers visualize better what they are doing.)

3. How can students be motivated to continue exploring, revising, and refining their designs—to do meaningful iterative design—when their common refrain is, "It works, so I'm done"?
4. What trade-offs do you see with the computer-based aids described in this chapter compared to doing strictly hands-on designing? (Two downsides to using CAD systems are that students never get a feeling for the objects and don't really know when the project is finished.)
5. When and how do teachers act as designers? (Do they revise lessons after teaching them? Adapt ideas from textbooks to the needs of the class?)

References

Adams, R. S., Turns, J., & Atman, C. J. (2003). Educating effective engineering designers: The role of reflective practice. *Design Studies, 24,* 275–294.

Bamberger, J. (2001). *Developing musical intuitions: A project-based introduction to making and understanding music.* New York: Oxford University Press.

Bamberger, J. (2003). The development of intuitive musical understanding: A natural experiment. *Psychology of Music, 31*(1), 7–36.

Bamberger, J., & Schön, D. (1991). Learning as a reflective conversation with materials. In F. Steier (Ed.), *Research and reflexivity.* Newbury Park, CA: Sage.

Bilda, Z., Gero, J. S., & Purcell, T. (2006). To sketch or not to sketch. *Design studies, 27*(5), 587–613.

Buchanan, R. (1995). Wicked problems in design thinking. In V. Margolin & R. Buchanan (Eds.), *The idea of design: A design issues reader* (pp. 3–20). Cambridge MA: MIT Press.

Churchman, C. W. (1967). Wicked problems. *Management Science, 14*(4), 141–142.

Clement, D. H., & Gullo, D. F. (1984). Effects of computer programming on young children's cognition. *Journal of Educational Psychology, 76*(6), 1051–1058.

Gurstelle, W. (2004). *The art of the catapult.* Chicago: Chicago Review Press.

Hutchinson, J. (2005). *Designing with PRO/Desktop.* Wall, NJ: Designed World Learning.

Johnson, S. D. (1988). Cognitive analysis of expert and novice troubleshooting performance. *Performance Improvement Quarterly, 1*(3), 38–54.

Jonassen, D. H. (2004). *Learning to solve Problems.* San Francisco: Pfeiffer.

Kafai, Y. B. (2005). Constructionism. In R. K. Sawyer (Ed.), *The Cambridge handbook of the learning sciences* (pp. 35–46). Cambridge, UK: Cambridge University Press.

Kimbell, R. (2004). Ideas and ideation. *Journal of Design and Technology Education, 9*(3), 136–137.

Mann, R. W., & Coons, S. A. (1965). Computer-aided design. In *McGraw-Hill Yearbook of Science and Technology* (pp. 1–9). New York: McGraw-Hill.

McCormick, R. (1998). Problem solving and the tyranny of product outcomes. *Journal of Design and Technology Education, 1*(3), 320–241.

McCormick, R., Murphy, P., & Davidson, M. (1994). Design and technology as revelation and ritual. *IDATER '94,* 38–42.

Miller, G. (1956). The magical number seven, plus or minus two: Some limits on our capacity for processing information. *Psychological Review, 63,* 81–87.

Papert, S. (1980). *Mindstorms: Children, computers, and powerful ideas.* New York: Basic Books.

Pea, R., Kurland, D. M., & Hawkins, J. (1985). Logo programming and the development of thinking skills. In M. Chen & W. Paisley (Eds.), *Children and microcomputers: Formative studies* (pp. 193–212). Beverly Hills, CA: Sage.

Schön, D. (1983). *The Reflective practitioner: How professionals think in action.* New York: Basic Books.

Turkle, S. (1995). *Life on the screen: Identity in the age of the Internet.* New York: Simon & Schuster.

Ullman, D. G., Wood, S., & Craig, D. (1990). The important of drawing in the mechanical design process. *Computers and Graphics, 14*(2), 263–274.

Vattam, S. S., & Kolodner, J. L. (2006). Design-based science learning: Important challenges and how technology can make a difference. *Proceedings of the International Conference of the Learning Sciences,* pp. 799–805.

Vygotsky, L. S. (1978). *Mind in society: The development of higher psychological processes.* Cambridge MA: Harvard University Press.

Welch, M., & Lim, H. S. (1999). Teaching sketching and its effect on the solutions produced by novice designers. *IDATER '99,* 188–194.

White, B. (1993). Intermediate causal models: A missing link for successful science education? In R. Glaser (Ed.), *Advances in instructional psychology* (Vol. 4, pp. 172–252). Hillsdale, NJ: Lawrence Erlbaum Associates.

Visualizing With Technologies

What Are Visualization Tools?

Humans are complex organisms that possess well-balanced sensorimotor systems, with counterbalanced receptor and effector systems that enable them to sense psychomotor data and act on it using complex motor systems. Likewise, humans have reasonably keen aural perception, allowing them to hear a large range of sounds. Those sounds can be replicated or at least responded to orally by forcing air through the diaphragm, palette, and lips to create an infinite variety of sounds. However, our most sophisticated sensory system, vision, where the largest amount and variety of data are received by humans, has no counterposing effector system. We receive massive amounts visual input, but we have no output mechanism for visually representing ideas, except in mental images and dreams, which unfortunately cannot be easily shared with others. Visual images are powerful mediators of meaning making. Many of us often have to visualize something before we can make sense of it, but sharing those images is problematic. Therefore, according to Hermann Maurer, humans need visual prostheses for helping them to visualize ideas and to share those images with others.

To some extent, draw and paint packages provide those visual prostheses, enabling us to visually represent what we know. They provide sophisticated tools that enable us to draw and paint objects electronically. However, to represent our mental images using paint/draw programs, we have to translate those images into a series of motor operations because it is not yet possible to dump our mental images directly from our brains into a computer. Skilled artists commonly use these tools to visualize ideas, which can help others to interpret ideas. But what we need are tools that help most of us to visualize ideas.

This chapter describes a new but rapidly growing class of technologies that allow us to reason and represent ideas visually without the artistic skills required to produce original illustrations. These tools help us interpret and represent visual ideas and to automate some of the manual processes for creating images. Visualization tools can have two major uses: interpretive and expressive (Gordin, Edelson, & Gomez, 1996). Interpretive tools help learners view and manipulate visuals, extracting meaning from the information being visualized. Interpretive illustrations help clarify difficult-to-understand text and abstract concepts, making them more comprehensible (Levin, Anglin, & Carney, 1987). Expressive visualization helps learners visually convey meaning to communicate a set of beliefs. Crayons, paints, and paper or paint and draw programs are powerful expressive tools that gifted learners may use to express themselves visually. However, they rely on graphical talent. Visualization tools go beyond paint and draw programs by scaffolding or supporting some form of expression. They help learners visualize ideas in ways that make them more easily interpretable by themselves and other viewers.

In this chapter, we present five kinds of visualization tools: scientific visualization tools, mathematical visualization tools, digital cameras and mobile phones, video productions, and video modeling and feedback.

Visualizing Scientific Ideas With Computers

So much of the scientific world is not easily visible to humans. The scale of scientific phenomena is too often so large or so small that we cannot observe those phenomena. From astronomy to atomic structures, science requires understanding dynamic visual relationships among things that are impossible to see. We briefly describe a couple of tools for visualizing atomic structures.

Imaging Molecules With Chemistry Visualization Tools

A number of visualization tools have been developed for the sciences, especially chemistry. Figure 9.1 illustrates a molecule of androsterone. Not only does the McSpartan program enable the learners to visualize molecules using five different representations (wire, ball and wire, tube, ball and spoke, and space filling), but it also enables the student to test different bonds and create ions and new molecules (Figure 9.2). Notice the phosphorus ion added to the molecule on the left. Understanding molecular chemistry is greatly facilitated by visualizing these complex processes. There has been a bit of research on these tools. High school students used eChem to build molecular models and view multiple representations of molecules. Students using the visualization tool were able to generate better mental images of chemicals that aided their understanding (Wu, Krajcik, & Soloway, 2001).

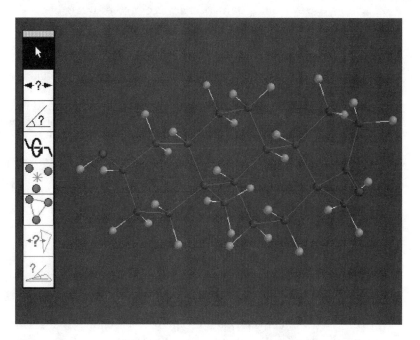

Figure 9.1 Visualization of a molecule of androsterone.

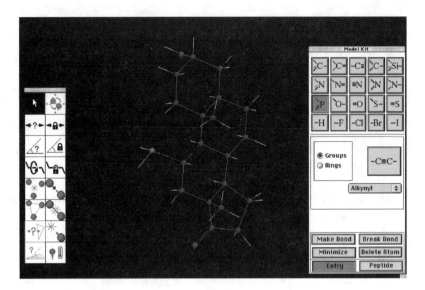

Figure 9.2 Manipulating molecules in McSpartan.

Students who engaged in discussions while building models benefited the most. Providing extra visualization, including colored drawing of experiments and ionic representations of reactions, facilitates concept acquisition in chemistry (Brandt, et al., 2001).

Another powerful chemistry visualization tool from the Concord Consortium (http://www.concord.org) is known as Molecular Workbench. Using Molecular Workbench, students create visual models of the interactions among atoms and molecules. The Workbench also provides learning activities to help clarify what is happening at the atomic level. This is especially effective for representing molecular problems. Figure 9.3 illustrates how benzene molecules may be used instead of proteins.

Visualizing Geography With Geographic Information Systems

Richard Audet and Gail Ludwig (2000) have written a wonderful book, *GIS in Schools*, in which they describe how geographic information systems (GIS) can be used to engage students in authentic problem solving. GIS is a system for storing, retrieving, displaying, analyzing, and manipulating geographic data. It is an excellent way to support students' spatial thinking, and geospatial data are widely available. ESRI is a major designer and developer of GIS technology (http://www.esri.com/). Using GIS requires a relatively fast computer with lots of available storage that can connect to large geographic databases that contain vast amounts of spatial databases related to population, land use, precipitation,

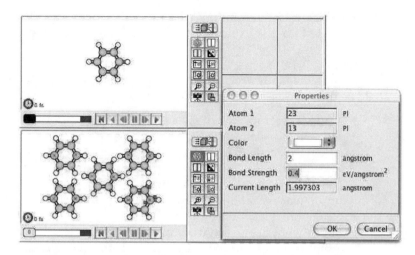

Figure 9.3   Benzene molecule represented in Molecular Workbench.
Source: Molecular Workbench website (http://mw.concord.org/modeler).
All copyrights are the sole property of the Concord Consortium.

vegetation, and other physical geography. GIS software enables students to query those databases to construct maps, create charts and tables to summarize data, and formulate specialized searches. Additionally, schools may purchase ready-made maps from companies or acquire them from local, regional, or state authorities (e.g., http://education.usgs.gov/).

Effective use of GIS also requires adventurous teachers and students. Teachers must be willing to let their students go while solving potentially complex social and environmental problems. Students must also be willing to engage in solving complex and ill-structured problems without single correct answers. When they are engaged, students learn to think spatially. In their book, Audet and Ludwig describe a number of classrooms in which students have used GIS systems to solve some fascinating problems, such as the following:

- Students in Chelsea, Massachusetts, High School worked with the local fire department and the Environmental Protection Agency to design and react to a simulated toxic chemical spill by tracking the spill, rerouting traffic, and warning the public.
- Students in Perham, Minnesota, used GIS and Global Positioning Systems (GPS) to help track newly reintroduced wolves into the Minnesota wilderness.
- Students in Raleigh, North Carolina, created a cultural anthropological view of the history of Raleigh by tracing annexations. They also created individual "life maps" showing the geographical progressions of individuals as they moved around the city. These students developed a new understanding of history.

- Students in Columbia, Missouri, investigate the economic impacts related to the concentration of businesses in the downtown area (Figure 9.4).

Among the many Web sites that offer maps and database information that could be used in classrooms are the following:

- Map Maker from Nationalatlas.gov
  http://nationalatlas.gov/natlas/Natlasstart.asp
- American FactFinder from the U.S. Census
  http://factfinder.census.gov/home/saff/main.html?_lang=en
- National Geographic Map Machine
  http://plasma.nationalgeographic.com/mapmachine/
- Geography Network (from ESRI)
  http://www.geographynetwork.com/
- Seamless Data Distribution Delivery from the U.S. Geological Survey (USGS)
  http://seamless.usgs.gov/website/seamless/viewer.php
- Terraserver
  http://www.terraserver.com

Students may also search for different types of maps at Find A Map! at the USGS Map Databases at http://education.usgs.gov/common/map_databases.htm.

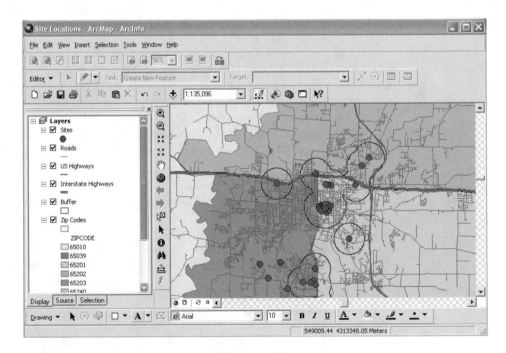

Figure 9.4   GIS graphic from Gail Ludwig.

Applications such as MapTap Atlas for PalmOS Mapping allow mapping to occur simultaneously with students' work in the field. This program creates one's choice of maps on a handheld, allowing maximum flexibility in fieldwork. http://www.mobilegeographics.com/maptap. Similar applications are offered through HandMap and Handango.

Google plays a major role in providing mapping information and tools to a broad segment of the population. Google Earth (Figure 9.5) is a free 3-D interface to the planet that combines satellite imagery and maps with Google Search. Clicking on the Earth begins a slow zoom in until distinct features can be viewed. Layers allow many types of information to be displayed. Categories such as transportation, terrain, and borders allow users to view and interact with the map in multiple ways. Using the inexpensive Google Earth Plus, users can import GPS data from select GPS devices.

Other Google tools include SketchUp, a free, easy-to-learn 3-D modeling program that enables users to create 3-D models of buildings that can then be placed in Google Earth. Google Maps combines directions, maps, and satellite imagery for searching locations. For example, when 10 Market St., San Francisco, is entered and the zoom feature used, the exact building at that location is visible. A mobile version of Google Maps works with cell phones that have a data plan.

GISs are used primarily in conjunction with a computer, including a laptop computer in a field equipment kit giving students the means to apply GPS data to maps as they are being collected. GISs are progressively being integrated into mobile technologies (e.g., PDAs), permitting students new opportunities to utilize global positioning data.

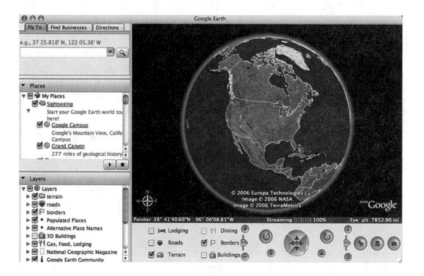

Figure 9.5 Google Earth's Interface. *Source:* Screenshot of Google Earth.
(c) Google Inc., and is used with permission.

Visualizing Mathematical Ideas With Technologies

Because of the abstractness of mathematics, visualization is an important strategy in helping learners understand mathematical concepts. Such visualization tools are not always computer mediated. For example, Cotter (2000) showed that using Asian forms of visualization (e.g., abacus, tally sticks, and place cards) advanced understanding of place value, addition, and subtraction. Mathematics educators have promoted the use of manipulatives and similar visual comparative devices for many years. Snir (1995) argues that computers can make a unique contribution to the clarification and correction of commonly held misconceptions of phenomena by visualizing those ideas. For instance, the computer can be used to form a representation for the phenomenon in which all the relational and mathematical wave equations are embedded within the program code and reflected on the screen by the use of graphics and visuals. This makes the computer an efficient tool to clarify scientific understanding of waves. By using computer graphics, one can shift attention back and forth from the local to the global properties of the phenomenon and train the mind to integrate the two aspects into one coherent picture (Snir, 1995).

Visualization tools have been developed primarily for mathematics and the sciences. Mathematics is an abstract field of study. Understanding equations in algebra, trigonometry, calculus, and virtually all other fields of math is aided by seeing their plots. Understanding the dynamics of mathematics is aided by being able to manipulate formulas and equations and observe the effects of that manipulation. Programs such as Mathematica (http://www.wolfram.com/products/mathematica/index.html), MathLab (http://www.mathworks.com/), Statistical Analysis System, and Statistical Package for the Social Sciences are often used to visually represent mathematical relationships in problems so that learners can *see* the effects of any problem manipulation. Being able to interrelate numeric and symbolic representations with their graphical output helps learners understand mathematics more conceptually. Those tools, because of their power and complexity, are seldom used with K–12 students. Most of the research on these tools has been conducted in universities.

Visualizing Formulas With Graphing Calculators (by Fran Arbaugh)

The National Council of Teachers of Mathematics (NCTM) recommends that mathematics instruction at all grades enable students to create and use representations to organize, record, and communicate mathematical ideas; select, apply, and translate among representations to solve problems; and use representations to model and interpret physical, social, and mathematical phenomena (NCTM, 2000, p. 360). Handheld graphing calculators (such as those made by Casio, Hewlett-Packard, and Texas Instruments) are portable tools that students can use in the classroom or at home to support their mathematical sense making.

Students often have difficulty distinguishing important features of functional relationships. For instance, to build understanding of linear relationships, students can use different representations, generated by the graphing calculator, to make connections between what is happening contextually, numerically, graphically, and symbolically for a particular mathematical relationship. Figure 9.6 contains four different representations of the same linear relationship.

Students using a graphing calculator can easily move between the symbolic, graphical, and numeric representations of the two functions. They can trace along both functions to find (x, y) values graphically. They can then compare those values to the (x, y) pairs in the table. Students can find x and y intercepts on the graph and table and discuss how to manipulate the symbolic representation to find the same information.

Research indicates that the use of graphing calculators has a positive influence on students' understanding of mathematics (Ruthven, 1990). In addition, Dunham and Dick (1994) report that students who use graphing calculators are more flexible problem solvers, are more persistent when faced with a new problem situation, and are highly engaged in the act of problem solving. As more and more mathematics textbooks incorporate the use of a graphing calculator in learning and

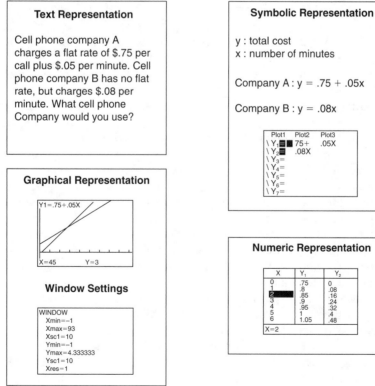

Text Representation

Cell phone company A charges a flat rate of $.75 per call plus $.05 per minute. Cell phone company B has no flat rate, but charges $.08 per minute. What cell phone Company would you use?

Symbolic Representation

y : total cost
x : number of minutes

Company A : y = .75 + .05x

Company B : y = .08x

Graphical Representation

$Y1 = .75 + .05X$

X=45   Y=3

Window Settings

WINDOW
  Xmin=−1
  Xmax=93
  Xscl=10
  Ymin=−1
  Ymax=4.333333
  Yscl=10
  Xres=1

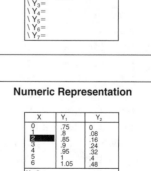

Numeric Representation

X	Y_1	Y_2
0	.75	0
1	.8	.08
2	.85	.16
3	.9	.24
4	.95	.32
5	1	.4
6	1.05	.48

X=2

Figure 9.6 Four different representations of linear relationships.

teaching high school mathematics, more research needs to be conducted on the impact of this technology on student understanding.

Tinkering With Data Sets

Data analysis and interpretation of statistics are key skills, according to standards published by the NCTM. The Technical Education Research Center in Cambridge, Massachusetts, created a simple-to-use database program called TableTop to support database construction and analysis by school-age children (Hancock, Kaput, & Goldsmith, 1992). Tabletop works with existing databases or with databases students create themselves. Data are visually represented by mobile icons that can be arranged into box plots, cross tabulations, histograms, scatter plots, and Venn diagrams. Students develop mathematical understanding of attributes, logical relationships, place value, and plotting and learn to perceive the stories and patterns that lie within the data they collect.

TableTop has been replaced by new data visualization software called TinkerPlots (http://www.umass.edu/srri/serg/projects/tp/tpmain.html). Developed with a grant from the National Science Foundation at the University of Massachusetts, TinkerPlots is data visualization software for grades 4 to 8 that enables students to see different patterns and clusters in statistical data. Students begin by asking a question that requires a prediction or inference (see chapter 3). They collect data (e.g., shoe size and height), assign units to the data (e.g., size and inches), and then represent the data graphically in many ways. With all the data points on a graph, students can group them in clusters, sort them by amount or other sequence, and display them in a seemingly infinite variety of formats. Students are able to use rich data sets or generate their own data sets based on problems they invent and construct their own graphical displays to help them solve the problem. Students learn to reason with data.

Cliff Konold (2006), the designer of TinkerPlots, introduces the use of the software by asking the class whether they think students in higher grades carry heavier backpacks than do students in lower grades. He has them explore a data set to see whether the data support their expectations. To help them answer the question, students can separate the cases into four bins according to the weight of the backpacks (Figure 9.7). To view the data in different representations, the icons representing each case can be stacked, then separated completely until the case icons appear over their actual values on a number line (Figure 9.8). By selecting the attribute Grade, the fifth-grade students were separated vertically from the other grades. By pulling out each of the three other grades one by one, students could then see the distributions of PackWeight for each of the four grades in this data set (grades 1, 3, 5, and 7). These different views enable students with different cognitive styles to find a mathematical representation that makes sense to them. TinkerPlots can also import Microsoft Excel spreadsheet files to enable students to visualize data in more ways than those afforded by Excel. Students can assign different icons to the data points and generate numerous comparative plots that Excel cannot.

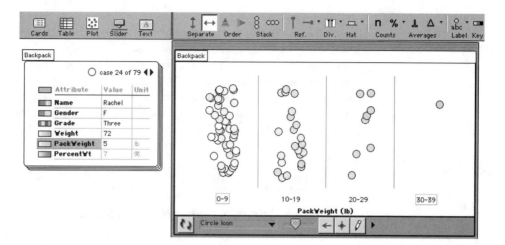

Figure 9.7 Separating cases into bins in TinkerPlots.

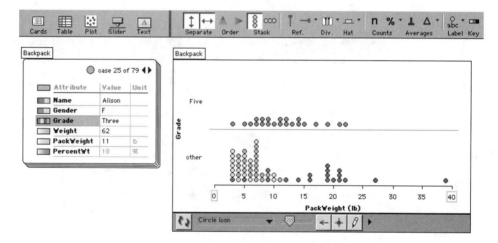

Figure 9.8 Stacked cases with fifth-grade students separated out.

The students in my multiage fourth- and fifth-grade classroom love TinkerPlots. I start off each year with a short demo of the software. Then I pose some questions about a data set that the students might find interesting and have them create plots that will answer their questions. That is all it takes. I find that any time we are working with a data set, the kids will ask if they can enter it into TinkerPlots. It is so powerful when a student can quickly try dragging a variety of variables to the axis and explore the data set without the frustration of having to draw and redraw the graph.

I am amazed at the questions students will ask about a data set. My favorite story is the day that we had free time in the computer lab and many of the students asked if they could use TinkerPlots. One student looked up the size of each of the planets and the number of moons each planet has and entered the data into TinkerPlots. He posed the question, "Do bigger planets have bigger moons?" After creating the plot he concluded that "bigger planets do have more moons because even though the biggest planet does not have the most moons, the four biggest planets do have the most." TinkerPlots is an open-ended tool that encourages creativity and develops students reasoning skills. Every school computer lab should have it!

Teri Hedges, Madison Metropolitan School District, Madison, Wisconsin

Fathom Dynamic Statistics Software (by Fran Arbaugh)

Like TinkerPlots for elementary and middle grade students, Fathom Dynamic Statistics Software (Finzer, Erickson, & Binker, 2001) allows high school students access to powerful tools for making sense of large data sets. The data set displayed in Figure 9.9 allows students to investigate questions regarding geographical patterns in demographic attributes of each state in the United States.

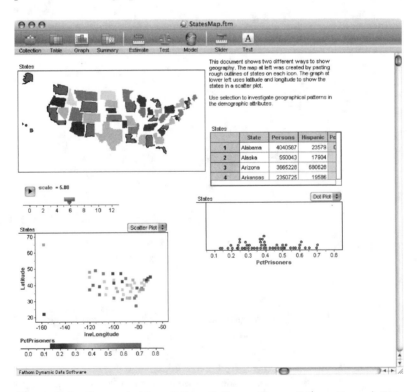

Figure 9.9 Screen shot from Fathom Software. *Source:* Fathom Dynamic Data (TM) software, Key Curriculum Press, Emeryville, CA, www.keypress.com/fathom.

Visual Geometry With Geometric Supposer

One of the best-known visualization tools is Geometric Supposer (http://cet.ac.il/
math-international/software5.htm), a tool for making and testing conjectures in
geometry through the process of constructing and manipulating geometric objects
and exploring the relationships within and between these objects (Schwartz &
Yerushalmy, 1987). Geometric Supposer allows students to choose a primitive
shape, such as a triangle, and construct it by defining points, segments, parallels
or perpendiculars, bisectors, or angles (Figure 9.10) (Yerushalmy & Houde, 1986).
The program plots and remembers each manipulation and can apply it to similar
figures. For example, if the students conjecture that "a median drawn from the
vertex of any triangle to the opposite side bisects the angle," they can test it easily
by asking Geometric Supposer to measure the angles or by applying the relationship to several other triangles. The students will learn immediately that the conjecture is not true. Constructing these test examples manually would require more
effort than students are likely to generate, but the computational power of the
computer makes this testing very easy.

Geometry instruction is traditionally based on the application of theorems to
prove that certain relationships exist among objects. This top-down approach
requires analytic reasoning, which a majority of students find difficult. Geometric

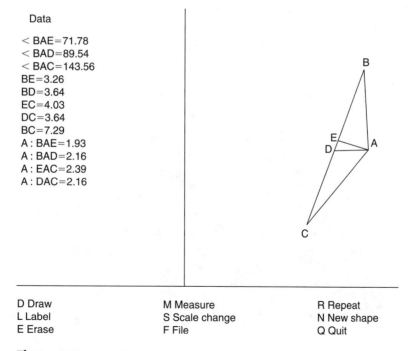

Data

< BAE=71.78
< BAD=89.54
< BAC=143.56
BE=3.26
BD=3.64
EC=4.03
DC=3.64
BC=7.29
A : BAE=1.93
A : BAD=2.16
A : EAC=2.39
A : DAC=2.16

D Draw	M Measure	R Repeat
L Label	S Scale change	N New shape
E Erase	F File	Q Quit

Figure 9.10   Investigating a triangle with Geometric Supposer.

Supposer supports the learning of geometry by enabling the student to inductively prove these relationships by manipulating the components of geometric objects and observing the results. Rather than having the student apply someone else's logic, Geometric Supposer makes explicit the relationships between visual properties and the numerical properties of the objects (Yerushalmy, 1990). Rather than using the computer to provide conclusive results, the computer calculates the results of students' experiments. The research results with Geometric Supposer have been consistently positive.

Visualizing With Digital Cameras and Mobile Phones

In the past decade, photography has been revolutionized by the use of digital cameras and mobile telephones. Each new generation of digital camera provides higher resolutions (up to 10 million screen pixels per picture) for less money (Figure 9.11). Excellent digital cameras can be purchased for $100. These cameras feature light weight, multiple megapixels for high-resolution pictures, zoom lenses with image-steadying functions, selectable color modes (black and white, natural, rich, and sepia), image storage on Memory Sticks, Compact Flash, Secure Digital Cards, automatic focusing, movie mode with up to 60 frames per second, image processors, built-in flashes, self-timers, and a host of other technical features. After taking high-resolution pictures, the pictures can be quickly and easily downloaded onto any computer, where the images may be pasted into any other kind of document (e.g., word processing, PowerPoint, or multimedia). They can also be printed, or they can be manipulated in an infinite variety of ways using photo manipulation software such as Photoshop. Novice photographers with

Figure 9.11 Modern digital cameras.

Figure 9.12 Modern mobile phones with picture-taking capabilities.

photo manipulation software can now create visuals that only 10 years ago were the domain of graphics artists.

Many modern mobile phones (Figure 9.12) also enable users to take pictures with their telephone. Although these images do not possess the picture resolution available from digital cameras, they can be immediately sent to other people who have phones with similar capabilities. The mobile phones are much lighter and more portable than digital cameras, but the picture quality is not as good.

Digital Documentaries

Digital cameras and mobile phones have become the tool of choice among modern reporters, storytellers, and ethnographers, or social scientists who study cultures using observation, interviews, and other qualitative methods. These people create documentaries that are usually accompanied by visuals. Pick up any newspaper or magazine, and you can easily see the importance of visuals to the stories being told. Students can create documentaries that examine local issues or controversies. In doing so, they observe and document real-world phenomena and become more concerned and productive members of society.

A good way to get students warmed up to the process of creating documentaries is to create personal documentaries. That is, they produce a documentary about themselves. They decide the most appropriate setting, the perceptions about themselves that they want viewers to have, and the format of the personal description. Personal documentaries have taken many forms. Some students create a personal diary. Others have taken viewers on a tour of their room, while others have played musical instruments, recited poetry, or acted out different personae. The self is the most interesting topic for most kids, so this can be an engaging activity.

An extension of the personal documentary is to conduct it in a foreign language. Pelletier (1990) recommends sending students in foreign language classes out with a camera to tape a short, 3- to 5-minute tour of their room, home, classroom, or library or a video synopsis of some activity, such as a family supper, miniature golf, bowling, or any other activity requiring them to conduct the tour in the language they are studying. Personalizing the use of language rather than treating it as an object to be studied is an important component in language acquisition. So students combine new words with previously learned vocabulary in order to express more meaningful ideas. Have the students be as verbally expressive in their narrations as possible.

Visualizing With Video

Today's children cannot imagine a world without television. The average child spends several hours per day parked in front of the television, inactively absorbing image after image. The results of excessive television viewing (e.g., lethargy, hyperactivity, social isolation, and obesity) have been well documented.

The premise of this book is that any technology, including television, can become a powerful learning tool when students are critical users and producers rather than consumers. Producing videos requires learners to be active, constructive, intentional, and cooperative—to solve numerous decision-making problems while solving design problems associated with production. Video production requires the application of a variety of research, organization, visualization, and interpretation skills. Producing videos engages critical and creative thinking in order to plan and produce programs. Additionally, there are a variety of social values of producing videos in schools (Valmont, 1994):

- Improving students' self-confidence by planning, producing, and sharing video productions in class
- Producing feelings of self-satisfaction
- Providing valuable feedback to students about how others perceive them
- Fostering cooperative learning while sharing ideas, planning and producing programs, and evaluating outcomes
- Providing great public relations at open houses and other school functions

In this chapter, we describe a number of learning activities where television can provide meaningful learning contexts that can engage learners when they identify a purpose for viewing the program to find information and solve problems. However, most of the activities described in this chapter make students television producers. Just consider the popularity of YouTube (www.youtube.com), where young people show the results of days worth of imagination and activity. As producers, teachers and students need to understand a little about video production hardware, which we describe next.

Using video to engage meaningful learning requires three things: imaginative students willing to take chances, ideas for how to engage them, and some equipment. The equipment may be the easiest part, so let's briefly describe some of the hardware that you will need first. Following that, we will provide numerous ideas for engaging learners. You will have to provide the students with the following technologies.

Camcorders

Camcorders (camera recorders) are portable electronic recording systems that are capable of recording live motion video and audio for later replay by VCRs or computers. Some newer models are also capable of taking still images. When they first arrived, camcorders recorded in analog format (VHS and Beta) onto reel-to-reel tape and later videocassettes for replay from VCRs. These camcorders produced less-than-ideal image quality, and the large video cameras had to be rested on the shoulder. As technology improved, other smaller analog formats became available, such as S-VHS, Hi-8, and 8mm. These formats produce better-quality images, were a fraction of the size of the original camcorders, and enabled longer recording times than previously. In order to transfer the images from an analog camera to a computer, the computer had to be equipped with a video board that would convert the analog signals into digital.

Most camcorders today record images digitally. Rather than scanning line by line, light values for each pixel on the screen are registered digitally in memory (Figure 9.13). Re-creating the image is a matter of lighting up each pixel on the screen. Most digital camcorders feature the following:

Figure 9.13   Digital video cameras.

- Zoom lenses with electronic zoom controls (up to 500 times magnification) and optical zoom (up to 25 times magnification) for a sharp, a clear image.
- LCD video screen for viewing the subject while recording as well as playback and the editing of previously recorded material.
- Videocassette recorder with record, playback, fast-forward, and rewind controls and playback through the viewfinder.
- High video resolution range (200K–500K pixels per frame).
- Built-in microphone, CD-quality sound (PCM stereo digital audio recording), and external microphone input jack. Some cameras have low base filters to eliminate the roar of the wind.
- Various shooting features, including time lapse (setting specific time intervals), slow motion, remote control, self-timer, still-image capture, and many others.
- Automatic and manual video controls for adjusting exposure (how light or dark the video will be), shutter speed (number of images per second), and white balance (for different sources of light, such as daylight, incandescent light, and fluorescent light).
- Separate connection jacks for inputting and outputting audio, video, or for playback through a regular television.
- Character generators, known as titlers, for adding titles or other text on your video; date and time stamp, which records the date and time on the video; and special effects (fade, dissolves, and wipes).
- Autofocus (allowing you to concentrate on the subject being recorded without having to worry about the quality) and image stabilization (minimizing the minute tremors of videoing by hand).

Recording with different camcorders will vary slightly, so we will not attempt to show you how to do these things. You should consult the manual that accompanies your digital videocamera and experiment extensively with your equipment before trying to use it for learning. We also recommend that for every camcorder you acquire you purchase a tripod to hold the videocamera steady while it is being used. The tripod also permits individuals to create videos of themselves.

Editors

Videocameras enable students to shoot video "on location." The compact size enables student to move around easily to get different shots. When all of the shooting in the various locations has been completed, you end up with a large number of disconnected scenes stored in the camera or on different disks. In order to arrange those disconnected scenes into the coherent production, those video sequences must be rearranged. Today, these editing functions are accomplished on multimedia computers with digital video editing software, such as iMovie. To make a video with iMovie, you need to follow the process illustrated in Figure 9.14. We will briefly explain the process.

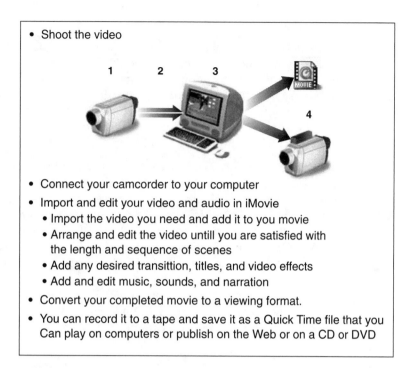

- Shoot the video

- Connect your camcorder to your computer
- Import and edit your video and audio in iMovie
  - Import the video you need and add it to you movie
  - Arrange and edit the video untill you are satisfied with the length and sequence of scenes
  - Add any desired transittion, titles, and video effects
  - Add and edit music, sounds, and narration
- Convert your completed movie to a viewing format.
- You can record it to a tape and save it as a Quick Time file that you Can play on computers or publish on the Web or on a CD or DVD

Figure 9.14   Process for editing a video with iMovie.

Figure 9.15   Selecting video.

Editing Video

a. Selecting video

To select a video clip, click the clip in the clip viewer or time-line viewer (Figure 9.15). If you want to select a section of a clip, select the clip, then click and drag just below the scrubber bar under the iMovie monitor. If the crop markers appear, drag them to mark the beginning and end of the selection.

b. Arranging video clips in a movie

To arrange video clips in a movie, drag a clip to a position before or after another clip in the clip view. You can also change the order of video clips in the clip viewer.

c. Transitions

Transitions add visual appeal through smoothing the cuts between clips. To add a transition to a clip, click on the Transition button. Then select a transition in the transition panel (Figure 9.16). You can modify the speed of the transition into or out of the clip using the speed slider.

If you want to change the transition direction, click an arrow to indicate the direction. After that, drag the transition from the Transition panel to the desired location in the timeline viewer.

When your masterpiece is completed you may want to export it so that you can share it with others. You can export back to the camera through the camera to digital video tape or as a QuickTime movie in various formats. When you want to distribute your movies electronically, you can convert them into QuickTime files so that you can play them on computers and put them on a Web page. To save your movie as a QuickTime file, choose Export Movie. Then select QuickTime and a movie format from the "Export to" pop-up menu. After that, click on the Export button, name your movie, and click on Save.

Digital video editing is fast and convenient. Our experience has shown that kids readily learn how to perform sophisticated editing. We describe one teacher's experience with using video in the classroom next section.

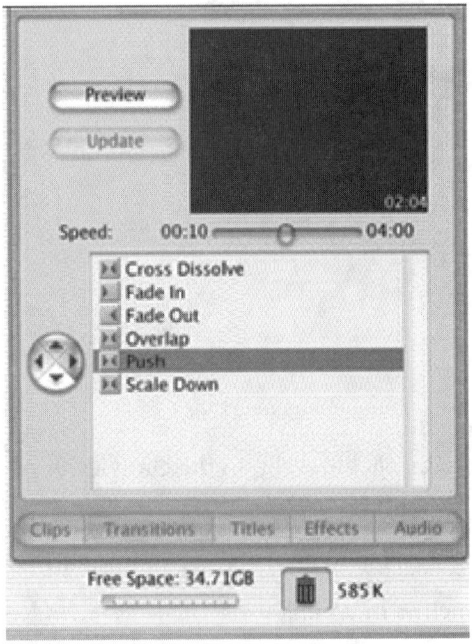

Figure 9.16 Selecting transitions.

Digital Storytelling (by Kate Kemker)

In digital storytelling, technology is not the focus of the activity but rather a tool used to create the story. With digital storytelling, students use their creative skills to create a storyboard on a paper, use a camera to shoot their video, and finally edit their video on a computer using some type of software. Through the combination of working with visual images, text, and sound, students develop their critical thinking skills in a number of different ways that are not necessarily dependent on computer hardware. To create digital stories, students must create a desktop movie.

In the first part of the activity (preproduction), students plan the story they will be telling. In preproduction, students research, write, and organize information about the structure of their story. It is during this portion of the activity that the majority of the work takes place, providing students with the opportunity to generate their ideas on paper before using the camera. The preproduction portion of the activity allows students to optimize their time when actually using the camcorder. An essential part of preproduction is storyboarding. The storyboard (Figure 9.17) is a document that provides students the opportunity to create a plan for their story from which they can begin filming. Storyboards can take on a number of formats combining verbal and/or graphic descriptions of screen shots. The storyboard includes specific information and the logistics for shooting the footage for the digital story.

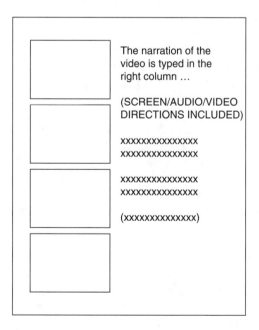

Figure 9.17 Video storyboard.

Students should also create a checklist that includes the basic elements of a story: exposition, rising action, climax, and falling action. Students should use the checklist to evaluate their project to ensure that their story is communicating to the viewer their intended message. Sample questions could be the following: What is the plot? Who are the characters? Does there appear to be conflict between the characters? Is there some kind of resolution?

During the production portion of the activity, students begin to shoot their video. Before students shoot their video, it is important to prepare them with a basic knowledge of how this digital medium works. Fundamentals that the students should understand include types of camera shots, camera angles, and camera movement. Some issues in digital filming that should be addressed include the difference between a close-up shot, a medium-range shot, and a long-range shot; framing a subject in the shot; camera angles not from an eye-level perspective; and creating action with the camera movement.

A digital storytelling activity provides students the opportunity to work collaboratively in a variety of roles, such as the director, actor, videographer, and editor. When shooting video, each student should be involved in the process. As one student uses the camera, another student should be directing the shots, other students acting, and another student logging the video to remember the shots taken. This type of project should lead to an understanding that each role in the production plays an important part in completing the project and that no role is more important than another. The director has the plan for how the video should be done, but he or she must communicate that idea effectively to the actor, the videographer, and the editor. It is a true team process.

The final stage, postproduction, is when students edit their video (described before). In this process, it is the role of the editor to bring to fruition what the director had envisioned for the project. In the postproduction process, students act as editors using nonlinear editing software to create the final product (Figure 9.18). We have used Apple iMovie as well as more powerful products like Final Cut Pro or Adobe Premiere.

At the conclusion of this activity, students should review their digital stories as well as those done by other students. At the movie premiere, all the movies' students take on the role not only of stars but also of critics to review the digital stories. A video production rubric can be used to assess students' progress based on guidelines set out for the given project. Students then write a critique for each movie, evaluating the structure, the fundamentals of digital media, and the editing.

Digital storytelling provides students with the opportunity to establish a connection between the creator and the viewer. Well-told stories can have a powerful effect on an audience, but the secret of their success is the structure of the story: how it is put together and the order in which events appear. A digital story involves the same structural components of any good story: a beginning, a middle, and a end. As with other types of narrative, digital storytelling also involves a sequence of events that follows characters in a particular context. Through the

Figure 9.18 Students in post-production editing of a digital story.

digital storytelling activity, students will begin to understand how all the elements work together and how you can manipulate video to create the effect you want for your story. Such an activity allows students to critically understand that the information they see and hear influences many of their thoughts and decisions as critical thinkers.

Video Modeling and Feedback

One of the most productive ways to use video for teaching is to model specific performances. Video models are used frequently in teaching athletics, where skilled performers show you how to improve your golf or tennis swing. However, video modeling is useful not only for psychomotor tasks. Any kind of performance can be modeled by the teacher or other skilled performer, such as public speaking or acting for theatrical performers, empathic behavior for counselors or social workers, interpersonal communication skills for personnel workers or librarians, and even thinking and research behaviors.

Teachers and students together might think about developing a study strategies video by acting out what a skilled learner would do to write a term paper or study for a test. Shoot the video from the point of view of the student—reading a book, looking in a catalog, searching the library stacks, or turning off the television. After shooting the video, dub in the voice, using an echo chamber to make it seem like the person in the video is talking to him- or herself. Find out what skills students possess and videotape them performing what they do best. Not only will you have a series of useful videos, but students will gain self-confidence as well. Getting students to articulate what they should be doing is usually a good idea.

When modeling performances for students, it is important to model not only the actual performance but also the mental processes (decision making, questioning, and resolving) involved with the performance. This think-aloud process can be very informative for the learners while watching the video performance, especially if the teacher conveys his or her uncertainties as well as solutions while thinking aloud. Although providing video models of any desired performance is one of the most powerful video teaching methods available, it is maximally successful if used in conjunction with video feedback (described later). Essentially, providing video models and then videotaping the learners' performances and using those tapes as feedback is probably the most powerful use of video possible.

Learning Through Video Feedback

Video can help learners reflect on their own performance primarily through video feedback—that is, the process of videotaping a performance and then viewing that performance with or without a teacher or expert accompanying you. For instance, Orban and McLean (1990) use videocameras for self-evaluations and teacher evaluations of French-speaking ability. "Video is like a mirror in which a magician practices his tricks, a way to evaluate his performance over and over" (Taylor, 1979, p. 28). You can use video to engage constructive (articulative/reflective) learning with the following activities.

Video feedback is perhaps the most constructivist use of video. Select virtually any meaningful performance task in schools (theatrics, foreign language usage, public speaking, or performing a chemistry experiment—anything but test taking) and assess the learners' performance by videotaping them while performing the activity. That performance can then be evaluated, and feedback about their performance can be provided to the student. Video feedback is one of the deepest, most incisive learning experiences possible. Having learners watch themselves perform provides them with an unfiltered, unbiased view of themselves. Caution needs to be exercised. Teachers should prepare students for using such feedback constructively because video feedback can be intimidating and demotivating if not used correctly. This method is often (though not often enough) used to help prepare preservice teachers for teaching. Teachers are videotaped teaching lessons to students. Reviewing the videotape with or without a supervisory teacher to provide feedback teaches new teachers more about teaching than all the textbooks they have read.

Visualizing Yourself With Video

In addition to providing performance feedback, video feedback can also be used to provide insights into the self. When people see themselves on a video, it often affects their self-perceptions (Jonassen, 1978, 1979). The video provides an unfiltered mirror into the self. Viewers become more evaluative and less role oriented in their perceptions of themselves. This experience is very powerful and should not be used with troubled individuals without proper care.

Things to Think About

If you would like to reflect on the ideas that we presented in this chapter, articulate your responses to the following questions and compare them with others' responses.

1. In this chapter, we have described how various technologies can function as visual prostheses. Can you think of other ways that technologies can help us "see things" in a new way? Are there scientific concepts that you had a hard time imagining in school?
2. Google Earth goes a long way toward mapping the world. How will that affect our perceptions of the world?
3. Mathematics is one of the most—if not the most—abstract subject-matter domains. Helping students visualize mathematical concepts is very useful in helping students make math real. What other methods suggested in this book will also help make math more real to students?
4. What kinds of reasoning/thinking are students performing when they think mathematically?
5. Is it ever possible to learn from television alone—that is, learn how to do something merely from watching television instruction? What meaning will it have after only watching the show? What meaning will it have after you try it yourself?
6. "Public television exists to enrich people's lives." What does that mean? In order to be enriched, what does the individual viewer have to contribute?
7. Video production is a constructivist activity; that is, students are learning by constructing an artifact. What other kinds of constructionist activities can you think of (using technologies or not)?
8. After the Watergate investigation that brought down Nixon's presidency, investigative journalism increased dramatically. What kinds of issues (personal, local, regional, and national) would be most likely to attract students to investigative reporting? How can you support that in your school?
9. Video feedback has been called a "mirror with a memory." Why is seeing yourself on television such a compelling and incisive experience? How do you see yourself? Why is that so powerful?

References

Audet, R. & Ludwig, G. (2000). *GIS in schools.* Redlands, CA: Environmental Systems Research Institute.

Brandt, L., Elen, J., Hellemans, J., Heerman, L., Couwenberg, I., Volckaert, L., & Morisse, H. (2001). The impact of concept-mapping and visualization on the learning of secondary school chemistry students. *International Journal of Science Education, 23*(12); 1303–1313.

Cotter, J. A. (2000). Using language and visualization to teach place value. *Teaching Children Mathematics, 7*(2); 108–114.

Dunham, P., & Dick, T. (1994). Research on graphing calculators. *Mathematics Teacher, 87*, 440–445.

Finzer, W., Erickson, T., & Binker, J. (2001). Fathom Dynamic Statistics™ Software [Computer software]. Emeryville, CA: Key Curriculum Press.

Gordin, D. N., Edelson, D. C., & Pea, R. D. (1996, April). *Supporting students' science inquiry through scientific visualization.* Paper presented at the annual meeting of the American Education Research Association, New York.

Hancock, C., Kaput, J. J., & Goldsmith, L. T. (1992). Authentic inquiry with data: Critical barriers to classroom implementation. *Educational Psychologist, 27*(3); 337–364.

Jonassen, D. H. (1978). Video as a mediator of human behavior. *Media Message, 7*(2); 5–6.

Jonassen, D. H. (1979). Video-mediated objective self-awareness, self-perception, and locus of control. *Perceptual and Motor Skills, 48*, 255–265.

Konold, C. (2006). Designing a data analysis tool for learners. In M. Lovett & P. Shah (Eds.), *Thinking with data: The 33rd Annual Carnegie Symposium on Cognition.* Hillsdale, NJ: Lawrence Erlbaum Associates.

Levin, J. R., Anglin, G. J., & Carney, R. N. (1987). On empirically validating functions of pictures in prose. In D. M. Willows & H. A. Houghton (Eds.), *The psychology of illustration, Vol. 1, Basic research.* New York: Springer-Verlag.

NCTM (2000). *Curriculum and evaluation standards for school.* Reston, VA: National Councils of Teachers of Mathematics.

Orban, C., & McLean, A. M. (1990). A working model for videocamera use in the foreign language classroom. *French Review, 63*(4); 652–663.

Pelletier, R. J. (1990). Prompting spontaneity by means of the video camera in the beginning foreign language class. *Foreign Language Annals, 22*(3); 227–232.

Ruthven, K. (1990). The influence of graphic calculator use on translation from graphic to symbolic forms. *Educational Studies in Mathematics, 21,* 431–450.

Schwartz, J. L., & Yerushalmy, M. (1987). The Geometric Supposer: Using microcomputers to restore invention to the learning of mathematics. In D. N. Perkins, J. Lockhead, & J. C. Bishop (Eds.), *Thinking: The second international conderence.* Hillsdale, NJ: Lawrence Erlbaum Associates.

Snir, J. (1995). Making waves: A simulation and modeling computer tool for studying wave phenomena. *Journal of Computers in Mathematics and Science Teaching, 8*(4); 48–53.

Taylor, C. B. (1979, January). Video to teach poetry writing. *Audiovisual Instruction,* pp. 27–29.

Valmont, W. J. (1994) Making videos with reluctant learners. *Reading and Writing Quarterly: Overcoming Learning Difficulties, 10*(4); 369–677.

Wu, H. K. Krajcik, J. S. & Soloway, E. (2001). Promoting understanding of chemical representations: Students' use of a visualization tool in the classroom. *Journal of Research in Science Teaching, 38*(7); 821–842.

Yerushalmy, M. (1990). Using empirical information in geometry: Students' and designers' expectations. *Journal of Computers in Mathematics and Science Teaching, 9*(3); 23–33.

Yerushalmy, M., & Houde, R. A. (1986). The Geometric Supposer: Promoting thinking and learning. *Mathematics Teacher, 79*; 418–422.

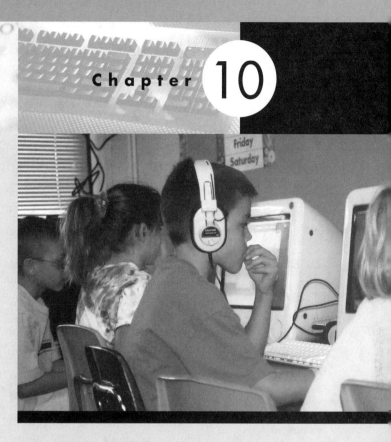

Assessing Meaningful Learning With Technology

This entire book has provided examples of how technology can support different types of complex learning outcomes. But technology can also be used to support another key aspect of learning: assessment. This chapter describes technology-based means of conducting learner assessment. As we will see, the line between an assessment activity and a learning activity can often be blurred when assessing meaningful learning with technology.

Assessing Meaningful Learning: Authentic and Performance Assessment

We have argued throughout this book that technology-supported meaningful learning should be authentic and therefore complex. Just as the learning activities we have described engage learners in meaningful experiences, so must our assessments as well. Educators are finally beginning to understand that in order to evaluate authentic learning, we must use *authentic assessments*. In the past decade, calls for authentic assessment have encouraged educators to discard outdated evaluative methods designed to *sort* students in favor of *assessment systems* designed to provide important information required to *improve performance*. Similarly, for our assessments to be "congruent" or in alignment with the activities we have described, we must adopt authentic and/or performance assessment practices.

Performance assessment refers to the process of assessing a student's skills by asking the student to perform tasks that require those skills. Performances in science might examine the ability to design a device to perform a particular function or to mount an argument supported by experimental evidence.

One source (Perlman, 2002) defines performance assessment as having these elements:

- Students must construct a response or a product rather than simply select from a set of predefined alternatives or answers. In chapter 9 we saw that students can create or "construct" a news broadcast rather than completing a multiple-choice test on current events.
- Assessment then consists of direct observation or assessment of student behavior on tasks or on the product that they produced, and, further, the tasks or products are designed to resemble activities commonly required for functioning in the world outside school.

In essence, the performance of the learning task and the assessment tasks are interwoven and inseparable. Rather than assessing an activity that is completely separate from the activity that learners engage in, we assess the product of that very same learning activity; we assess the learners' performance.

Other terms—authentic assessment and alternative assessment—are sometimes used for performance assessment. These terms, however, are not interchangeable. *Alternative assessment* generally refers to assessments that are in opposition to standardized achievement tests (e.g., the SAT or ACT exam) and to objective test item formats. On the other hand, *authentic assessment* is a term that is closely related to performance assessment and means that learners engage in educational tasks that are meaningful and directly related to real tasks they may need to perform in the future. For instance, having social studies students engage in an activity to poll public opinion on a local issue would be an authentic assessment task as compared to having these same social studies students taking a closed-book exam on principles of democracy.

Many of the technology-supported activities described in this book can become performance assessment activities when accompanied with a set of performance criteria and a scoring rubric. In all cases, the students should be aware of the scoring system and the criteria used to determine the scores for the assessment of the activity.

Technology-Based Assessments

Assessment is the process of gathering and analyzing data to determine if intended learning outcomes have been achieved (Gagne, Bridges, & Wayne, 1998). As described in this book, it makes sense to harness technology for assessment, particularly because at least one aspect of assessment is the management of data—potentially large amounts of data. Because of this, educators have begun to harness technology to make assessment more feasible and more effective. Beyond the simple fact that technology can make assessment data easier to manage, it may also allow teachers to assess more frequently and provide more and better feedback to learners to improve their performance. Before you dismiss this idea because it means more data for you to manage, more grades to record, and more student anxiety, consider that an easy-to-use technology-based assessment can allow a teacher to *formatively* assess—that is, gather assessment data quickly and easily *only* to determine if learners are "getting it" (not to record a "grade"), potentially revise instruction, and then move on.

Technology-based assessment could also address another need presented by implementation of learning environments to support complex learning outcomes. Such outcomes cannot effectively be assessed by any *single* means of assessment. Using technology-based assessments may provide teachers with the ability to assess these outcomes in multiple ways, thus providing a more complete and arguably valid assessment picture.

Although most readers are familiar with computer-based testing, quizzes, or surveys, the use of technology to support assessment has developed beyond simply placing traditional forms of assessment in a digital format. This chapter describes applications of technology to the assessing of higher-order learning outcomes. Finally, we discuss the kinds of assessments for which technology is not well suited.

Assessing Growth Over Time with Electronic Portfolios

As more and more teachers are having students create digital artifacts of their learning (e.g., presentations, word processing documents, and Web sites), they are also asking them to put these artifacts together in a coherent way to represent a body of work that addresses certain learning outcomes. These are often called electronic portfolios, or "e-portfolios." For instance, a visual/performing arts high school teacher had students keep digital portfolios of their artwork for later use in other projects, such as theater backdrops, calendars, and so on. The purpose of the portfolio was to have students work with multimedia programs, learn to organize information coherently, and collaborate with one another. Digital pictures of traditionally created pieces were mixed with digitally created artifacts. Students used a variety of technologies, including digital cameras, graphics programs, and Web page programming tools (KITE, 2001).

E-portfolios are a collection of digitized artifacts that may include video clips, graphics, sound, writing samples, artwork, and multimedia presentations, to name a few. Taken together, they can represent the accomplishments of an individual or group of learners (Lorenzo & Ittelson, 2005). E-portfolios are meant to be more than simply a collection of student work stored in an electronic format. Rather, they are intended to purposefully exhibit students' efforts, progress and achievements (Paulson, Paulson, & Meyer, 1991).

Portfolios (either as electronic or in hard-copy form) are part of the move toward performance assessment and away from teacher-centered forms of assessment as portfolios can provide more autonomy to students as they make their own choices on which artifacts to include and how to present them (Tombari & Borich, 1999). Generally, portfolios can be used to demonstrate students' ability to create a certain type of product (e.g., a newspaper article that describes a recent PTA meeting), demonstrate their ability to follow a process (e.g., reconcile income and expenses in an accounting ledger), or, by using a variety of products over a period of time, demonstrate student growth in a learning domain.

Portfolios can be classified in three types associated with the intended purpose of the portfolio, and any of these can be implemented as e-portfolios. Notice that an important distinction between the types of portfolios is how much control students have over choosing portfolio content:

- *Working portfolios* show student's best performance or performance over time in specified learning areas. Such portfolios tend to be more formative in nature, and students would have the chance to get feedback and improve their portfolio over time.
- *In standards-based portfolios,* teachers are likely to define the content based on meeting certain curricular requirements. In Missouri, a fifth-grade teacher might ask students to put together a portfolio that demonstrates the "grade-level expectations" for understanding the water cycle.

- *External evaluation portfolios* are generally summative and are used for an *external* audience, such as an accrediting body to demonstrate that your school or grade has met this external body's requirements.

Why Use Them?

There are many reasons to use e-portfolios. To begin with, they can be useful for assessing many types of learning outcomes. In fact, the range of learning outcomes one can assess is essentially limitless, is defined by the portfolio designer, and will vary based on the types of products included in the e-portfolio. For instance, e-portfolios that include documents containing narratives might demonstrate writing or literacy skills. A video clip of a student-generated news editorial might demonstrate the learner's ability to develop a persuasive argument as well as oral presentation and technology literacy skills. Or a spreadsheet containing data collected at a local stream might be used to demonstrate an ability to perform simple descriptive statistics as well as to draw and present conclusions from data. This list could be endless; the key is in defining what the goal of the e-portfolio is—we'll discuss that soon. Here are some more reasons for using e-portfolios.

E-portfolios offer teachers flexibility in terms of how they are implemented:

- E-portfolios can be developed over varying periods of time (e.g., a 3-week earth science unit on streams or an over an entire 15-week semester of earth science content). A longer-duration format offers students the opportunity to get peer or teacher feedback, make modifications, and create an improved product and demonstrate student growth on learning outcomes.
- E-portfolios can also be developed by individual students or student groups. When done in groups, different group members can contribute different artifacts to meet portfolio requirements. Having group members negotiate which artifacts best fit the portfolio task can be another means for helping students engage in deep or evaluative thinking about artifacts.
- E-portfolios have logistic advantages, as the electronic nature of them makes them searchable, transportable, and more easily modifiable (Batson, 2002). This is an advantage both for teachers and for students.

E-portfolios offer a way to encourage meaningful learning outcomes. As previously described, e-portfolios can be used to demonstrate an endless set of learning outcomes. An additional benefit is that the task of assembling an e-portfolio can offer students a chance to reflect on their work (e.g., What did I learn from this activity? What does this product demonstrate? What would I do differently next time?). The act of reflection on one's work can contribute to modifying one's thinking based on comparisons of one's own work with that of experts and peers (Lin, Hmelo, Kinzer, & Secules, 1999). It is important to specifically include such reflective components in portfolio guidelines and to offer students chances to practice self-reflection in order for this task to be meaningful. Finally, but certainly not insignificantly, e-portfolios can be compelling from a student point of view, as students can take pride in their assembled products, and certain types of portfolios may allow students some autonomy in their choices about what to include.

How Do I Define an E-Portfolio Task for Students?

The components of an e-portfolio task will vary depending on what your goals are for the students as they complete the e-portfolio. To help you define your e-portfolio, here are some questions you should consider (Tombari & Borich, 1999):

- What is the purpose of the portfolio?
  Do you want the portfolio to show growth over time? Exemplify students' best work?
  Is the portfolio intended to show that students have achieved a particular set of standards?
- What learning outcomes should the portfolio demonstrate?
  Then, for each outcome, what tasks or artifacts from your students will you require or suggest?
- What audience is intended for the portfolio (teachers only, other students, parents, or other stakeholders)?

Once the initial design is specified, you will need to consider the following:

- What organizational structure should the portfolio use?
      The organization of e-portfolios refers to how a reader finds or accesses the products in the portfolio. E-portfolio organization becomes particularly important when the e-portfolio addresses more than one learning outcome or a collection of student work over time. One commonly used organizational strategy for portfolios is by learning outcomes or the competencies the portfolio measures. Just as a paper-based portfolio might contain individual file folders each containing work that represents a particular learning outcome, an e-portfolio can be organized as a "home" page that provides an overview of the portfolio and a list of links to content organized by learning outcomes. For instance, Figure 10.1 shows a second-grade student's portfolio arranged by content areas. Of course, using an electronic format means that there can be multiple paths to individual portfolio products—perhaps not only by learning outcome but also by content domain or the time frame in which the product was produced (e.g., first attempt at designing a science experiment or third attempt). Other e-portfolio organizations are possible; the important point is to consider portfolio organization and either define the organization for your students or work with them to negotiate an organization that is appropriate for the portfolio's purpose.
- What sorts of synthesizing documentation or reflection will you require from students in the portfolio?

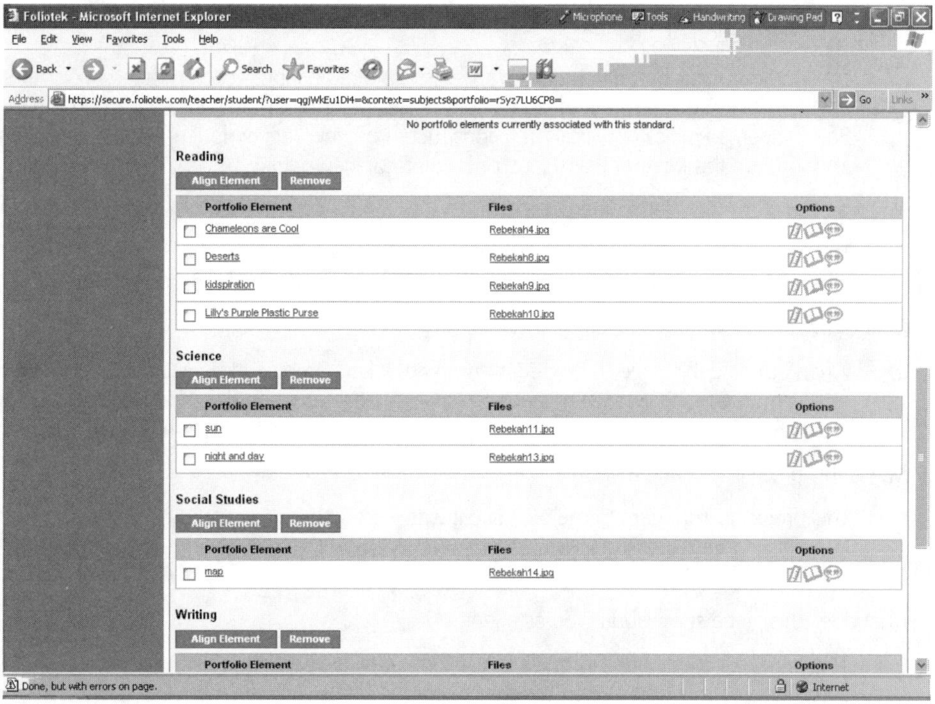

Figure 10.1 Second grader's portfolio home page example.

An e-portfolio is intended to be more than simply a collection of digital artifacts. It must be a cohesive body of work that represents students' ability for a defined set of learning outcomes. In some cases it may be self-evident how a particular product meets a portfolio requirement, but in others, students may need to annotate or reflect on their work to explain what aspects of the product meet a learning outcome, their understanding of the strengths and weaknesses of the work, or how they might improve a similar product in the future. Researchers in the field of student writing report that having students annotate their own writing can increase a student's autonomy in initiating feedback and lead to improvements in student performance (Cresswell, 2000).

Figure 10.2 shows an excerpt of a sixth-grade student's annotations or reflections on the social studies portion of her portfolio. This student's teacher structured the reflections or annotations by a series of questions. Such structuring may be necessary to help students learn to reflect on portfolio products.

Another important aspect of e-portfolio design is assessment criteria. As with all the meaningful learning tasks described in this book, students should be

Give a brief description of the piece.

> This portion of my portfolio provides an example of a final project completed in Social Studies. It contains a written report on the state of New Jersey, a Bibliography of the sources used in the report, a "Facts in Brief" sheet, a Political/Physical map constructed of New Jersey done in ClarisWorks, and examples of clip art found on the Internet that relate to the State of New Jersey.

Why was this piece included in the portfolio?

> The New Jersey report was included in my portfolio because I felt that it showed that I knew how to use technology as both a research and productivity tool and because it demonstrates my writing skills.

What did you learn when you created this piece?

> When I created this project I learned many things. I learned how to download clip art from the Internet as well as from a CD-ROM. I learned how use search engines when doing research on the Internet. Writing was the most difficult part for me, but I was able to learn that I could complete it if I worked on it after school.

Why is this piece important to you?

> This project is important to me because it was the first time that I was able to use the computer and the Internet to do a research project. Usually we have had to look only at books. I am proud of the way it turned out.

What does this piece show about you as a learner?

> This project shows that I can persevere as a learner. It also shows that I know how to do research and communicate that information to other people.

How will what you learned creating this piece help you in the future?

> Now that I was able to complete this research project, I will be able to use these skills when I go to intermediate school and high school. I would like have a career in technology.

Figure 10.2 Sample student portfolio reflections (http://www.k12.hi.us/~cmin/tethree/learning/portfoliosample.htm).

aware of the criteria that will be used to assess their work. Thus, establishing assessment criteria for the e-portfolio should be considered *before* students begin the portfolio task. We refer readers to our discussion of creating criterion-based rubrics in this chapter's section on electronic rubrics. However, Table 10.1 lists a few criteria one would often consider in a rubric for e-portfolios (Vandervelde, 2006). Applying an e-portfolio rubric will allow teachers to create a score for the portfolio, but even if creating a numeric score is not necessary for a particular portfolio (e.g., a portfolio that is intended simply to show students' best work), providing students with criteria will guide their portfolio construction.

What Technology Do I Need to Implement in E-Portfolios?

Although the technology basis of e-portfolios offers many advantages (e.g., reduced physical storage requirements, flexibility of editing, and updates), one may be unfamiliar with the actual technologies employed to create e-portfolios.

Table 10.1 Sample E-Portfolio Rubric Criteria and Performance Ranges

Criteria	Performance Ranges				
Selection of artifacts	Artifacts meet defined portfolio purpose.				Artifacts do not meet defined purpose (or artifacts are missing).
	X	X	X	X	X
Student annotations	Describe clearly reason for artifact inclusion.				Annotations are missing or do not describe reason for artifact inclusion.
	X	X	X	X	X
Student reflections	Illustrate ability to self-evaluate artifacts.				Reflections are missing or do not demonstrate ability to self-evaluate artifacts.
	X	X	X	X	X
Navigation	Portfolio is easy to navigate; finding artifacts is easy.				Site navigation is confusing or does not work.
	X	X	X	X	X
Text design (use of white space, font size, etc.)	Text layout is clear and easy to read and enhances portfolio's goals.				Text layout is sloppy or misleading; detracts from portfolio purpose.
	X	X	X	X	X
Use of multimedia	Demonstrates appropriate use of multimedia that enhances how the artifacts and portfolio show student competencies.				Multimedia are distracting or do not work; detract from overall portfolio purpose.
	X	X	X	X	X
Writing mechanics	Writing is correct grammatically; clearly communicates to reader; no spelling errors.				Writing contains many grammatical errors, misspellings, or incorrect punctuation.
	X	X	X	X	X
Audience	Contains materials and is presented in manner appropriate for specified audience.				Materials, design, and/or content are inappropriate for specified audience.
	X	X	X	X	X

Developing an e-portfolio can be as simple as using HTML editors or commonly available tools like Microsoft Front Page or Macromedia Dreamweaver to develop simple Web-based portfolio sites (simple Web sites). However, e-portfolio specific software packages such as Foliotek (http://www.foliotek.com) have also been created. These packages provide features such as the ability to accept a full range of file types and content: text, graphics, video, audio, photos, and animation (Batson, 2002) as well as secure storage and portfolio management (Figure 10.1).

Your choice of e-portfolio software will invariably depend on the resources available at your institution. In addition to the Web page development of multi-media software you use to create a complete e-portfolio, you may also need a digital camera and/or a scanner for creating images, software such as Adobe Photoshop for manipulating images, and other commonly available software packages, such as word processors, spreadsheets, and presentation packages, all of which can be used to create e-portfolio individual artifacts.

Assessing Performance With Technology-Based Rubrics

By definition, a *rubric* is a code or a set of codes designed to govern action. In educational settings, the term has evolved to mean a tool represented as a set of *scales* used for assessing a complex performance. In recent years many technology-based tools for rubric creation, implementation, and management have become available. We begin this section with a brief overview of rubrics in general and then describe the functions, benefits, and applications of technology-based rubric tools.

Rubrics and Meaningful Learning

Many terms are used to name the documents or methods we use to assess learner performance. These include scoring grids (because they are often in grid form), scoring schemes, rating scales, and, perhaps the most commonly used term, rubrics. In schools, rubrics often take the form of a scale or set of scales. Applying a rubric to a complex learning process or product (such as an e-portfolio) provides a means for systemically assessing the degree that certain criteria are demonstrated in the product or process. In essence, a rubric helps the scorer consistently apply a set of valid criteria to the product. The process of developing and applying a rubric addresses the problem that both teachers and learners often face when it comes to grading complex learning products.

For instance, in a typical classroom, oral reports are mysteriously *graded* (neither students nor teachers can really tell you where the grades come from), and a few comments generally accompany the grade. Little substantive feedback about the performance is made available to the student, who cares only about the grade received. On the other hand, using a rubric, perhaps jointly developed by students and teachers, can promote intentional learning by identifying important aspects of the performance, gathering information about the learner's performance, and using the information to improve learner performance.

Technology-Based Rubric Tools

There are a variety of technology tools for creating and supporting the use of rubrics. They fall into two basic categories: rubric banks and rubric generation tools (Dornisch & Sabatini McLoughlin, 2006). Online rubric banks offer already created rubrics for a wide array of learning tasks. One impediment to using rubrics is that the task of creating a high-quality rubric is not trivial in any circumstances and even less so when one is creating a rubric for a complex learning task. We refer the reader to the section "Characteristics of a Good Rubric" later in this chapter.

So creating such a rubric may be a time-consuming task—although the authors would argue that it is a beneficial one, as it requires that teachers clearly and precisely articulate the characteristics of a high-quality learning activity (e.g., what characteristics does a really good oral presentation have?), which in turn can help them design their instructional activities toward those characteristics. Nonetheless, teachers are undoubtedly short on time, so banks of existing rubrics certainly have potential. Figure 10.3 shows a sampling of rubric banks available at this writing.

We caution users of rubric banks for several reasons. First, before using any rubric, the user needs to evaluate its appropriateness for the intended learning task. Just because you are in need of a rubric for a group discussion and you find one (or a dozen), none of these rubrics may align with the learning outcomes you had intended for your classroom group discussion. We perused several rubrics on class discussions and found that they addressed a broad range of activities, including consensus building, speaking and listening, conflict resolution, facilitation skills, summarization skills, keeping track of time, and on and on. Which of these (if any) are you interested in? Our point is that finding a rubric that fits your learning outcomes, even if the "task" is the same, is quite unlikely. Be prepared to both examine many rubrics that match your task and then modify them to meet your needs (perhaps by combining several of them).

In many cases, the rubrics you find may not clearly state the intended outcomes they are to assess, so you will need to glean these outcomes from the content of the rubric—which may or may not be feasible, depending on the rubric's clarity. We suggest that the better rubrics will in fact clearly state the outcomes they intend to assess, and teachers can use this as a way of sorting through the many rubrics they may find.

Finally, as Figure 10.3 shows there are a lot of rubric banks out there (and this is only a sampling). The main argument for using them is that they could save teachers time. You may wish to consider that by the time you search all these

---

Discovery School:

http://school.discovery.com/schrockguide/assess.html

Provides a fairly comprehensive set of domain-specific and general rubrics.

Rubrician:

http://www.rubrician.com

Offers a collection of rubrics by subject-matter area and, under the "general" category, offers links to other rubric banks. It is not clear how the quality of submitted rubrics is maintained on this site.

Figure 10.3   A selection of online rubric banks.

banks, you may have had time to create your own rubric that can avoid some of the problems of using or having to modify someone else's conception of your learning task.

The other category of technology-based rubric tools is rubric generators. As the name implies, a rubric generator helps the user actually create a rubric. As a user, you can create a rubric that is customized to your learning task, and you can avoid some of the issues discussed pertaining to the use of rubric banks. However, since you are creating your own rubric, what do rubric generators offer over sitting down with a word processor? Rubric generators can scaffold or support the user through the rubric generation process. A good rubric generator will force you to address the critical components of a high-quality rubric.

For instance, the Rubric Processor (http://ide.ed.psu.edu/ITSC/RubrProc/) steps users through a series of screens that each represent a critical step in creating a rubric. In addition to asking you for a rubric title, the tool requires you to define up to seven "elements" (criteria) you wish to assess in your rubric, and then for each element you are prompted define the different performance levels or "ratings" for that element. Keeping with our "group discussion" activity example, one "element" or criteria might be "activity level." As prompted by the rubric processor, we would define "activity level" as the amount of participation an individual contributes to the discussion during one class period. Then the processor prompts us to define the different performance levels and their definitions for this criterion. Figure 10.4 shows the three rating or performance levels we defined. Users continue this process, defining each criterion and their associated performance levels. Once completed, your rubric is stored for later use.

The rubric processor is an example of a technology-based rubric tool that also provides support for using rubrics with students. As you define the performance levels for each criterion, you create the stem of a sentence that would be used in combination with your performance level definition, which can be used in creating a feedback report for a student as you apply the rubric to his or her product. So student Juan—who demonstrated adequate activity level during the discussion— would see on his report "Juan participates as much as other group members." This focus on creating qualitative feedback for students is a positive aspect of this particular tool. Other rubric generation tools offer similar features, but the step-by-step approach of the Rubric Processor can offer valuable support to the novice rubric writer. Figure 10.5 provides information on a sampling of other rubric generator tools.

Performance Level	Definition
Inadequately:	Never participates; quiet/passive
Adequately:	Participates as much as other group members
Exceptionally:	Participates more than any other group member

Figure 10.4   Performance levels for criteria activity level during group discussion.

Rubricator:

http://www.rubrics.com
Commercial software designed to help teachers create rubrics. Provides step-by-step prompting for rubric elements and rating levels or allows user to select from their bank of existing elements and ratings.

Tech4Learning Tools RubricMaker:

http://myt4l.com/index.php?v=pl&page_ac=view&type=tools
Provides scaffolded interface for creating rubrics. Features include pull-down menus for types of learning outcomes and four definable levels-of performance for each criterion/component defined.

Rubric Builder:

http://landmark-project.com/classweb/tools/rubric_builder.php
Creates/scaffolds creation of online rubrics. Supports rubric generation by prompting users for number of objectives (meaning ratable elements and rating (performance levels), each associated with a point value.

Rubistar:

http://rubistar.4teachers.org/index.php Users do not create a rubric from scratch but rather customize rubric templates that are available in a variety of subject area domains.

Figure 10.5 Sample rubric generators.

Characteristics of a Good Rubric

Whether you are trying to decide if the rubric you found online is high quality or whether you are using an online rubric generator to create your own, you need to know the characteristics of a good rubric. The most effective and useful rubrics tend to display certain important characteristics. We will discuss these characteristics briefly, along with the most common pitfalls experienced by novices.

In an Effective Rubric, All Important Elements Are Included If something is important enough to assess, consider it an element and develop a scale with ratings that describe it. By definition, the rubric identifies (both for the assessor and for the student) the aspects of the performance that are considered important. Consider the rubric a sort of contract between educator and student and resist the temptation to assess anything not included in the rubric. If you forgot an important element, then renegotiate the rubric.

In an Effective Rubric, Each Element Is Unidimensional Avoid using elements that are really *molecules*. In chemistry, an *element* is irreducible. Water is a molecule, composed of both hydrogen and oxygen—it can be separated into these elements, which cannot be further separated. Likewise, in the preliminary example presented in our first rubric, the so-called element "voice qualities" is really a combination of things that should be broken down more completely, perhaps into separate elements of "volume" and "intonation." The penalty for attempting to assess molecules rather than elements is that assigning ratings is more difficult, as is deriving specific feedback on which to base attempts to improve performance. Just what was it about the voice quality that was not adequate?

In an Effective Rubric, Ratings Are Distinct, Comprehensive, and Descriptive   The ratings should cover the range of expected performances. Some elements are best assessed in a simple, two-rating scale—a yes/no distinction—while others might require as many as seven distinct ratings. For example, the "volume" element in an oral report might simply be assessed as "too quiet" or "loud enough," while an element like "social interaction" might justifiably involve five or more ratings.

A common problem in rubric design involves an attempt to use a similar scale for all elements, such as using a standard five-point scale of weak, poor, acceptable, good, and excellent. Although it might seem simpler and cleaner to use such a scale for each element, can you really describe the difference between ratings of "weak" and "poor" or between "good" and "excellent," say, for the pace of an oral presentation? Would these assessments be defensible or too subjective? In addition, when a standard scale is used for multiple elements, you lose a lot of information that is better transmitted by descriptive ratings rather than generic labels. For instance, a student might learn more from a presentation that had been rated as "boring" than from one that received a "weak" rating in an element titled "motivation." Use labels that make sense and describe the behaviors and use just enough of them to cover the range of possibilities.

An Effective Rubric Communicates Clearly With Both Students and Parents   The ultimate purpose of a rubric is to improve performance. This is accomplished by clarifying expectations and by providing important information about progress toward the desired goal states. Rubrics convey the complexity of the task and focus intentional learning. The feedback their use provides serves as an important baseline for reflection by both learners and educators. For these purposes to be realized, the rubric must communicate clearly with those it is to serve. Make sure that all who use the rubric (learners, parents, and educators) share a common understanding of all the terms used. This common understanding is often achieved as educators and students develop the rubric collaboratively, after which students explain it to their parents. This is a great way to develop metacognition (understanding of cognitive processes used), and it helps students regulate their learning as they proceed through the complex tasks offered by meaningful learning environments. Avoid educational jargon and words with weak or several meanings. Consider developing, preferably with students, descriptions of each element and each rating or using elaborate, full-sentence rating labels instead of single terms.

An Effective Rubric Provides Rich Information About the Multiple Aspects of the Performance and Avoids the Temptation to Create a Contrived Summary Score   Despite the fact that the real value of a rubric lies in its ability to provide information on the separate elements that make up a complex task, novice users (especially teachers in the public schools) seem compelled to turn the ratings given on individual *elements* into *scores* for each element and then to combine these scores to form a total score and then, worse yet, a *grade*.

When individual elements are combined, information that could improve performance is lost. When ratings are treated as numeric scores and combined, elements of more and less importance are generally treated as if they were of equal value, and an inaccurate picture of the performance is created. For example, suppose that ratings for "organization" and "intonation" are combined after using a rubric to assess an oral presentation. Generally, the scores are added in a way that makes the two appear equally important. Even when the different elements are combined using some sort of weighting system that assigns different numbers of points based on the importance of the element, when scores are combined, attention is paid to the total at the expense of the information about how to improve performance on each element.

Clicker Assessment Tools

Clicker technology, also called "student response" or "audience response" systems, consists of small wireless keypads with alphanumeric keypads that are linked to a computer (Duncan, 2005; Hafner, 2004). Clickers are being used in elementary through college-level classes to support assessment and engage students. The clickers look a lot like a television's remote control (Figure 10.6). It has several buttons labeled with letters or numbers. You use them with your class

Figure 10.6 Clicker student remote (CPSOnline Higher Ed http://www.einstruction.com/).

by distributing them to your students to allow them to respond to questions not by raising their hands but by selecting buttons, and the results can appear on a screen in the front of the class.

Student responses are transmitted to a receiver connected to a computer at the front of the classroom. The computer tabulates and analyzes and can display the results if the machine is hooked to a projector. Results can also be posted to a Web site or loaded into a spreadsheet. The responses are anonymous among the student participants, but the teacher can link responses to students through the clicker serial numbers (which are associated with the answers transmitted). Students need to be aware of this, but teachers using the technology don't report that this concerns students (Hafner, 2004).

One may wonder how these devices can be beneficial to learning, but those who have used them report that clickers do offer legitimate ways to support assessment in the classroom. Here are some strategies:

- Use them as a quick "pretest." Design a few items that contain distracters that represent common misconceptions to find out what students do and do not know. Because the responses are anonymous (and quick), you can get a more accurate picture of what misconceptions students have and directly address them.
- After instruction, use them to gauge whether you are getting your points across; you get immediate feedback about what misconceptions students still have.
- Have students predict the outcome of a class demonstration or experiment you are about to perform (Duncan, 2005). Create an item(s) that includes common misconceptions about the phenomenon you are investigating and ask students to predict the outcome (Figure 10.7). You can hold a peer-to-peer discussion before and/or after to have students provide an argument for their prediction or for the outcome.
- Assess conceptual knowledge and other higher-order learning outcomes. Clickers can be used to respond only to "forced response" types of items (e.g., true/false or multiple choice). We often think that such items can

---

We will drop feather and a marble from the exact same height and at the exact same time. Which one will hit the floor first?

a. the marble

b. the feather

c. at the same time

Figure 10.7   Sample "prediction" question.

assess only recall and recognition knowledge, but with some thought, these items can also be used to assess conceptual understanding and other higher-order learning outcomes. For example, the item in Figure 10.7 assesses a learner's conceptual understanding of gravity and mass.

Beyond their ability to support assessment—gathering data about students' performance or knowledge—clickers are described as being intrinsically motivating, having the added potential of increasing student interaction (among themselves and teachers) and actively engaging students. Research has shown that engaging students actively in learning can increase retention and performance on various measures. The following clicker strategies can facilitate active learning. We note that most of these strategies are effective only when used in combination with a clicker question that involves more than simply recall and recognition:

- Using clickers can "even the playing field," allowing (and expecting) all students to respond to the posed question. Systems enable teachers to see a count of responses so that they can encourage all students to respond. This allows those learners who need more time to respond—and who normally lose the opportunity to answer questions to those who raise their hands quickly—to have that time and thus participate in the answer-giving activity.
- "I'm not the only one who got it wrong." Students who don't normally actively participate may be reticent for fear of getting a wrong answer. That student may or may not answer a posed question correctly, but it is unlikely that he or she is the only one who didn't get it right. By displaying the class distribution of responses, such learners see they are not alone, and teachers can reinforce this with their comments. This could eventually lead to a more confident student.
- Use clickers to provide a learner-centered, active component in a class with a large number of students. Technology can be used in effective and ineffective ways. In chapter 1 we argued that we should take advantage of what each component of the learning system (e.g., human learners or teachers versus technology) does best. Using technology in large classroom settings often has the potential to b effective because the technology enables a large number of students to participate in a complex or meaningful learning task in the same way. In the case of clickers, it allows all students to respond *and* the teacher to keep track of responses and trends. Even in a classroom with many students, this activity enables teachers to have students discuss or defend their choices. Teachers don't have to be involved in each of these paired or small-group discussions; the discussions don't have to be very long—in fact, you will probably maintain more engagement and energy if you make them stop before they are actually finished—and teachers can still quickly debrief with a sampling of students to find out what they discussed. Better yet, the teacher can design a follow-up clicker question that asks them to choose which justification they used for their answer. So the

follow-up question to figure X might be as shown in figure Y. We don't argue that such a technology is the *only* way to actively engage a large number of students, but they do facilitate such engagement.

      Which justification did you use for your response about the marble and the feather?

a) The marble weighs more, so it would fall faster.

b) Gravity works the same way regardless of weight.

c) Neither.

Clicker System Logistics and Technology

There are numerous clicker systems available, and, as with most technologies, the cost is dropping and the features are growing. To run a clicker system, you need the following:

- A PC to run the clicker data collection software, preferably running a spreadsheet and presentation software packages. One does not need a particularly powerful PC to run the software, and the software is generally free when other clicker system components are purchased.
- An LCD projector to display the clicker question and the class's response results. Two projectors can be useful, as one can be used to continue to display the question while the other provides an updated read out of student responses.
- Clicker remotes for students to respond to questions. Each clicker has a unique ID or registration number associated with it. Students look for their ID number on the response display to ensure that their response has been received and recorded by the system. Clickers range in price from $6 to $60 each, depending on the system and the features incorporated (Gilbert, 2005). Discounts may be available when purchasing large numbers of clickers or when purchased in association with specific textbooks.
- Receivers in the classroom to receive students' response transmissions. The receivers are part of the clicker packages available from vendors. Depending on the technology your system uses, you will need about one receiver for every 25 to 40 students; otherwise, students may experience a "jam" where their responses are not initially detected.

To locate potential vendors, type "clicker," "classroom response system," or "audience response system" into your favorite Internet search engine.

      To use a clicker system, the teacher projects the question to the class. Teachers can compose questions using their preferred word processing or presentation software. Students then select their answers using their clickers. The response system software includes a status screen that indicates when each registered clicker's response has been recorded (Figure 10.8). Students are aware of their registration number. When their number shows up on the screen, they know that their response has been recorded.

Question 3	Time: 09:43				
000		002			004
005	006	007			
010		012	013		014
	016	017			019
020	021		023		024

Figure 10.8 Data collection status screen components.

When the responses are collected, the teachers can see the results using the clicker system software and display them if they wish—generally in the form of bar chart showing percentages of the class that responded for each possible answer.

Clicker systems are becoming cheaper as manufactures replace infrared technology with radio frequency. They are also easier for students to use, as they don't have to aim the remote at anything in particular. Beyond the basic functionality described, new features are being incorporated into clicker systems. Here are a few you may wish to consider or seek out:

- *Two-way receivers*. Systems have traditionally included receivers that can only "receive" input from the students. With two-way receivers, students' clickers receive a transmission from the receiver indicating that their response has been received and recorded.
- *Confidence levels*. Some systems are now incorporating a confidence level feature where students indicate not only their response but also how confident they are that their response is correct. Such data can help teachers know if students are primarily guessing the correct answer. Of course, constructing high-quality questions can help prevent this from consistently occurring.
- *Seamless interfaces between presentation and clicker software*. Some manufacturers are creating built-in interfaces between their clicker software and commonly used presentation packages such as PowerPoint. This allows teachers to easily create and display questions in PowerPoint and then associate the created questions with the results in the clicker software.

Clicker Closing Comments

Clickers are a relatively new phenomenon, and although some teachers are raving about them (see Duncan, 2005) and their potential to revolutionize the dynamics of the classroom, there isn't much research yet to support that these systems actually improve learning (Gilbert, 2005). Good sense and prior experience indicates, however, that effective use of clickers—particularly if one hopes that clickers will have the "engaging" effects on students that we discussed—requires that teachers set the stage for their use. Students must understand that, in general, you are *not* "grading" their responses bur rather using their responses to find out what they do or don't understand so that you can modify your instruction to be most beneficial.

For younger students, teachers might present the use of clickers as a game—something fun to do.

Further, clickers rely on the use of well-written questions. We've argued that some of the most effective uses of clickers are in diagnosing student learning and in the process creating an activity around which teachers can build student-to-student interaction and discussion. Such applications require that clicker questions engage students in more than simply recall and recognition. After all, how much discussion can you really have about the definition of an isosceles triangle? Further, writing forced-response questions that assess more than recall and recognition can be hard work. So teachers should be prepared to put a bit of preparation into clicker lessons to reap the potential benefits discussed.

Assessing Learning With Computer-Based Tests and Surveys

Computerized tests, computer-scored tests, and computer-based surveys have been available for many years. Computerized tests or surveys are completed by students directly on a computer, and with computer-scored tests, students record their responses on a "bubble" or scan sheet that can be scanned and scored by a computer. Recognizing that tests and surveys generally have different purposes—tests and for assessing knowledge or performance relative to learning outcomes and surveys for gathering opinions or descriptions of behaviors—we treat them both of them in this section, as both technologies are similar and can be used for assessment purposes.

In the past, computer-based testing has been used to simplify the testing process for teachers and administrators and to enable, through scan sheets and tests actually completed by students on a computer, a faster turnaround on scoring students' work. Unlike many of the other technology applications we address in this book, a student's experience of a computer-based test or quiz is not terribly engaging or motivating. Other than selecting a response to the posed item, students are passive recipients of what is being shown on the computer screen. Clearly, this use of technology does not embody the student-centered nature that the technology applications throughout this book promote.

Even so, computer-based tests can have meaningful applications in learning. Computerized adaptive testing (CAT) is one such application (Clark, 2004). Although the fairly sophisticated domain of "item response theory" underlies most CAT system designs (see Wainer & Dornas, 2000), in essence CAT relies on educators creating a pool of potential items of varying difficulty level; difficulty levels could be based on the types of thinking required to correctly answer the item (e.g., recall or recognition versus application or analysis) or the degree of transfer required. Learners are presented with differing items based on their prior answers or even on an "ability level" that is determined before they begin to use the test. The potential to adapt the sequence of items answers a difficulty long expressed about standardized tests—that they test those who are of "average" ability level quite well but do not work well for learners at either end of the spectrum. A test that adapts can answer this concern and also increase learner engagement and persistence, as the level of items is appropriate for the learner to be challenged but not overly frustrated. Software that creates adaptive tests is relatively sophisticated (and consequently expensive) because of the need to support item banks and the underlying item-response theories. However, Assessment Systems Corporation (http://www.assess.com/software/FTP16main.htm) does offer a free 30-day trial of their software as well as a comparison of CAT tools.

Although they are called tests, such software does not have to be used for testing in the traditional sense (e.g., take a test and record the grade that impacts your overall school performance). Districts such as Meridian in Idaho report that they are using them as diagnostic tools to help assess learner skills and adapt instruction to better meet learner needs (Clark, 2004). We argue that any use of an assessment process, computerized or not, that is used to modify instruction to improve learner performance is a good use of assessment.

Computerized testing and surveying tools are finding a home on the Internet. Any Internet search for "online test" or "online survey" will literally produce hundreds if not thousands of hits. To say that the number of tools out there to support online tests or surveys is growing rapidly is an understatement. Although these tools vary significantly both in features and in price (from free to several thousand dollars), one major distinction between tools is those that are stand-alone test or survey tools versus tools that are embedded within an overall online course management system (e.g., Blackboard) (Figure 10.9). Readers interested in a comparative review of online survey and testing tools may wish to refer to NPower's review of these tools (NPower, n.d.).

Online instrument development tools allow users to easily create an online test or survey that is hosted on the Internet. Respondents complete tests or surveys at a computer, and their responses are stored by the tool provider. Then test givers can download the results for their own records or provide feedback and/or scores to the respondents. Features of these systems vary, but the following is a set of features that are generally available in these tools:

- Support of a variety of formats of forced-response items (Figure 10.10).
- Ability to implement "logic" or branching in the instrument based on responses to prior items.
- Inclusion of graphics and, in some applications, animation within test or survey items.

SurveyMonkey (http://www.surveymonkey.com)	Zoomerang (http://www.zoomerang.com)
Blackboard*	WebCT*

Figure 10.9   Sample of online testing and surveying tools.
* Indicates course management system that includes quiz or survey tool.

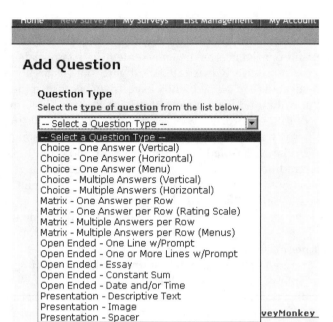

Figure 10.10 SurveyMonkey screen showing question type supported.

- Ability to identify an instrument URL that can be included in other course materials or in an e-mail message.
- Some packages allow tracking of respondents (who has completed this test or quiz, and who has not?).

Users may also wish to consider features that vary based on the pricing structure, such as the number of questions, responses, and/or participants that are allowed. Fee-based tools are more likely to allow unlimited instruments, customizing options, and data analysis tools that filter results to help users find patterns in the data. Other features include sharing of results, downloadable files for export to spreadsheets, randomizing the order of answer choices to reduce bias, and requiring responses to questions that the instrument creator specifies.

We normally assume that such item types can assess only lower-level learning outcomes, such as recall and recognition. While this is often how such items are *used*, in the spirit of maintaining our focus on assessing meaningful learning, we want to remind readers that a well-structured forced-response item paired with well-crafted response choices can indeed assess complex learning outcomes, such as knowledge of concepts, analysis, and application. For instance, an item such as the one shown in Figure 10.7 could easily be implemented in these online packages.

Online testing tools are prevalent, and thus we felt we should include them in this chapter. We see their main value not in being able to generate lots of extra testing for students (although they do enable one to do that) but rather in that they can be used for collecting formative feedback on student progress. Free tools such as SurveyMonkey allow teachers to easily gather data on student progress and use it for monitoring and adapting instruction as indicated by the results. Such tools can also make it possible for teachers to gather data from parents that may impact student activities. For instance, a quick survey could be constructed to determine how parents feel about the possibility of a planned field trip or parents' observations of how much time students spend doing homework each evening.

The downside of these tools is that teachers can quickly generate *poorly* constructed items; the tools make it easy to create online items, but nothing can change the fact that writing good assessment (or survey) items is a difficult task. The online nature of the tool should not tempt teachers into shortchanging good item creation practices that include creating items in alignment with desired learning outcomes, pilot testing, and revising items.

Conclusion

Assessment in schools is a necessity. Assessing students learning takes time and in some cases creates anxiety for both teachers and students. Lately, certain types of assessment—generally standardized tests—have been mandated by state and national governments. Consequently, teachers and administrators may be scrambling to "teach to the test" for fear of the repercussions of students not performing up to the standards. All these factors culminate in "assessment" getting a bad wrap these days in schools. But it is necessary.

In this chapter we have offered ideas for assessing what students know using different applications of technology. All these applications have the potential to assess meaningful learning (e.g., more than recall and recognition) and, perhaps most important to provide a window into discovering what learners really know while providing rich information that can be organized into meaningful feedback to learners that can improve performance. We argue that such assessment applications help us know more about what students know, and whenever we can attain that knowledge, we can help students learn more and better.

Things to Think About

We suggest that you can use the following questions to reflect on the ideas that we presented in this chapter.

1. Is assessment really a separate activity from learning? What circumstances may impact whether it is or isn't?

2. How do you use assessment activities as a way to generate feedback that can improve learner performance? After reading this chapter, are there ways you can see how technology can contribute to this?

3. How can you use technology to make assessment activities less threatening to learners or maybe even a positive experience?

4. What processes do you use to generate your assessment items and activities? Are there other teachers you can collaborate with to pilot test your assessments, help develop forced-response items that assess higher-level thinking, and share the development of technology-based assessments?

5. Does the use of technology-based assessments impact validity and reliability? Does technology help address these? Does it make any difference at all?

References

Batson, T. (2002). The electronic portfolio boom: what it all about? *Syllabus*. Retrieved 26 February 2007 form http://www.syllabus.com/article.asp?id=6984

Clark, L. (2004). Computerized adaptive testing: Effective measurement for all students. *T.H.E. Journal, 31*(10), 14, 18, 20.

Cresswell, A. (2000). Self-monitoring in student writing: Developing learner responsibility. *ELT Journal 54,* (3), 235–244. Retrieved August 3, 2006, from http://eltj.oupjournals.org/cgi/content/abstract/54/3/235

Dornisch, M., & Sabatini McLoughlin, A. (2006). Limitations of web-based rubric resources: Addressing the challenges. *Practical Assessment, Research and Evaluation, 11*(3). Retrieved August 5, 2006, from http://pareonline.net/pdf/v11n3.pdf

Duncan, D. (2005). *Clickers in the classroom.* San Francisco: Pearson.

Gagne, R. M., Bridges, L. J., & Wayne, W. W. (1998). *Principles of instructional design.* Orlando: Holt, Rinehart and Winston.

Gilbert, A. (2005). New for back-to-school. *CNET News.com*, August 5, 4:00AM PDT.

Hafner, K. (2004). *In class, the Audience Weighs In.* Retrieved March 15, 2004, from http://www.nytimes.com/2004/04/29/technology/circuits/29hand.html?pagewanted=allposition=

KITE (2001). Case 8119-1. Kite Case Library. Retrieved August 22, 2006, from http://kite.missouri.edu

NPower. (n.d.). *Online survey tools.* Retrieved February 13, 2006, from www.austinfix.net/seminar/files/survey/guide+to+online+survey+tools.pdf

Lin, X. D., Hmelo, C., Kinzer, C., & Secules, T. (1999). Designing technology to support reflection. *Educational Technology Research & Development, 47*(3), 43–62.

Lorenzo, G., & Ittelson, J. (2005). *An overview of e-portfolios.* Retrieved March 27, 2006, from http://www.educause.edu/ir/library/pdf/ELI3001.pdf

Paulson, L. F., Paulson P. R., & Meyer C. (1991). What makes a portfolio a portfolio? *Educational Leadership, 48*(5), 60–63.

Perlman, C. (2002). "An Introduction to Performance Assessment Scoring Rubrics". In C. Boston's (Ed.), Understanding Scoring Rubrics (pp. 5–13). University of Maryland, MD: ERIC Clearinghouse on Assessment and Evaluation.

Tombari, M., & Borich, G. (1999). *Authentic assessment in the classroom.* Upper Saddle River, NJ: Merrill.

Vandervelde, J. (2006). *Rubric for electronic portfolio.* Retrieved August 25, 2006, from http://www.uwstout.edu/soe/profdev/eportfoliorubric.html

Wainer, H., & Dornas, N. (2000). *Computerized adaptive testing: A primer.* Mahwah, NJ: Lawrence Erlbaum Associates.

Epilogue

Implications of Learning With Technology

The purpose of this book has been to demonstrate ways that technology can be used to engage and support meaningful learning. In each of the chapters, we briefly described how different environments or applications can be used to engage different activities. In many of those examples, we described specific software applications. If you do not have those applications or the specific applications will not run on your computer, don't despair. There are likely other, similar applications that can be used. These are examples of how to use technologies to engage meaningful learning. Our purpose was not to show you how to use these technologies. That is impossible, as we do not know what kinds of hardware, software, students, teachers, administrators, and support materials you may or may not have in your school. If you wish to try out some of these examples, it is likely that you will have to find your own software. Our goal is that you generalize the ideas that we present, not replicate the activity.

New Roles for Technology

As stated in chapter 1, we believe that although technologies can be used to provide additional testing practice, when they are used to engage students in active, constructive, intentional, authentic, and cooperative learning, then students will make more meaning. Throughout this book, we have contended that learning takes place in environments where students truly understand the nature of the tasks they are undertaking. Only then, when individuals understand and freely divest the effort needed to complete a task or activity, does meaningful, authentic learning occur. When learning tasks are relevant and embedded in a meaningful context, students see them as more than simply busywork.

Using technologies to engage meaningful learning assumes that our conceptions of education will change, that schools or classrooms (at least those that use technologies in the ways that we describe) will rethink the educational process. Although few people would ever publicly admit that schools should not emphasize meaningful learning, meaningful learning is not engaged or assessed using standardized tests. Meaningful learning presupposes that parents, students, and teachers will realize the implications and demand change, so that meaningful learning is valued as much as memorizing. Technologies will not be the cause of the social change that is required for a renaissance in learning, but they can catalyze that change and support it if it comes.

Implications for Teachers

In order for students to learn *with* technology, teachers must accept and learn a new model of learning. Traditionally, teachers' primary responsibility and activity have been directly instructing students, where teachers were the purveyors of knowledge and students the recipients. That is, the teacher told the students what they knew and how they interpreted the world according to the curriculum, textbooks, and other resources they have studied. Teachers are hired and rewarded for their content expertise. This assumes that the ways that teachers know the world are correct and should be emulated by the students. Students take notes on what teachers tell them and try to comprehend the world as their teachers do. Successful students develop conceptions more similar to those of teachers. Learners will not be able to learn *with* technology in this kind of learning context. They will not be able to construct their own meaning and manage their own learning if the teacher does it for them.

So, first and foremost, teachers must relinquish at least some of their authority, especially their intellectual authority. If teachers determine what is important for students to know, how they should know it, and how they should learn it, then students cannot become intentional, constructive learners. They aren't allowed. In those classroom contexts, there is no reason for students to make sense of the world—only to comprehend the teacher's understanding of it. We believe that the students' task should not be to understand the world as the teacher does. Rather, students should construct their own meaning for the world. If they do, then the teachers' roles shifts from dispensing knowledge to helping learners construct more viable conceptions of the world. We said earlier that we believe that not all meaning is created equally. So the teacher needs to help students discover what the larger community of scholars regards as meaningful conceptions and to evaluate their own beliefs and understandings in terms of those standards. Science teachers should help students comprehend the beliefs of the scientific community. Social studies teachers should examine with their students the values and beliefs that societies have constructed. In this role, the teacher is not the arbiter of knowledge but rather a coach who helps students engage in a larger community of scholars.

Teachers must also relinquish some of their authority in their management of learning. They cannot control all of the learning activities in the classroom. If teachers determine not only what is important for students to know, but how they should learn it, then students cannot be self-regulated learners. They aren't allowed.

Finally, teachers must gain some familiarity with the technology. They must gain skills and fluency with the technology. However, they will be most successful in helping students to learn *with* technology if they do not learn about the technologies in order to function as the expert. Rather, they should learn to coach the learning of technology skills. In many instances, teachers will be learning with the students. We have worked in many school situations where the students were constantly pushing our understanding of the technology. Often, we were barely keeping ahead of the students. They can and will learn *with* technologies, with or without the help of the teacher. That does not mean that as a teacher you can abdicate any responsibility for learning the technologies. Rather, teachers should try not to be the expert all of the time.

These implications are very problematic for teachers. They require that teachers assume new roles with different beliefs than they have traditionally pursued. Most teachers in most schools will find these implications challenging. We believe that the results will justify the risks. And just as teachers must assume new roles, learning *with* technology requires that students also assume new roles.

Implications for Students

If teachers relinquish authority, learners must assume it. Learners must develop skills in articulating, reflecting on, and evaluating what they know; setting goals for themselves (determining what is important to know) and regulating their activities and effort in order to achieve those goals; and collaborating and conversing with others so that the understandings of all students is enriched. Many students are not ready to assume that much responsibility. They do not want the power to determine their own destiny. It is much easier to allow others to regulate their lives for them. How skilled are students at setting their own agendas and pursuing them? Many students believe in their roles as passive students. However, our experience and the experiences of virtually every researcher and educator involved with every technology project described in this book show that most students readily accept those responsibilities. When given the opportunity, students of all ages readily experiment with technologies, articulate their own beliefs, and construct, coconstruct, and criticize each others' ideas. When learners are allowed to assume ownership of the product, they are diligent and persevering builders of knowledge.

Constructivist approaches to learning, with or without technology, are fraught with risks for students, parents, teachers, and administrators. Change always assumes risks. Many of the activities described in this book entail risks. We encourage you to take those risks. The excitement and enthusiasm generated by students while they construct their own understanding using technology-based tools is more than sufficient reward for taking those risks.

Standards

Teachers are challenged to ensure that students meet a myriad of required national, state, and local standards. It was impossible to tie each of our recommended activities to these myriad standards. The most relevant national standards, National Educational Technology Standards (NETS), are provided by the International Society for Technology in Education. NETS are designed to provide educators with frameworks and standards that guide them in creating rich, technology-supported learning environments. Teachers often become overwhelmed by the numerous indicators students are required to demonstrate in meeting state standards, see each of these indicators as discrete, and subsequently design disconnected instruction that isolates individual objectives. Instead, teachers should think broadly, recognizing that rich project-based learning that incorporates problem-solving and authentic tasks can meet many standards simultaneously. Rather than structure this book around specific, grade-level lesson plans, we have offered ways that several types of technologies can be used to enhance a variety of learning activities and outcomes. The six general standards that make up the NETS for students are demonstrated through 10 separate, specific grade-level performance indicators for students in prekindergarden through second grade, third through fifth grade, sixth through eighth grade, and ninth through twelfth grade.

Using the Arbor Day/Earth Day Tree Exploration field experiment in chapter 2 as an example, let's examine how Suzanne Stillwell's fourth-grade students could meet the NETS standards and performance indicators for third through fifth graders. Each performance indicator (PI) is followed by the general standard being meet in parentheses.

First, students spent time exploring technology, giving them an opportunity to meet PI-9: *Determine which technology is useful and select the appropriate tool(s) and technology resources to address a variety of tasks and problems. (5, 6)*

Students then used handhelds and digital cameras to capture and record data about trees. PI 8: *Use technology resources (e.g., calculators, data collection probes, videos, educational software) for problem solving, self-directed learning, and extended learning activities. (5, 6)*

Next, students shared data with each other by beaming among handhelds and uploaded the data to computers, where they created graphs. In this process, they demonstrated PI 1; *Use keyboards and other common input and output devices (including adaptive devices when necessary) efficiently and effectively (1),* and PI 4; *Use general purpose productivity tools and peripherals to support personal productivity, remediate skill deficits, and facilitate learning throughout the curriculum. (3)*

The Arbor Day/Earth Day project could easily be extended to include student creation of a Web site, meeting PI 5: *Use technology tools (e.g., multimedia authoring, presentation, Web tools, digital cameras, scanners) for individual and collaborative writing, communication, and publishing activities to create knowledge products for audiences inside and outside the classroom. (3, 4)*

The activity might also be one component of a larger project involving Internet research, with the potential of meeting PI 10: *Evaluate the accuracy, relevance, appropriateness, comprehensiveness, and bias of electronic information sources. (6)*

Students used resources from their state Department of Conservation; by connecting with experts at that organization, they would engage in the kind of activities indicated in PI 6: *Use telecommunications efficiently and effectively to access remote information, communicate with others in support of direct and independent learning, and pursue personal interests. (4)*

An interesting means for bringing additional collaboration into this project is by connecting with other classrooms in different parts of the country to share findings and create a joint product, such as a wiki, to publish results. In this way, students would meet PI 7: *Use telecommunications and online resources (e.g., e-mail, online discussions, Web environments) to participate in collaborative problem-solving activities for the purpose of developing solutions or products for audiences inside and outside the classroom. (4, 5)*

As you can see, it is possible within one well-designed, rich instructional activity to meet nearly all the performance indicators and standards required for a grade level. With thoughtful planning, it is also just as feasible to simultaneously meet a number of content standards. This results in efficient use of students' time, but most important, it helps pull teachers away from an isolated standards model to teaching, where instruction is more likely to be prescriptive and disconnected from authentic learning activities. With a deeper focus, not only will teachers be helping students meet a multitude of standards, but they will also be offering rich, interesting learning opportunities that engage students and compel them to think beyond the superficial. Challenging students' cognitive skills by providing motivating instruction that fulfills multiple standards is a worthy accomplishment—one that all teachers should strive for.

We encourage you to consider the complex learning outcomes described in this book as you design instruction for your students. Although authentic, complex, technology-supported activities may seem to be the antithesis of what is needed to prepare students for high achievement on tests, they are not. On the contrary, the meaningful learning that results from this work can not only encompass the knowledge needed for successful test taking but also develop individuals who are capable of real thinking.

Index